Knowledge about Language and the Curriculum:
The LINC Reader

Edited by Ronald Carter

Hodder & Stoughton
LONDON SYDNEY AUCKLAND TORONTO

British Library Cataloguing in Publication Data
Carter, Ronald, *1947–*
    Knowledge about language and the curriculum: the LINC
    reader.
    1. Great Britain. Schools. Curriculum subjects: English
    language
    I. Title
    420.7104121

    ISBN 0 340 54010 9

First published 1990
Fourth impression 1991

Typeset by Rowland Phototypesetting Ltd
Bury St Edmunds, Suffolk
Printed for the educational publishing division of
Hodder and Stoughton Ltd
Mill Road, Dunton Green, Sevenoaks, Kent by
Clays Ltd, St Ives plc

Contents

Acknowledgments

The Publishers would like to thank the following for permission to reproduce material in this volume:

The Australian Council for Educational Research Limited for 'On Literacy and Gender' by Janet White; North London Language Consortium for 'What do we mean by knowledge about language' by John Richmond; *Language and Learning* for 'What do we know about reading that helps us teach?' by Margaret Meek; *Language Issues*, the journal of the National Association of Teachers of English and other Community Languages to Adults (NATECLA), Vol. 2, No. 2 for 'Critical Language Awareness in Action' by Roz Ivanič; Multilingual Matters Limited for 'Young Children's Writing: From Spoken to Written Genre' by Frances Christie from *Language and Education*, Vol. 1, No. 1, 1987; National Association for the Teaching of English for 'What Katy knows about language' by Heather Lyons; JMB for extracts from exam papers in chapter 4; Open University Press for 'Grammatical differentiation between speech and writing in children aged 8 to 12' by Katharine Perera from Wilkinson (ed.) (1986) *The Writing of Writing*, Open University Press.

Every effort has been made to trace and acknowledge ownership of copyright. The publishers will be glad to make suitable arrangements with any copyright holders whom it has not been possible to contact.

List of Contributors

Ronald Carter is Professor of Modern English Language in the Department of English Studies, University of Nottingham. He is National Coordinator of the LINC Project.

Fran Christie is Professor of Education, Northern Territory University, Darwin, Australia.

Beverly Derewianka is Senior Lecturer in the Centre for Studies in Literacy, University of Wollongong, New South Wales, Australia.

Yetta Goodman is Professor of Education and Co-Director of the Program in Language and Literacy, University of Arizona.

Roz Ivanič is Lecturer in the Department of Linguistics and Modern English Language, University of Lancaster.

Nick Jones is seconded from the post of English Adviser for Devon to be LINC Consortium Coordinator for the South West.

George Keith is seconded from Cheshire College of Higher Education to be LINC Consortium Coordinator for the North West (Cheshire, Lancashire and Wigan). He is Chief Examiner for the JMB English Language A Level.

Heather Lyons was until recently Lecturer in the Faculty of Education, University of Reading. Heather Lyons died early in 1990.

Margaret Meek is Emeritus Reader in the Department of English and Media Studies, University of London Institute of Education.

Pat O'Rourke is LINC Coordinator for the East Midlands Consortium and was previously Head of English in a comprehensive school in West Glamorgan.

Mike O'Rourke is Lecturer in the Language Centre, University of Exeter.

Katharine Perera is Senior Lecturer in Linguistics at the University of Manchester. She was a member of the English Working Party (Cox Committee).

John Richmond is joint LINC Coordinator for the North London Language Consortium. He was formerly English Adviser for Shropshire and a Project Officer for the National Writing Project.

Helen Savva is joint LINC Coordinator for the North London Language Consortium. She has worked on a DES Oracy Project in Shropshire and on the National Writing Project in ILEA.

Alison Sealey is the Primary Advisory Teacher for the LINC Project in Birmingham. She has extensive experience of primary phase teaching.

Mike Taylor is seconded from Anglia College of Higher Education and is LINC Coordinator for the Eastern Region Consortium.

Janet White is LINC Coordinator for the Central Southern Consortium. She is part-seconded from her post in the Centre for Research in Language and Communication at the National Foundation for Educational Research.

Introduction

Particularly in a language education perspective, we need to take a dynamic view of language in all three dimensions of its variation: dialectal *(regional/social),* diatypic *(functional) and* diachronic *(historical). To put this in less technical terms: for any theory of language in education, it should be seen as the norm, rather than the exception, that the community of learners use a variety of codes (languages and/or dialects), that they use a variety of language functions (or registers), and that none of these ever stands still. (Michael Halliday, 1987)*

USING THIS READER

This reader has two main purposes:

1 It is related organically to the LINC (Language in the National Curriculum) Project. The articles printed in this Reader are chosen as supplements to the LINC materials for professional development published by HMSO initially in December 1990. They are chosen for their suitability as pre- or post-reading support for individual LINC units. There are twelve LINC units covering a range of areas of the language curriculum and each unit contains specific guidance for the use of articles in this Reader.

2 The articles collected in this Reader have also been selected with a view to contributing to the general field of language in education. In keeping with the aims of LINC the articles have a particular focus on knowledge about language for teachers and for pupils.

It is hoped that the articles in this collection stand in their own right as a coherently organised body of material on topics of considerable current interest, not just within Great Britain but internationally too, where in a number of different contexts the relevance of more language-based approaches to English teaching and national curricula generally are being explored.

To this end, there is a mix both of previously published articles, recognised for their contribution to the field of language in education, and commissioned articles which address the specific inflections of knowledge about language in relation to the National Curriculum in England and Wales. Several of these articles are written by members of the LINC Project themselves and result from recent first-hand experience of the issues involved.

WHAT IS LINC?

LINC stands for *Language in the National Curriculum*. It is a project funded by the Department of Education and Science under an ESG (Education Support Grant). The main aim of the project is to produce materials and to conduct activities to support implementation of English in the National Curriculum in England and Wales in the light of the views of language outlined in the Kingman and Cox Reports on English language teaching and English 5–16 respectively (DES, 1988, 1989) The LINC project was designed to operate from April 1989 until March 1992.

The LINC professional development materials (DES, 1990–1), to which this reader relates, were prepared in the first year of the project (April 1989–April 1990) and were used as a basis for training of key project personnel. For the duration of the LINC programme the materials are included in LEA in-service courses and teachers are supported in considering the development needs of their own schools with regard to language in the National Curriculum. The primary aim of the materials is to form a basis for the immediate training requirements of the project; however, a further aim is to produce materials which are of use to providers of both in-service and initial teacher training over a much longer period of time.

The LINC materials (HMSO, 1990) are characterised by the following main features:

◇ There are twelve main units in the package; each unit is designed for approximately 1–1½ days of course time or its equivalent. The units are supported by BBC TV and Radio programmes.

◇ Each unit is organised around a sequence of activities to support users 'doing' things with language.

◇ Each unit is designed to be maximally flexible and can be supplemented or extended according to need. The loose-leaf ring binder format means that units can be easily detached and/or combined with other material.

◇ Units are grouped under main headings of development in children's talk, reading and writing together with a block devoted to language and society.

◇ Each unit has at its centre complete texts, usually drawn from recognisable classroom contexts; the activities promote analysis of language but scrutiny of decontextualised language is normally eschewed.

◇ The training package draws on the many available examples of good practice in language teaching and recognises that teachers already know a lot, particularly implicitly, about language.

Why is KAL (Knowledge About Language) important to teachers?

A primary aim of the LINC project is further to enhance teachers' understanding and knowledge about language in relation to processes of teaching and learning. In this respect LINC pays particular attention to the requirements of the National Curriculum for English. The project, together with this reader which supports it, operates with the following main assumptions:

1 Language is central to the processes of teaching and learning. Explicit knowledge about language can sharpen teachers' appreciation of children's achievements with language as well as broaden the language opportunities they provide for pupils in the classroom. It can also help teachers understand the nature of children's difficulties or partial successes with language.

2 More conscious attention to language provides tools which can enable teachers, for example, to:

◇ develop their pupils' already impressive ability to talk and to comprehend spoken language;
◇ help pupils to read more confidently (for example, through miscue analysis) and become autonomous readers;
◇ understand how to intervene constructively at various stages in their pupils' writing – in preparation, in drafting, in final product, in commenting and evaluating;
◇ help pupils to develop further insights into how they use language in their day-to-day lives for many purposes;
◇ better understand what to make explicit and what to leave implicit in pupils' own knowledge about language.

3 KAL helps teachers to distinguish between casual reactions to ways of speaking (responses to, for example, accent, dialect or the use of forms by the speaker of a second language which show the influence of a first) and more informed professional judgements.

4 In discussing language there are certain dangers in undue abstraction and in the perception of an associated *meta-*

language as threatening or inhibiting (especially to teachers with little previous background in the study of language). LINC believes that shared frames of reference are more important than terminologies *per se* but that some selected meta-language can enable us to talk about language more precisely and economically.

5 KAL assists teachers to present achievements in language in a positive light to parents and governors; it can enable them to be better equipped to discuss such questions as Standard English, 'grammar' and policies concerning marking.

6 The school is a fundamentally *social* language-using community. Deepening insights into the social functions of language and into the relationships between language and society can unlock for teachers important insights into the relationships between language and learning.

What does knowledge about language mean for pupils?

The National Curriculum for English in England and Wales includes a requirement that pupils demonstrate knowledge about language. Pupils' knowledge about language should take place within the context of reading, writing and speaking/listening development.

Members of the LINC project believe that there are many positive benefits to supporting in pupils a fuller and more explicit knowledge about language. The team is committed to the following main principles for KAL in primary and secondary schools:

1 There can be no return to formalist, decontextualised class-room analysis of language, nor to the deficiency pedagogies on which such teaching is founded.

2 Language study should start from what children can do, from their positive achievements with language and from the re-markable resources of implicit knowledge about language which all children possess.

3 A rich experience of using language should generally *precede* conscious reflection on or analysis of language. Language study can influence use but development of the relationship between learning about language and learning how to use it is not a linear one but rather a recursive, cyclical and mutually informing relationship.

4 Being more explicitly informed about the sources of attitudes to language, about its uses and misuses, about how language is used to manipulate and incapacitate, can *empower* pupils to see through language to the ways in which messages are mediated and ideologies encoded.

5 Metalanguage should be introduced where appropriate to facilitate talking and thinking about language but children

should be allowed to come to specialist terms as needed and in context.

6 Teaching methodologies for KAL should promote experiential, exploratory and reflective encounters with language; transmissive methods are usually inappropriate for the study of language in schools.

What general assumptions about the nature of language are adopted in the LINC materials for professional development?

LINC stresses above all the richness and variety of language: the uses and functions of language over the forms of language; the description of texts in social contexts over the description of isolated decontextualised bits of language. Its main assumptions are that:

1 As humans we use language primarily for social reasons, for a multi-variety of purposes.

2 Language is imbued with dynamism and varies from one context to another and from one set of uses to another. Language also changes over time.

3 Language is penetrated with social and cultural values and also carries meanings related to each user's unique identity.

4 Language reveals and conceals much about human relationships. There are intimate connections, for example, between language and social power, language and culture and language and gender.

5 Language is a system and is systematically organised.

6 Meanings created in and through language are often problematic; they can constrain us as well as liberate us. Language users must constantly negotiate and renegotiate meanings.

LINC strongly supports the view of language expressed by the English Working Party in paragraph 6.18 of its report (the Cox Report, DES, 1989):

> Language is a system of sounds, meanings and structures with which we make sense of the world around us. It functions as a tool of thought; as a means of social organisation; as the repository and means of transmission of knowledge; as the raw material of literature, and as the creator and sustainer – or destroyer – of human relationships. It changes inevitably over time and, as change is not uniform, from place to place. Because language is a fundamental part of being human, it is an important aspect of a person's sense of self; because it is a fundamental feature of any community, it is an important aspect of a person's sense of social identity.

THE LINC PROJECT: THEORETICAL PERSPECTIVES ON LANGUAGE AND EDUCATION

What specific underlying theories of language are influential in the LINC programme?

The LINC programme was designed to develop the model of language recommended in the Kingman Report (DES, 1988). The Kingman model of language is a descriptive and analytical model. As such it is helpful and it certainly reflects current developments in linguistics. However, an analytical model is not a pedagogic model. The approach to language developed by LINC is true to the spirit of the Kingman model but it develops that model in order to make it pedagogically sensitive. A diagrammatic version of the Kingman model of language is given in Figure 1.

The LINC group noted in particular the statement in the Kingman Report that there can be no one model of the English language and that the sequence in which the parts of the Kingman model were set out should not imply pedagogic priorities. Accordingly, the LINC group has re-aligned the Kingman model of language in order to give special emphasis to the third and fourth 'parts' of Kingman – the development of language and language variation – with greater emphasis than in Kingman given to the variation of language in different social and cultural contexts. In fact, a principal and underlying motivation for the LINC project is a concern with *language variation*.

A concern with social, cultural and textual variation does not preclude a concern with the *forms of language* (contained in Part 1 of the Kingman model of language). However, such forms should be examined not in and for themselves but in relation to functional variation. In educational contexts functional variation manifests itself in particular in the kinds of talk, writing and reading produced in schools and classrooms. Within the LINC model language form is systematically focused where it is judged to be relevant and enabling for teachers and pupils; but the broader social functions and parameters within which all forms are embedded operate as a constant check against decontextualised analysis of language.

The LINC approach to language is much influenced by functional theories of language. The main proponent of such theories – over a period of almost 30 years – has been Professor Michael Halliday, and the LINC model of language owes much to Halliday's work. Halliday has always placed meaning at the very centre of theories of language and LINC supports that position.

It is important, however, that a view of language in educational contexts should not only be systematic and detailed but should also be able to account for more than the most minute or 'lower-level'

Part 1: The forms of the English language

The following boxes, exemplify the range of forms found in English. If norms are combined in regular patterns, following the rules and conventions of English, they yield meaningful language.

1. *speech* • vowel and consonant sounds • syllables and word stress • intonation and pause • tone of voice	2. *writing* • vowel and consonant letters (the alphabet) • spelling and punctuation • paragraphing and lay-out

3. *word forms*
  • inflected words (plurals, comparatives, etc.)
  • derived words (e.g. *fair, unfair*)
  • compound words (e.g. *melt-down, play-boy, mouth-watering*)
  • idioms (e.g. *put a stop to, take care of, lose touch with*)
  • productive metaphors (e.g. *time is money, lose time, save time, spend time, waste time, run out of time*)
  • frozen metaphors (e.g. *kick the bucket, curry favour*)

4. *phrase structure and sentence structure*
  • verbs: auxiliaries, tense, aspect, mood
  • nouns: noun classes, number, gender, definiteness, pronouns, demonstratives
  • adjectives, adverbs, adjuncts, disjuncts and conjuncts
  • simple sentence structure, co-ordination, apposition
  • complex sentence structure, subordination
  • substitution and ellipsis, negation and quantification

5. *discourse structure*
  • paragraph structure, reference, deixis, anaphora, cohesion
  • theme, focus, emphasis, given and new information structure
  • boundary markers (in speech and writing)
  • lexical collocation (i.e. drawn from the same vocabulary area)

Part 2(1): Communication

Speakers and writers adapt their language to the context in which the language is being used. The boxes below indicate some of the main features of context which are relevant in conversations where the speaker and listener are talking face to face. In this section we shall also indicate how this model needs to be adapted to account for written language. (Note that in literature we often find *representations* of speech which rely on our experience of the spoken language.)

Context
  • place/time
  • topic
  • type of discourse
  • what has already been said in the discourse

Speaker • intention in speaking • attitude in speaking • perception of context	↔	Listener • intention in listening • attitude to speaker • attitude to topic (interest) • background information on topic • understanding of what has already been said • perception of context

Figure 1 The Kingman model of language

Part 2(II): Comprehension – some processes of understanding

In Part 2(I) we showed the context of communication which is of course the context in which comprehension takes place. We understand language in a context of use. Some of the prossesses involved in understanding are indicated in this figure which, like Part 2(I), is orientated to the speaker/listener relationship; In the notes on this section we shall show how these figures can be adapted to give an account of reading with understanding

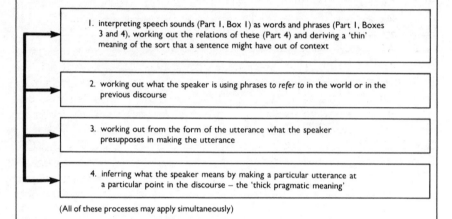

1. interpreting speech sounds (Part 1, Box 1) as words and phrases (Part 1, Boxes 3 and 4), working out the relations of these (Part 4) and deriving a 'thin' meaning of the sort that a sentence might have out of context

2. working out what the speaker is using phrases *to refer to* in the world or in the previous discourse

3. working out from the form of the utterance what the speaker presupposes in making the utterance

4. inferring what the speaker means by making a particular utterance at a particular point in the discourse – the 'thick pragmatic meaning'

(All of these processes may apply simultaneously)

Part 3: Acquisition and development

1. Children gradually acquire the forms of language identified in the boxes of Part 1. Whereas some aspects of acquisition are fairly rapid (most children have acquired a full range of vowels and consonants by the time they are 6 or 7), other aspects develop much later (for example, control of spelling patterns and conventions of punctuation).

2. Children gradually develop their ability to produce and to understand appropriate forms of language (both spoken and written) in a wide range of contexts (Part 2(I)). This development does not cease in the years of schooling but continues throughout life.

Part 4: Historical and geographical variation

1. Language changes over time – all forms of language are subject to change, to inception, modification and to decay sometimes rapidly and sometimes immeasurably slowly. Changes continue to take place in our own time.

2. As populations are dispersed and separated, they typically develop regular regional changes in their language forms. These changes may mark different dialects (or eventually different languages.) If one of these dialects is used for writing, that dialect may emerge as the standard language; it will, of course, share many characteristics with the other related dialects.

Figure 1 (continued) The Kingman model of language

operations of language. Language studies in the 1960s and 1970s were characterised by attention to lower-level forms such as phonemes, morphemes and clauses, usually out of context. In the 1980s, however, developments in text linguistics, discourse analysis and functional grammar have provided a basis for examining higher-level patterns of language across complete texts. The LINC programme recognises the importance of this work and its relevance to education – where written and spoken texts are generated in a range of contexts and for a range of purposes. Accordingly, a *text-based* view of language is adopted and complete texts are the usual focus of attention.

A functional theory of language is a natural complement to influential theories of language development constructed in the 1970s by Professor James Britton and others working to similar principles. These theories make clear the centrality of context, purpose and audience in language use and the salience of this understanding for children's learning. Such theories culminated in *The Bullock Report* (DES, 1975) – a very influential forerunner of the Kingman and Cox Reports – and are now central to the National Curriculum for English.

The following Hallidayan diagram (Figure 2) illustrates the extent to which a functional model of language can be integrated with

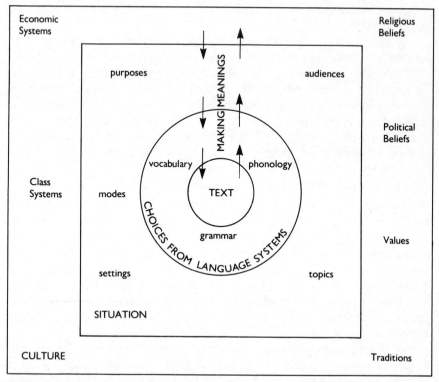

Figure 2 Integration of a functional model of language with Britton's theories of language development

Britton's theories of language development. It illustrates the following main features of functional theory:

◇ The making of *meaning* is the reason for the invention, existence and development of language.
◇ All meanings exist within the context of culture. Cultural values and beliefs determine the purposes, audiences, settings and topics of language.
◇ Texts, spoken and written, are created and interpreted by making appropriate choices from the language system according to specific purposes, audiences, settings and topics.

Functional accounts of language stress the importance of the *variation* of language at all levels within this model, both from the broadest parameters of cultural variation to variations in grammatical or phonemic form. The aim is to allow constant explanation and inter-pretation of all layers of variation in relation to one another. The model therefore prevents generalised discussion of situations for language at the same time as it prevents decontextualised discussion of language; forms and the making of meanings are shown to be inextricably interrelated in the creation of complete texts. The LINC approach to language in education is to promote precise and systematic discussion of language in the context of established theories of language learning and development.

LINC has a special responsibility to focus on language with descriptive precision. It recognises the contribution of linguistics to our understanding of language, but also that of educationists, philosophers of language, sociologists, psychologists, cultural and literary theorists, whose insights also have a continuing relevance to the central role of language in education. A functional theory of language allows us to embrace such perspectives, particularly those concerned with the making of textual meaning in social and cultural contexts.

What do we mean by variation theory?

A functional theory of language is, as we have seen, predicated on the fact that language varies. There are three main dimensions to this variation: language varies according to the uses to which it is put; it varies over time; it varies according to the language user. Variation over time is termed *diachronic* variation; variation according to the user is termed *dialectal* variation; variation according to use is termed *diatypic* variation. In all components of variation the social context of language use is a crucial, indeed sometimes determining, factor in the nature of the variation.

For example, changes in language over time are regularly the result of socio-cultural or socio-economic changes. From the mid-seventeenth to the nineteenth century the growth of the East Midlands dialect into the standard English dialect of Great Britain, and subsequently internationally too, can be attributed largely to the economic and political power of London and to the social attitudes which associate with such power, particularly in respect of 'non-standard' dialects with other geographical locations.

Contemporary uses of dialect forms are also often directly dependent on the social position of the user and on his or her attitudes towards it. A whole body of sociolinguistic research (e.g. Trudgill, 1983) confirms that dialectal variation occurs according to a range of largely socially constructed parameters. Such work also demonstrates that dialects are not fixed entities but rather continua with users making choices along the continua according to their social status, their perception of their own and their interlocutor's social status, their assessment of the nature of the context of their language use as well as such factors as their own gender or ethnicity and their perception of their interlocutor(s) in relation to such factors. Geographical factors are also relevant and for some users a sense of belonging to a particular community will be a crucial factor in choices along the continua of dialectal variation, not least because such choices will involve expressions of their identity as individuals. A further marker of individuality resides in the *idolects* which each speaker possesses, which are particular choices of words or phrases or particular phonological characteristics which single out one user from another. Such characteristics are largely regular over time. In more senses than one, however, dialectal variation reveals who you are.

Diatypic variation is also deeply embedded in different social contexts of use. A fundamental component of this variation, particularly in educational contexts, is a continuum between spoken and written *modes*. Differences and distinctions between speech and writing result in different diatypes with different communicative functions. For example, a written report is usually different from a spoken report. We need to remember, however, that different degrees of rehearsal or planning can underlie the same function within the two modes. A planned spoken report, which can even have been written to be spoken, will contain different forms of language from an unplanned one and for this main reason poles of 'planned' and 'unplanned' may be more significant than choices in spoken and written modes, however fundamental such choices are. Also significant in this variation will be the audience and the formality of the relations between the user and the audience; and the very subject-matter, as well as assumptions of familiarity with the general topic, will determine choices of mode and judgement of appropriate reception of the language. Such judgement will, of course, involve conscious or unconscious perception of the power relations which obtain in the socio-cultural context of this use of language as well as the relation of the choices of particular language forms to the ideologies, beliefs and value systems of the participants.

The diagrams in Figures 3 and 4 (based on Gregory and Carroll, 1978) illustrate some of the above points. Diachronic variation is not

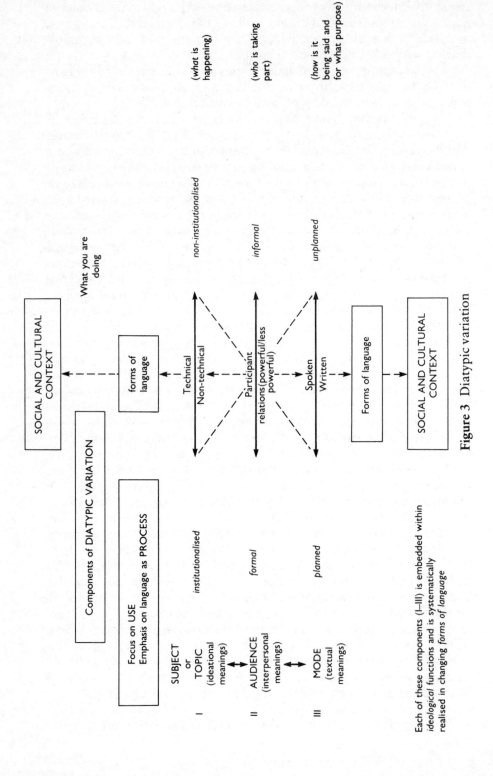

Figure 3 Diatypic variation

Each of these components (I–III) is embedded within *ideological* functions and is systematically realised in changing *forms of language*

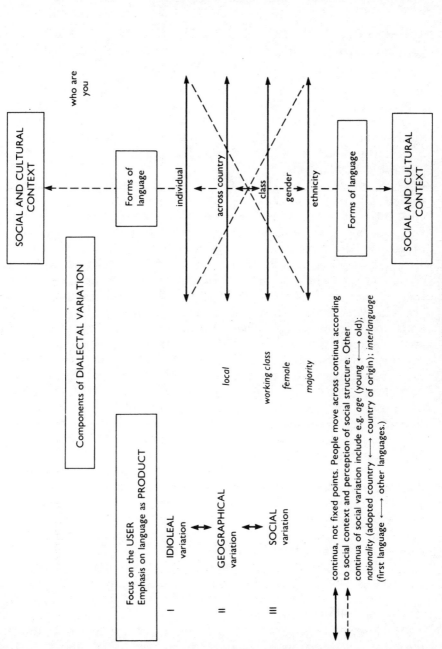

Figure 4 Dialectal variation

represented as it is of less specific relevance in educational contexts; instead there is a main focus on dialectal and diatypic variation although the separate figures for each should not suggest that the components are separate or discrete. There is a necessary *interpenetration* of dialectal and diatypic functions in language variation. A summary of the main variational parameters is given in Figure 5.

What is the relevance of these theories to classroom language development?

The pay-off for any applied linguistic theory of language is not its power as a theory; what counts is its relevance to classroom practice. To what extent can the above theories help teachers in their task of fostering language development? To what extent can such theories inform the kind of knowledge about language which serves pupils' understanding of language both in its own right and in generating their own more effective use of language?

There is obviously insufficient space in this introduction to explore all these parameters and a number of specific illustrations are given both in the articles in this volume and in the LINC training package. In general terms it can be said that an ability to manipulate a range of styles of language is crucial to success within any curriculum. Teachers therefore need to have a quite explicit knowledge about all components of variation in order that their own practice can support such a goal of development. The more opportunities that can be provided within teacher education for teachers themselves to explore and experience language variation, to reflect on its functions and to analyse some of the forms by which such functions are realised, then the better it will be for pupils' acquisition and development of language.

As far as pupils are concerned it is a matter of judgement on the part of the teacher how far to make such things explicit, at what stages of development and in what classroom contexts. Pupils possess considerable resources of mainly implicit knowledge about the way language changes according to purpose, audience and context. They acquire such knowledge at relatively early ages and can even explore such issues in the infant class. The National Curriculum for English in England and Wales specifies that explicit knowledge about language should be developed after Key Stage 2 (after 11) and become an integral component both in language learning and in the *study* of language as a phenomenon in its own right, though such study should always be in the context of use of the language modes of speaking, writing and reading.

The Cox Report (DES, 1989) provides two main rationales for knowledge about language for pupils: a *cognitive* rationale and a *social* rationale. The cognitive rationale underlines the intellectual benefits which can follow from disembedding implicit awareness of language and making it more explicit through a process of sustained reflection on the nature and functions of language; the social rationale underlines the

Summary

The following summary is based on Halliday and Hasan (1989):

Language Variation

Dialectal Varieties	Diachronic Varieties	Diatypic Varieties (or registers)
Variety 'according to user': dialect is 'what you speak (habitually)' i.e. determined by who you are geographically or socially (region &/or social class of origin &/or adoption)	Variety according to user and use. diachronic variation reflects social processes working against the social order diachronic variation shows how diatypes and dialects have evolved	Variety 'according to use': register is 'what you are speaking (at the time)' i.e. determined by what you are doing (nature of activity in which language is functioning)
dialect reflects social order in sense of social structure (types of social hierarchy)		register or diatypes reflect social order in sense of social process (types of social activity)
Hence in principle dialects are saying the same thing differently So dialects tend to differ in: phonetics phonology vocabulary grammar (to a certain extent) but not in text or discourse organisation		Hence in principle diatypes are saying different things So diatypes tend to differ in: text and discourse organisation and therefore in grammar and vocabulary (as expression of meanings) but rarely of phonology (some require special voice qualities)
Sample cases are: subcultural varieties caste or social class provenance (rural/urban) generation (parents/children) age (young/old) sex (male/female)		Sample cases are: institutionalised varieties technical (scientific, technological) occupational (e.g. doctor-patient) other contexts having special structures & strategies (e.g. classroom) In educational contexts competence in a range of diatypic varieties is crucial. The emphasis must therefore by on text-types or genes: e.g. narrative; argument; report; description; instruction etc.
Note: Members of a community often hold strong attitudes towards its dialects, owing to the function of dialect in the expression and maintenance of social hierarchy. One dialect may acquire special status as symbolising the values of a community. Dialects are best analysed from the lower levels of language up.		Note: Registers or diatypes are the semantic configurations that are typically associated with particular social contexts (defined in terms of topic, audience and mode). Diatypes are best analysed from the higher or discourse levels of language down.

BUT there is close interconnection between diatypes and dialects: so there is no very sharp line between the two. There is 'division of labour': different members have different social roles – so certain diatypes demand certain dialects (e.g. bureaucratic register: standard dialect), and on the other hand different social groups may tend to have different conceptions of the meanings that are exchanged in particular situations (Bernstein's 'codes'). Certain groups (e.g. English teachers) give high priority to the *aesthetic* functions of language. The aesthetic functions of language embrace dialects and diatypes.

N.B In this diagram as well as in Figures 3 and 4, the usual Hallidayan terminology is replaced by terms which are more widely in use in National Curriculum documents in England and Wales. (For example, the terms field, tenor and mode are substituted by *subject* or *topic, audience* and *mode*)

Figure 5 Some main variational parameters of language use

benefits in enhanced social tolerance and understanding which can follow from greater awareness of language diversity and of the necessary variations which occur within and across languages, often for social reasons. Pupils' knowledge about language should therefore include substantial components of both dialectal, diachronic and diatypic variation – and, indeed, this is recommended in the Cox Report.

A major unanswered and unexplained question in knowledge about language for pupils concerns the relationship between knowledge about or reflection on language and a development of competence in the use of language. Such a connection is plausible, but in the absence of evidence of the kind required by extensive longitudinal studies, it cannot be demonstrated. What can be said is that pupils are likely to benefit from detailed consideration being given to the forms and function of language variation. Such is the importance of an ability to control language in all its many variations that the more angles that can be provided on those variations the better.

Most important of all is the focus for pupils on written or *diatypic variation*. Much is made, particularly in National Curriculum documents, of the need for pupils to extend their spoken repertoire and in some cases this will involve incorporating standard English forms for use, where appropriate. A key phrase here is *where appropriate*, for the idea of standard English being serviceable for all purposes assumes that there are no contexts where variation along dialectal continua is appropriate. There are, of course, contexts such as formal interchanges with a large or an unknown audience where standard English is applicable; but for many speakers the same dialect would be quite inapplicable in an informal context interchanging with friends on topics where the expression of ideas and feelings is intimately a part of the speaker's individuality and identity.

It should be a universal educational goal to empower pupils to use as wide a range of language varieties as competently as possible. Such a goal of language learning equips pupils to meet the linguistic demands of adult society and to work effectively within that society and, where necessary, *against* forces within that society which might operate to disempower individuals and the communities of which they are part. To this particular end competence in diatypic variation is more likely to be empowering than is competence in a range of dialects. Changes to social realities as well as to one's position within society are more likely to be brought about not by the replacement of one dialect by another, even if that dialect is Standard English, but by a developed capacity to deploy and reflect on the deployment of as wide a range of varieties as possible.

The model of language adopted for the LINC programme is rooted in a theory of linguistic variation. The main educational application of this theory is to empower pupils to deploy language more effectively by learning to use and to reflect on the use of a variety of complete spoken and written texts. Of particular significance will be those spoken and especially written varieties of language which are central to achievement both in schools and within the broader social and cultural community. In this sense a theory of *linguistic variation* is highly relevant to classroom language development.

Some limits to linguistic approaches to language education

This introduction and the LINC materials for professional development support a view that a greater degree of linguistic awareness than has been available in much teacher training can be of real benefit and value to teachers. A stronger view still is that if teachers have no formal training in linguistic awareness then they will lack categories and frameworks for thinking about and analysing crucial elements in learning and will therefore draw such categories from a common store of half-belief in which prejudice and fact combine indistinguishably. To this end LINC training materials and the supporting articles in this reader promote a rigorous and systematic approach to language and its place in educational networks.

In spite of this strong belief it would be wrong not to end this introduction with some notes of caution. It is true that linguists and educational linguists together know a great deal more than they did 20 years ago. There is a lot, however, that is not known or which is currently being investigated; additionally, there are some aspects of language use which will resist systematisation or which can only be explained by reference to knowledge or contexts which are essentially non-linguistic in character.

For example, because it conveys *meanings*, language can be played with, distorted and used to reflect any meaning associations, however personal, that individual users create. In a related sense, too, language is subject to socially shared meaning conventions which are tacitly agreed for most of the time and which therefore can be systematically described; however, all conventions can be called into question and renegotiated – hence language and its conventions of use are permanently and unavoidably unstable and in flux. Much of the richness, pleasure and creativity of language use inheres in such play with these conventions.

Furthermore, there are areas of language which remain un-explained by linguists, while some areas are better explained by others. For example, in the case of reading development, knowledge about language drawn from linguistics can assist teachers in recognising the kinds of cueing systems used by children to make texts mean, their expectations based on genre, their anticipation of structures familiar to them from their knowledge of the spoken language, their awareness of the specific features of 'book language', or of grapho-phonemic correspondences in relation to 'sight vocabulary'. But knowledge about language drawn from work in the sociology and psychology of language is more likely to assist teachers with a fuller understanding of author–reader relationships, reading as a socio-cultural practice, the role of pictures in texts, the nature of text processing or the specific strategies of text comprehension. In this instance, specific knowledge drawn from linguistics together with broader understanding of the nature of language can be usefully integrated and deployed to recognise and divert children from counterproductive reading strategies.

Finally, we need to question just what it means to *know* about language. This introduction has stressed the need for conscious knowledge about language and argued for the advantages to teachers of being able to describe language explicitly. It is, of course, possible to know about language in more than one way and implicit, intuitive knowledge has an important part to play. All teachers and pupils possess considerable knowledge about language and this knowedge has to be valued, worked with, and built upon. It would also be wrong to assume that conscious knowledge operates independently of unconscious knowledge; there is a constant interplay and interaction between different modes of knowing and explicit, analytical attention to language can and should serve to deepen intuitions. There is a continuum from intuitions about language, reflection on language and analysis of language which is not linear in any simple way but rather cyclical, recursive and mutually informing. As we have already recognised, there is in the LINC programme a main emphasis, where appropriate, on explicit knowledge about language and on the contributions of linguistics to this understanding; but other emphases and other academic traditions have an important part to play in fostering the kinds of broad understanding of the nature of language which enables the full complexity and richness of language as a human resource for meaning making to be appreciated.

SUMMARY

The LINC approach to language variation in educational contexts:

1 is *functional* and Hallidayan in orientation;
2 is an educationally *relevant* model;
3 is close to the theory of language implicit in the Cox report but sufficiently broad to subsume a *re-aligned* Kingman model;
4 is a broad descriptive framework which allows *systematic* analysis and *principled* pedagogic questions to be generated;
5 provides a basis for a mainly discourse-driven account of language. Its functional, socio-semantic thrust ensures *ideological* issues are quite central;
6 has complete *texts* at the centre of interest;
7 is a natural complement to influential theories of language in

education development in the 1970s by, for example, Britton and others – culminating in the Bullock Report – with their emphasis on categories of *audience*, *purpose* and *context*;

8 accommodates both linguistic perspectives (e.g. phonemic variation) and more holistic perspectives on language (e.g. language as cultural practice);

9 recognises that some aspects of language resist systematisation;

10 (potentially) renders distinctions between linguistics in education/language in education passé.

ORGANISATION OF THE READER

The Reader is divided into two main parts. Part 1 contains six essays which directly address issues of knowledge about language for pupils in both primary and secondary contexts. Five of the essays are published here for the first time. The aim is to explore key issues in the development of increased knowledge about language such as: the interface between implicit and explicit knowledge; the content of a language syllabus; appropriate methodologies for KAL; the relationship between increased knowledge about language and critical insights into uses and functions of language in the exercise of power in society. The material here complements the LINC unit devoted to Pupils' Knowledge about Language.

Part 2 of the Reader contains a balance between newly published and previously published essays. All these essays, which are more directly concerned with teachers' knowledge about language, relate to particular LINC units. For example, the essays cover: early language development; reading, writing, speaking and listening; multilingualism; language and social groups; spoken and written language. However, such essays also aim to be of general support for understanding of the place of language and the curriculum and can be read independently of LINC units. Some essays have a more general orientation, for example, the essay on historical variation and the history of English, which can be read as support for the unit on Accent, Dialect and Standard English or as an extension to the essays in Part 1 concerned with Pupils' Knowledge about Language.[1]

---

[1] At the time of writing and editing this Reader, LINC training materials are still being prepared. Changes may occur to the design and structure of the materials, and there may be modification to the models and diagrams discussed in this Introduction. However, any changes which are made are unlikely to affect the usefulness of this collection as support reading material for the LINC training materials. It is in any case hoped that the Reader will also be of sufficient interest to stand in its own right as a contribution to the field of language and education and to the specific part played by knowledge about language within that field.

REFERENCES

DES (1975) *A Language for Life* (the Bullock Report). London: HMSO.

DES (1988) *Report of the Committee of Inquiry into the Teaching of the English Language* (the Kingman Report). London: HMSO.

DES (1989) *Report of the English Working Party 5–16* (the Cox Report). London: HMSO.

DES (1990–1) *Language in the National Curriculum (LINC): Materials for Professional Development.* London: HMSO.

Gregory, M. and Carroll, S. (1978) *Language and Situation: Language Varieties and their Social Contexts.* London: Routledge.

Halliday, M. A. K. and Hasan, R. (1989) *Language, Context and Text: Aspects of Language in a Social-Semiotic Perspective.* Oxford: Oxford University Press.

Halliday, M. A. K. (1987) 'Some Basic Concepts in Educational Linguistics', in Bickley, V. (ed.) *Languages in Education in a Bi-lingual or Multi-lingual Setting.* Hong Kong: ILE, pp. 5–17.

Trudgill, P. (1983) *On Dialect.* Oxford: Blackwell.

ACKNOWLEDGMENTS

Thanks are due to Beverly Derewianka and to Richard Bain for the basis of the diagram in Figure 2. The LINC national team of consortium coordinators have made many contributions to the thinking outlined in this introduction. John Richmond has helped to clarify much in the rationale for functional theories of language, has commented perceptively on numerous draft documents and written material himself which I have drawn on. Particular acknowledgment is made to Leslie Stratta who contributed much to earlier draft documents and who co-authored an introductory statement on the LINC project on which this introduction is in part based. The particular views expressed in this introduction and any flaws in associated argument are, however, my own and no other member of LINC should be held responsible for them.

Ronald Carter
Department of English Studies and
Centre for English Language Education
University of Nottingham

Part 1

Knowledge about Language: Some Key Issues

1

What Do We Mean by Knowledge About Language?

JOHN RICHMOND ——————————————————————◇

As a phrase, it is like many another in education. People have started to slip it into their conversation with that beguiling confidence which suggests that, of course, they understand perfectly well what they mean by knowledge about language. You stand there hoping that sooner or later they will accidentally drop a clue as to what it means without you having to undergo the embarrassment of actually asking. You search your memory: perhaps people have always been talking about knowledge about language – it is just that you never really caught the phrase before. After all, it is a pretty common-or-garden trio of words, isn't it? Knowledge about language. Knowing things about langage. Being interested in and informed about language. Seems harmless enough: in fact, it seems like something that every teacher of language or English should have in some measure. There is one worrying thing: the phrase has begun to be written with capital letters (Knowledge about Language) or even abbreviated to KAL. A few people – the sort who are always doing this kind of thing – actually use a new word, kal, to rhyme with pal, in their everyday vocabulary. More seriously still, it is in the National Curriculum. It seems that we shall have to attend to it.

A BIT OF HISTORY
In tracing the history of the phrase, we need to go back as far as the HMI booklet, *English from 5 to 16*, published in 1984. It proposed that teachers should be promoting children's development as speakers and listeners, readers and writers. It said, fourthly, that teachers should:

> *teach pupils about language, so that they achieve a working knowledge of its structure and of the variety of ways in which meaning is made, so that they have a vocabulary for discussing it, so that they can use it with greater awareness, and because it is interesting.*

From the perspective of 1990, this proposal, quoted in isolation from the rest of the booklet, interpreted generously, sounds like something we could live with and even in some respects (discussing the variety of ways in which meaning is made, for example) get excited about. Reading the booklet as a whole at the time, however, weighing up what its author might really have in mind as the more important things to teach pupils about language, and putting these thoughts next to worries about other aspects of the booklet (its proposals for age-related objectives for pupils at seven, 11 and 16, its narrow, muddled and often backward-looking collection of statements about what a language or English curriculum should contain), most people came to the conclusion that the booklet was once again proposing something which had been vigorously debated for the previous 20 years and rejected. This is the tempting idea that, in order to help children get better at using an element of language, they need to be given a set of rules, definitions and distinctions about that element in advance. We can put the tempting idea in a diagram, clearly marked for what it is:

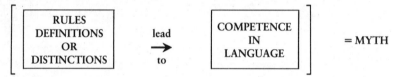

The particular topic of dispute in this part of *English from 5 to 16* and in people's responses to it was, of course, grammar teaching and whether we need to get back to it. Overwhelmingly, those who wrote down their responses to the booklet and sent them in to HMI said: no. When HMI published *English from 5 to 16: the Responses to Curriculum Matters 1* in 1986, they acknowledged the degree of dissent from the original booklet on this and other topics. They suggested that it might be a good idea to have an enquiry, 'with the ultimate object of drawing up recommendations as to what might be taught [about language] to intending teachers, to those in post and to pupils in schools.' (It might have been an even better idea, instead of leaving *English from 5 to 16* and the responses booklet dangling as two contradictory documents for teachers to pay their money and take their choice, to provide a single revised booklet which really did aim to summarise the best recent thinking about what the language and English curriculum should look like. That, after all, was the aim of the series of which *English from 5 to 16* was the first number.)

GOOD IDEA BECOMES COMMITTEE

The reader may be tiring of this ancient history. We will move on quickly. The good idea about an enquiry became the Kingman Committee, which produced its report in March 1988. On the particular question of grammar teaching, it declared:

Nor do we see it as part of our task to plead for a return to old-fashioned grammar teaching and learning by rote. We have been impressed by the evidence we have received that this gave an inadequate account of the English language by treating it virtually as a branch of Latin, and constructing a rigid prescriptive code rather than a dynamic description of language in use. It was also ineffective as a means of developing a command of English in all its manifestations. Equally, at the other extreme, we reject the belief that any notion of correct or incorrect use of language is an affront to personal liberty. We also reject the belief that knowing how to use terminology in which to speak of language is undesirable.

This statement, quoted from chapter 1 of the Kingman Report, was greeted by a large sigh of relief all round, although there was some puzzlement that the Committee had apparently discovered groups of teachers who refused to accept that there was such a thing as an incorrect use of language and never used any terminology in their teaching, and had felt that this tendency was as dangerous as 'old-fashioned grammar teaching and learning by rote'. The report then devotes the whole of chapter 2 to a discussion called 'The importance of knowledge about language'. In fact chapter 2 is not principally about the importance of knowledge about language: it is principally about the importance of language. The chapter says some fine and true things in a general kind of way. For example:

People need expertise in language to be able to participate effectively in a democracy . . .
The acquisition of new and difficult concepts, which is integral to education in any subject, is dependent above all on language . . .
. . . language plays an important role both in exploring and defining responses and feelings and in shaping the kind of people we become.

NOT ENOUGH MAIN VERBS . . . TOO MANY PRONOUNS

Chapter 2 is at its weakest, interestingly enough, when it has to commit itself to examples in the section on 'The teaching of language'. We are introduced to a pupil who 'keeps on omitting main verbs from sentences' and told that the pupil would start including main verbs in sentences if he or she were taught the definition and function of a verb. Another pupil, who makes excessive use of pronouns, would be helped to check this habit if similarly taught the definition and function of a pronoun. These are unfortunate examples. I would be glad to meet a pupil who kept on omitting main verbs from sentences. A pupil who had used a verb incorrectly in a sentence would be helped to spot and overcome that difficulty by being asked to read the sentence back and compare the form of the verb as written with the form which he or she, as an experienced user of the language, knows to be correct. The likely cause of the incorrect usage in the first place is that pressure of production of writing has caused a temporary derailment of the trains of grammatical connection between brain and pen. If the writer, guided by the teacher, becomes a critical reader of his or her writing, he or she will solve the problem quickly enough. Similarly, the user of over-frequent pronouns is a type I have not so far met. Much more common is the opposite case: children who, for a while, make repetitive use of nouns in writing because they are not yet confident of the job that pronouns can do in their place. Here again, the advance abstract knowledge of the definition and function of a pronoun will not help. We shall come back to this example later, with some suggestions about what might help. We should just note here, however, the central point that when children compose texts − when they write − they should concentrate on meaning, not on pronouns.

A LANGUAGE MODEL

The Kingman Report proposed, in chapter 3, a model of the English language. In detail, there is much to criticise in it on the grounds of obscurity, confusion or omission. It would not be especially interesting to the reader to do that here. In the broadest of terms, the model does, to its credit, say that if we are going to talk about language, we must remember that language is more than just forms. Language *is* to do with forms ('verb' and 'pronoun' are ways of talking about two particular kinds of word doing particular jobs in sentences or other groups of linked words) but it is also to do with the ways that speakers and listeners, readers and writers behave towards each other in different contexts; it is also to do with how people acquire and develop a repertoire of competence in language from infancy onwards; it is also to do with the fact that there are variations − of accent and dialect, for example − within any language. We might add that there are variations between languages, important relationships between them, as well as variations within a language. The Kingman Committee was obliged to confine itself to the discussion of English. In fact, the categories it proposes in its model − forms; speaker/listener, reader/writer relationships; acquisition and development; variation − are equally relevant to any language. It would, furthermore, have been good to see multilingualism (a key element, after all, of the language experience of about 70 per cent of the world's population, including many of the children we teach) presented as an integral part of a model of language as a whole.

The dissemination of Kingman's model is, strictly, the purpose for which the government found £15.2 million to be spent by LEAs in England and Wales between 1989 and 1992. Hard on the heels of the Kingman Report, however, has come the National Curriculum for English. It was recognised that any attempt to disseminate a set of ideas about language which failed to notice that teachers' overriding preoccupation at the moment is with the introduction of the National Curriculum would, to put it mildly, have a credibility problem. It is also the case that the Cox Report discusses knowledge about language, in the chapter with that name and also in the chapters on Standard English and on linguistic terminology, and that the Cox Committee has proposed elements of knowledge about language which will be part of the statutory curriculum for English for pupils working at level 5 and above, and has suggested that opportunities for pupils to develop their knowledge about language should be available from the beginning of schooling. So, in addition to the need to discuss teachers' knowledge about language in ways that will seem relevant to teachers amid all their current concerns, we should try to clarify what we mean by pupils' knowledge about language, and see how the two things interact – as of course they must – and what the similarities and differences between them might be. Let us look at some examples of classroom language use to help us do this.

THE DEVELOPMENT OF IMPLICIT KNOWLEDGE

First, let us look at the piece of writing by Leanne, aged six, which appears on page 28.

Next, on page 29 there are the first four pages, in reduced size, of a book produced by a class of infants, called *Would you be Scared?*. (The teacher has written out the text at the children's instruction.)

The most important kind of knowledge about language is implicit knowledge. Language is such a complex network of meanings and symbols, and the knowledge which users of a language share is so detailed and so vast, that the learning brain, engaged from birth on its enormous task, necessarily operates mainly using the powerful levers of unconscious learning. It could only be that way, for life is not long enough for the conscious acquisition of language to the degree that human beings require and employ it. The gear would be too low, the pace too slow. Much mystery still surrounds the exact mechanisms by which the brain experiences language in the world, and remembers, selects, sorts, extrapolates, generalises; in short, how it draws on experience to develop its own competence, and how experience and competence grow together. The most important job for the adults who care for the child is to help the child's implicit knowledge develop. For teachers, this means providing a classroom environment which supports and affirms the child's achievements, while continually proposing

24th march Tuesday   my mummy is
on the 25 of march thats tomore to
today my mummy is going in
to hospidil I will Be loney
with out my mammy. the
BaBy that She is going to
have is going to Be called
Sadie and its going to Be
a girl. we ate all atsitde
Me and My mummy
wanted a girl and my
Dammy wonted a Boy. My
mummy has got a lucky
dip For me and you have
to pick a number betwen
1 and 11 and you get a
paper Bag with a present in

it. And She has Bourt me the
Book of the little prinsess
so that She can read it to
Me So that I dont get
Bord. When She is Born
I will read here a
Story and it mite go like
this. once down a Dark
oark hole in a Dark
hall there lived a
Bager he was gray
on top Black.....

Leanne
Top Infant

activities calling forth greater powers of articulation and understanding. The essential business of the language and English curriculum is, in
fact, to provide opportunities for pupils to compose, communicate and
comprehend meanings, their own and other people's, in purposeful
contexts. Within these contexts, pupils' competence as users of language develops. Pupils' language competence is their implicit knowledge put to work, as in our two examples. Thousands of examples of
implicit knowledge put to work are produced in classrooms every week.
The reader will perhaps, however, have noticed some features about the
examples presented here which can extend our understanding of implicit knowledge. Leanne offers us a story within a story. At the point when

the *she* of her own story changes from a reference to her mummy to a reference to her expected sister (would lessons on pronouns help at this point?) she decides to draw on an event in her own reading, with the proper sense that what has been good for her is likely to be good for Sadie. Of course, simply to repeat *Funnybones* word for word would lack ingenuity (or perhaps frighten one so young) so Sadie is to hear of badgers down holes instead of skeletons in cellars. Leanne's pleasure in reading or hearing *Funnybones* is finding a practical application in her writing. The application 'shows', in a way that we find charming. Older writers learn how to cover their tracks.

Would you be Scared? has its origin in a genre of children's book which, starting from a simple but large question (as here) or statement ('If I could have my favourite wish I would . . .', 'I'm happy/unhappy when I . . .'), branches out into many possibilities. The children who produced this book have encountered some of this genre. In producing

their own book, they have realised or furthered their understanding that:

◇ books are 'made' by authors engaged in a common pursuit. There is nothing essential that divides the children from the authors of commercially published and widely distributed books;

◇ authors borrow ideas from each other and work within conventions which they find effective;

◇ texts and images need each other;

◇ the world is multilingual, and many languages have highly developed written forms, greatly different from each other;

◇ different languages can do a similar job equally well.

In other words, the book, whose primary purpose is to tell truths and explore fantasies in an entertaining way, and which is first and foremost another example of implicit knowledge put to work, causes us to imagine a whole collection of conversations where implicit knowledge was advanced by moments of explicit comparison and reflection.

COMPETENCE AND REFLECTION

We can explore further the relationship between competence and reflection, looking at ways in which children's language use is helped forward by reflection, in some more examples.

Fiona and Neil, two reception-class children in a Shropshire school, have already appeared in *Responding to and Assessing Writing*, one of the collections of the work of the National Writing Project (published by Thomas Nelson, 1989). Quoted here is an account of a series of dialogues between them.

> *Fiona and Neil were invited by their teacher, Sheila Hughes, to help each other to write, once a week. Fiona wrote herself and Neil dictated to the teacher. Fiona and Neil also produced pictures to accompany the text. Each week they exchanged their writing, read each other's work, and made comments which the teacher wrote underneath. These are some extracts.*

Week 1

Fiona wrote: 'I like black because I had a toy black dog and I have always wanted a real life black dog.'

Neil commented: 'She could have made it better if she'd put legs on the dog.'

Neil wrote: 'I like yellow wallpaper and I am going to ask my dad if I can have some.'

Fiona commented: 'He should have put "wallpaper" at the end of his story.'

Week 2

Fiona wrote:	'Red makes my Mummy happy. She has a red Renault 5 car and there is a lot of room in the boot.'
Neil commented:	'She should have put spokes on the wheels and two lights front and back.'
Neil wrote:	'This is a red lorry and I like it.'
Fiona commented:	'He should have said where the lorry was going and why he liked it.'

The teacher was, at first, a little discouraged. The children seemed rather negative in their comments and Neil seemed to be concerned only with the drawing. However, they were revealing considerable knowledge about the needs of text and drawings, and they wanted to continue. After six weeks observable changes had occurred.

Week 6

Fiona wrote:	'The bear is trying to get some honey out of a tree. He looks very cuddly but really he is dangerous.'
Neil commented:	'Draw a bigger tree. It is a good story.'
Neil wrote:	'My teddy bear is sitting by a tree thinking about doing something naughty.'
Fiona commented:	'Ears and paws on the bear. I would like to know what naughty things this bear was going to do.'

Flickering into life (stronger so far in Fiona – the more advanced writer – than in Neil) is a critical awareness of a writer's responsibilities and choices. The children are interchanging, productively, the roles of writer and reader. Reflection of this kind on writing, if sustained throughout a writer's development, will significantly help that development; the eye of the reader informing the voice of the writer.

CINDERELLA AND THE FIVE VERSIONS

A year 6 class consider *Cinderella*, in several versions. It is part of a sequence of work in which the class is studying 'stories as travellers'. The teacher hopes to bring about an understanding that we have a rich variety of story from different times and cultures, and that there are links between versions of the same story told or read across the world. She also wishes pupils to re-write, re-tell and dramatise some of the stories used. On several occasions during the work, the teacher wants pupils to focus on the structure, themes and conventions of fables and folk-tales: an aspect of knowledge about texts. *Cinderella* provides one of these occasions.

The class is shown a drawing, taken from a book of folk-tales, of a young Chinese woman, dressed in traditional clothes, putting on a slipper. Pupils are asked what the drawing reminds them of. After some discussion, a pupil offers 'Cinderella'. The class discusses their surprise that Cinderella is presented as Chinese.

The teacher divides the class into four groups. She gives each group one of four other drawings, all of which, in different ways and using different cultural references, suggest Cinderella. The teacher asks each group to invent a story from the drawing, making notes if they wish. When they have done this, each group tells their story to the whole class. The class discusses similarities and differences between them. The teacher guides discussion towards the consideration of structure, themes and conventions in the groups' stories. She brings the children's attention back to the drawings. What influence did they have on the stories invented? What cues and clues did they contain?

The teacher gives each group tapes and scripts of the story of which the drawing they received was an illustration. For the first time, she tells the children directly that they are looking at versions of the story of Cinderella of which there are hundreds across the world. Each group listens to and reads their story. The teacher hands out a sheet on which each group is to write answers to six key questions about their story: 'Who is the main character?' 'Who is bad?' 'What is the big problem?' 'Who helps with the problem?' 'How many times does a similar thing happen?' 'How does the story end?' Groups study their scripts and discuss the answers.

Groups give their answers to the whole class. Answers for the four versions are combined on a large sheet. The class discusses similarities and differences. The teacher builds on the previous consideration of structure, themes and conventions. Naturally, she uses terminology as she does so.

Groups go back to their invented stories and complete a written version of them as prose or dramatic narrative, for presentation to the class. In fact, all the groups choose dramatic portrayals using puppets. Pupils take photographs of the portrayals. The groups' scripts and illustrations will be published together with the four illustrated versions of *Cinderella* which groups have studied and the Chinese version with its illustration, as a short anthology. The teacher reads to the class the Chinese version of *Cinderella* from which the original drawing was taken.

The teacher makes careful choices about the composition of groups. She has decided on single-sex groups, two of boys and two of girls, because she thinks this might produce more vigorous discussion about the roles of men and women in the four versions (which she has selected to be somewhat different in this respect). The groups contain a range of personalities and degrees of attainment in reading and writing. The teacher expects that the more successful readers and writers in the groups will support the less successful, particularly in coping with some quite demanding language in the versions of *Cinderella*. The tapes will help here too. The teacher has a long-term plan that every pupil will work with every other pupil on a significant sequence of activity at least once in the year.

The teacher intends to devote around six hours to the work on *Cinderella*. This is about a quarter of the time the class will spend on 'stories as travellers' as a whole. The complete work will be spread over four weeks in the primary school. (If the work were being done by a year 7 class in a secondary school, for example, it would be spread over a seven-week half term.)

The class contains nine children who are bilingual in English and in one of two Asian languages. The teacher makes sure that there are at least two of these pupils, speaking the same home language, in each group. The class understands that the teacher is interested in children's knowledge of story and their abilities as tellers, whatever cultural and language background they have to draw on. She expects that bilingual pupils will sometimes use their home language in conversation with each other, and is prepared for the possibility that there will be bilingual elements (perhaps some dual-language text or a bilingual character) in some of the presentations.

There are fables and folk-tales in the class library as background for the work, and to take pupils' interest further. Pupils need equipment for writing, illustrating, and making puppets. There is a small collection of costumes and props. Furniture in the class can be moved to allow for performance. There is a computer available for word processing.

At the end of the work on 'stories as travellers', the teacher discusses with the children what they have enjoyed most in the work, what they would like to do again soon, which parts they found difficult, which groupings they found productive or otherwise.

In discussion with a colleague, she considers how the work might be adapted and improved in a future year. A broader range of versions and smaller groups? More demanding questions on structure, theme and conventions (the pupils found the answers to the six provided rather obvious)? A decision to introduce a film version of *Cinderella* as an extra element of the work? An offer to involve the colleague's class as an audience for the presentations?

We can see clearly here, amid a wide variety of language activities, children reflecting on texts. Their knowledge of structure and convention, of similarity and difference, in a certain kind of text, not to mention their understanding of the social and moral assumptions made or questions raised in the different versions, are likely to be enhanced by what they have done. Reflection will help them forward as readers (and quite possibly as writers, speakers and listeners too.) But, to go back to our myth equation on page 24), how inappropriate it would have been to teach children the 'rules' of the genre in advance, as if they would not know how to read the stories without them. No better than giving Leanne lessons in the 'rules' of the pronoun.

EVACUEES ON BEST BEHAVIOUR

One more example of the relationship between doing and reflecting. A group of 60 pupils, with two teachers plus a visitor working together, is considering the wartime evacuation of children as part of a sequence of work on the second world war. The children divide into groups of four. Two take on the role of evacuee 'parents' and two the role of evacuated children. The scene for their improvisation is the railway station in a small Welsh village where 'parents' and children meet for the first time. The groups work on this for 15 minutes, while the teachers move round, listening, helping when asked and noting down observations. Then some of the groups perform their improvisations.

At this point, the teachers ask the children how they felt in role. The children give general answers: 'all right', 'good', 'fine'. Up to now, they have not had any experience of reflecting on their role-play. The teachers want to prompt the children to be more specific in their reflection. The visitor role-plays being a child at home talking with a friend or sibling. The children agree that the teacher's speech style was authentic for that situation. The teacher then mimics the careful, precise speech used by the children in role as evacuees. The children are asked why they spoke in that way. Now they reply: 'for politeness', 'to show that we had good behaviour', 'so that they (the new 'parents') would choose and accept us', 'to make a good impression'. The teachers point out to the children how easily they slid from an everyday speech style to more formal language use when they were in role.

As a result of this activity, which depends, it will be noticed, on a crucial and exposed piece of adult intervention in role, children's understanding of an aspect of the way speech varies according to situation is very likely to develop. Both the teachers and I, however, would hesitate to claim that the activity would certainly produce, in any direct sense, children who varied their own speech according to situation more appropriately and skilfully. It might; but even if it did, that was not the main purpose of the activity, which was to enhance the children's understanding of an important aspect of human language behaviour (and to teach persuasively about evacuees).

So, in discussing the relationship between competence and reflection, we need first to reverse the equation on page 24, and then to introduce a degree of variation and honest doubt. The nature of the relationship depends on the language activity in which learners are engaged and upon the stage of development which individuals have reached. For example, a pre-school child learning to talk is acquiring and demonstrating large amounts of implicit knowledge, but there would be no point in engaging the child in reflection on the psycholinguistic processes involved. But the same young child, introduced to picture books, will immediately be reflecting on the organisation of words and images there. Meanwhile, older pupils reading poetry are likely to benefit as future readers of poetry if the teacher provides opportunities for reflection on the structure, content and background of the poems being studied, and on the particular characteristics of poetic language.

Figure 1.1 attempts to visualise the relationship between competence and reflection.

TERMINOLOGY AND UNDERSTANDING

The reader will notice the phrase 'appropriate use of terminology' on the diagram. There has been much misunderstanding of this issue and false accusation of teachers on the subject. It has been suggested that teachers are afraid to call a spade a spade (a metaphor a metaphor, speech marks speech marks) because they have some hypersensitivity about pupils' ability to make sense of technical terms or, worse, because they don't know what such things are any more. (Once upon a time they did, of course.) I presume that no reader of this article is afraid, in principle, of the word *word* (a metalinguistic category which, at an early point in their language development, children have to come to understand) or *sentence* (though to use the term *sentence* in purposeful

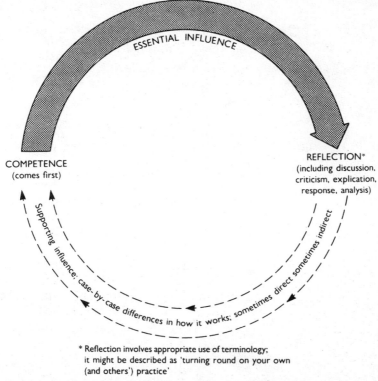

Figure 1.1 The relationship between competence and reflection

discussions with pupils is a very different thing from defining in an abstract way that thing which comes between a capital letter and a full stop) or *story* or *play* or *character* or *chapter* or *rhyme* or *text* or *image*. The central principle that should guide teachers in their decisions as to the use of terminology with pupils is that the introduction of terminology must be based on some prior conceptual understanding of what the terminology refers to.

I promised to return to the case of the writer who is in a phase where he or she makes repetitive use of nouns when pronouns could help out (the opposite condition, it will be remembered, to that which Kingman purports to have discovered). I choose this example for closer attention because sentence grammar is one of the areas of language and metalanguage (that is, language about language) in learning which has been most fought over in recent decades; because top-level disagreement over this small (in relation to the major concerns of the language and English curriculum) but highly charged area is the main reason why the project of which this publication is a part exists; and because a provision in the Programme of Study for Writing at Key Stage 1 unrealistically requires teachers to teach pupils 'grammatical terms such as . . . pronoun' (admittedly 'in the context of discussion about their own writing') by the age of seven. We noticed in passing Leanne's immature use of *she* which does not acknowledge that a new person is being referred to (hardly an example of 'scattering words such as *she . . .* throughout a text', to quote Kingman). I would challenge anyone to insist that, even if the teacher decided that it would be appropriate to draw Leanne's attention to this usage, the introduction of the term *pronoun* itself would help this confident six-year-old writer. But let us take a somewhat older writer, and see how a teacher, in discussion with the writer, might proceed.

Let us say that teacher and pupil are discussing a draft of a piece of personal writing about the writer's family. There has already been some conversation about the content and organisation of this piece – about what it is telling the reader. The teacher then says: 'You see where you've put *my aunty* all these times here . . . three, four times? Can you think of another word to put instead of some of the later ones, to make it less repetitive?' At this point, the pupil will respond in one of two ways. In the one case, he or she will say: 'I could put in *she*', in which case the teacher knows that the child understands implicitly the function of a pronoun in writing in those places in the text, and suggests that the child should put some in where they would help. The teacher also remarks: 'Words like *she* are pronouns. They stand in for words or phrases (like *my aunty*) which they refer to.' In the other case, the child will not make sense of the teacher's question, because it is pitched conceptually too far in advance of the child's current stage of development as a writer. In that case, the teacher's best professional judgement is a decision *to do nothing*. The child needs more experience of writing and of reading. In the first case the teacher did discover a piece of implicit knowledge which he or she was able to help the child turn into an explicit operation on the text. But even in that case, the teacher made an important distinction between helping the child to see the need to put in *she* (the first priority) and teaching the term *pronoun* (the second priority). The analytical statement about pronouns had a chance of making sense; interestingly, its principal use in the future will be to the child as a talker about texts, as a reader (the texts will, certainly, include some of the child's own writing) rather than directly to the child as a composer of texts, a writer. The learning of terminology from one mode of language often proves most useful to the learner in another mode.

All areas of the language and English curriculum carry terminology, of course; it is not confined to grammar, nor to writing conventions nor to literary terms. There is no need for teachers to be intimidated by terminology, as long as they are satisfied that it will help pupils to reflect more effectively on language in use. We could set the terms we have used so far within a potentially endless list: *word, sentence, speech mark, metaphor, text, noun, pronoun, genre, paragraph, intonation, accent, alphabet, improvise, role, fiction, database, script, caption, camera angle*; an assortment of terms, some little and some large, all signifying important concepts or referring to potentially valid activities in the language curriculum. The Cox Report sensibly resisted pressure to insist on a roll-call of terms that pupils must have been introduced to during particular Key Stages (with a few exceptions such as the grammatical terms for Writing at Key Stage 1). If we ask ourselves, when in doubt, 'Will this piece of terminology serve meaning?', that will help us in the fine judgements we have to make.

KNOWLEDGE ABOUT LANGUAGE AND LANGUAGE STUDY

The Cox Report recommended: 'Knowledge about language should be an integral part of work in English, not a separate body of knowledge to be added on to the traditional English curriculum' (*English for ages 5 to 16*, 6:2). This means that opportunities for the development of knowledge about language should be found throughout the whole language and English curriculum: speaking and listening, reading, writing, drama, media education and information technology. Such opportunities exist laterally across this range for children of a particular age. They also exist vertically, 'from play activities in pre-school to explicit systematic knowledge in upper secondary education' (ibid., 6:16). In addition to all these opportunities (of which we have already looked at several examples), where children's knowledge about language is being developed, as it were, in the course of other enquiries, the Cox Report said that there ought to be occasions on which children study aspects of language itself, in its own right. Certainly, the requirement in the Programme of Study for Speaking and Listening at Key Stage 2 that pupils should discuss vocabulary specific to local communities, local usages, particular age groups and certain occupations will probably best be met satisfactorily by the teacher devoting a series of lessons to that topic, although the requirement is likely also to be met to an extent in the course of pupils' wider learning. The same would be true of the requirement in the Programme of Study for Reading at Key Stage 4 that 'Pupils should consider not only the extent to which English has changed from the earliest written records, but also ways in which it is changing now.'

Requirements like these are the legal minimum of what might constitute language study: formally, they apply only to pupils working at levels 5 to 10. It would be useful to have some headings for language study, including but not confined to the legal minimum, of potential use throughout all the Key Stages. Suppose we settled on:

◇ variety in and between languages;
◇ history of languages;
◇ language and power in society;
◇ acquisition and development of language;
◇ language as a system shared by its users.

This list corresponds closely with the Cox Report's discussion of language study in paragraphs 6:6–6:18, and could fully exemplify the principles laid out in paragraph 6:18:

> *Language is a system of sounds, meanings and structures with which we make sense of the world around us. It functions as a tool of thought; as a means of social organisation; as the repository and means of transmission of knowledge; as the raw material of literature, and as the creator and sustainer – or destroyer – of human relationships. It changes inevitably over time and, as change is not uniform, from place to place. Because language is a fundamental part of being human, it is an important aspect of a person's sense of self; because it is a fundamental feature of any community, it is an important aspect of a person's sense of social identity.*

Interestingly, our five headings closely resemble Kingman's four headings for teachers' knowledge about language. We have given 'history of languages' a category of its own; 'language and power in society' would take speaker/listener, reader/writer relationships and put them in a broader context, including consideration of mass uses of language; 'language as a system shared by its users' is a bigger and better way of talking about forms. It goes without saying that all these headings overlap, and that their realisation in the curriculum would be through actual examples and experiences of language in use, not through their presentation *as* categories.

Let us look at two sequences of work which have an aspect of language itself as their organising principle.

LANGUAGE TO PERSUADE

A teacher of upper-secondary pupils is considering with a class a wide range of texts, written, oral and visual, whose common purpose is to persuade a reader, listener or viewer to accept a certain point of view or adopt a certain course of action. He or she will use authentic texts from the past as well as the present, and will ask the pupils to produce their own persuasive texts as well as consider other people's.

The teacher shows the class the following texts: a party political broadcast on television, an advertisement on television for a modern consumer product, a group of didactic poems, songs or ballads on a particular theme, a wartime propaganda poster, a letter to a newspaper strongly stating a point of view, a tape of a lawyer's summing-up speech in court, an opinion article in a newspaper. In groups, pupils consider the texts, with an instruction from the teacher along these lines:

> *All these texts are out to persuade someone to do or think something. How successful do you think each of them is? What techniques (of language, image and sound) does each employ? Using these to start you off, make a list of all the examples you can think of where language, images or sounds (often working in combination) are used to persuade. Who is the persuasion aimed at (it could be anyone; it could be one person only, with various particular groups in between) and what was the person or group being urged to think or do?*

When the groups of pupils have produced their lists, these are pooled in the whole class. The teacher suggests ordering the lists according to four categories: what kind of text? what use of language, image, sound? aimed at whom? persuading them to do or think what? By the end of this session, pupils have some sense of the variety of kinds of persuasive text in the world, and of their techniques, audiences and purposes.

The teacher has four small collections of texts which exemplify each of the four categories. In other words, he or she could, for example, have a collection of posters promoting good causes (kind of text), or of texts where music is used in combination with words to build up a rhetorical effect, or of texts aimed at young adults, or of texts urging a group to demonstrate their discrimination and independence by buying certain products. Each group takes one of these collections, examines each of the texts closely, discussing similarities and differences, using the questions which are relevant from the first group activity, and also asking the question: 'What do we think of the intentions of the producers of these texts? Is the language – and images and sound where appropriate – being used for a purpose we admire?' The outcome of this discussion could be a piece of writing, produced individually or collectively (in the second case, the group would decide on particular sections for individuals to write).

As a final activity, groups produce their own persuasive text(s). The teacher encourages a variety of forms (video, leaflets, posters, live simulation, audiotape for radio transmission, newspaper advertisements, campaign magazines) and a variety of specific intentions (to sell, to request financial and other support for a cause, to promote a political party or pressure group, to debate an issue of contention). Building on the invitation in the previous activity to groups to make judgements on producers' intentions, the teacher suggests as an option some kind of campaign of opposition to persuasive texts groups have considered whose intentions they disapprove of and wish to challenge.

ALPHABETS AND PICTURE-WRITING

Our second example takes us to a middle infant class where the children are making alphabet friezes. Three languages (all with alphabetic scripts) are represented in the class, so the teacher suggests to the children that there should be three friezes. These are designed with the help of alphabet books for each of the languages, and advice from parents of children with home languages other than English. While the friezes are being made, there is discussion of the names of the letters in each alphabet. By the end of the activity, everyone is familiar with the English alphabet, the bilingual children have reinforced their existing knowledge of two alphabets, and all the children, monolingual and bilingual, have some knowledge of the alphabets of languages which they do not speak.

A way of extending this work with the children perhaps a year later would be to introduce the idea that, when languages were first written down, there were no alphabets; people used pictures. The teacher shows the class three sets of pictures (in fact, some early pictographs for Chinese, Egyptian and Sumerian). The pictures are on cards. Each group takes a set of cards, and is asked to construct a story or a message using them; the children can invent their own pictures to add to those they have received. Groups then tell their story or message to the class, holding up their cards as they do so. Finally, the teacher shows the class how the pictographs for the three languages changed over the centuries, until they became unrecognisable as representations of the thing they referred to. The class sees how some of the Egyptian symbols became letters of the alphabet which English and other languages now use; the children also look at some modern Chinese characters and their meanings.

KNOWLEDGE ABOUT LANGUAGE IN THE WHOLE CURRICULUM

In this article, we have considered pupils' implicit knowledge of language, their reflection on language use (their own and other people's) and the study of language itself. Figure 1.2 attempts to relate these three things within a whole language curriculum. It is not of course, 'to scale' as an indication of the amounts of time which might be spent on each of its elements; and it should not be forgotten that the development of competence and implicit knowledge remains the fundamental purpose of the language and English curriculum. The area of greatest overlap in the middle of the diagram is not, by that token, the most important thing in the curriculum.

Four notes on the diagram:

1   The shaded areas in the diagram will often involve use of appropriate linguistic terminology.
2   The areas of reflective learning will also provide significant opportunities to teachers and pupils for assessing pupils' developing language competence; identifying their achievements and needs.

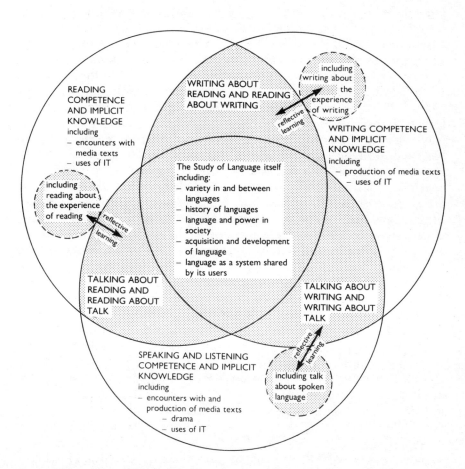

Figure 1.2 Knowledge about language in the whole curriculum

3 The Knowledge about Language requirements of Programmes of Study in English all fall within the shaded areas: the areas of reflective learning and the area of language study. The diagram also relates these requirements to the wider elements of the English curriculum as identified in Programmes of Study.

4 The inclusion of drama, media texts and information technology within speaking and listening, reading and writing is intended to suggest the broadest definition of these language modes. The diagram does not mean to suggest, however, that drama, media texts and information technology can be confined within the modal categories. For example, drama is of course more than speaking and listening (and sometimes, as in mime, something other than speaking and listening).

PUPILS AND TEACHERS: THE CLASSROOM AND THE WORLD

Finally, let us try to summarise the relationship between *pupils'* and *teachers'* knowledge about language. Teachers, like pupils, already have much valuable knowledge about language derived from their experience as human beings in the world. There is no hard line dividing teachers' 'human' knowledge from their 'professional' knowledge, any more than it is possible to divide pupils' classroom language development from their experience of language in the world. Moreover, teachers' knowledge cannot simply be communicated in transmissive ways. A large part of the knowledge about language teachers should have will be realised, first, in the creation of *contexts* in which the pupils' implicit knowledge, that is, their competence, is enabled to develop. A second role for teachers' knowledge about language is in their *interventions* in language use with pupils in order to give advice, offer formative assessment, suggest lines of further development. The effectiveness of these interventions, as we have seen, will depend on teachers' sensitivity and skill in applying this kind of knowledge about language, including their understanding of when to deploy information and when not. Thirdly, there will be some aspects of teachers' knowledge about language which will form appropriate and interesting *content* for pupils' learning; in language as in any other area of knowledge, the teacher's own enthusiasm for the topic is likely to generate enthusiasm among pupils. Contexts for and content of knowledge about language may sometimes be linked, as for example when a class which contains users of a diversity of languages and dialects is given the opportunity to explore that diversity and relate it to information about language variety in modern Britain.

The three categories of teachers' knowledge about language proposed here make a close match, it will be noticed, with the categories of pupils' knowledge about language presented in Figure 1.2. However, it would be wrong to insist that they are simply a replica for teachers of pupils' knowledge about language, or are always realised in identical ways. They involve a degree of worked-out understanding which is, at least potentially, explicit; the teacher can, if necessary, explain why he or she has acted in a particular way. Teachers' knowledge about language is, in fact, their working theory of language in learning. It should continually develop in interactions with pupils' knowledge about language. These interactions in the classroom depend on teachers' and pupils' human experience – joint or distinct – of language in the world.

We have described four sets of relationships which, between them, make up knowledge about language. These are the relationships between:

◇ pupils' implicit knowledge, reflection on language use and language study;
◇ teachers' knowledge of how to provide contexts for language development, their knowledge of how and when to intervene in and respond to language use, and those aspects of their knowledge which could be used as content in the curriculum;
◇ pupils' and teachers' knowledge;
◇ pupils' and teachers' language use in the classroom and their experience of language in the world outside.

Figure 1.3 (on page 44) attempts to visualise these relationships interacting in a classroom where pupils and teachers compose, comprehend and communicate meanings in purposeful contexts, drawing on their experience of language in the world.

ACKNOWLEDGMENTS

I thank the following people for their contributions to this article. Susie Rosenberg was Leanne's teacher at Newington Green Primary School, ILEA. Richard Ray provided me with the example of her writing. Sarah Kingham taught the class which produced *Would you be Scared?* at Bounds Green Infants' School, Haringey. Ned Ratcliffe was co-ordinator of the National Writing Project in Shropshire, and encouraged Sheila Hughes, Fiona's and Neil's teacher, to encourage the children to collaborate on their writing. Helen Savva designed the 'stories as travellers' sequence, including the work on *Cinderella*, and used it with a class at John Wilkinson School, Broseley, Shropshire, whose teacher was Marlena Hotchkiss. Caroline Bishop and Shirley Whitehand taught the class at Scargill Junior School, Havering, who were role-playing evacuation. Maureen Harriott, advisory teacher in Havering, was the visitor, and wrote the description of the work. Figure 1.2 is principally the work of Margaret Wallen, advisory teacher in Dorset, who designed its original version. Several sections of the text and the revision of Figure 1.2 are the result of my collaboration with George Keith in writing non-statutory guidance on knowledge about language. Rebecca Bunting and Ron Carter contributed to the design of Figure 1.3.

INTERACTIONS BETWEEN PUPILS' AND TEACHERS' KNOWLEDGE
ABOUT LANGUAGE IN THE CLASSROOM DEPEND ON AND DERIVE FROM
THEIR EXPERIENCE (JOINT OR DISTINCT) OF LANGUAGE IN THE WORLD

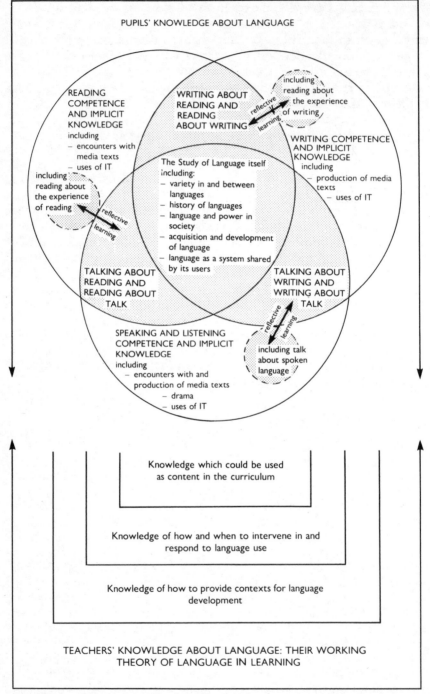

PUPILS' KNOWLEDGE ABOUT LANGUAGE

including
reading about
the experience
of writing

READING
COMPETENCE
AND IMPLICIT
KNOWLEDGE
including
– encounters with
  media texts
– uses of IT

WRITING ABOUT
READING AND
READING
ABOUT WRITING

reflective
learning

WRITING COMPETENCE
AND IMPLICIT
KNOWLEDGE
including
– production of media
  texts
– uses of IT

including
reading about
the experience
of reading

reflective
learning

The Study of Language itself
including:
– variety in and between
  languages
– history of languages
– language and power in
  society
– acquisition and development
  of language
– language as a system shared
  by its users

TALKING ABOUT
READING AND
READING ABOUT
TALK

TALKING ABOUT
WRITING AND
WRITING ABOUT
TALK

reflective
learning

SPEAKING AND LISTENING
COMPETENCE AND IMPLICIT
KNOWLEDGE
including
– encounters with and
  production of media texts
– drama
– uses of IT

including talk
about spoken
language

Knowledge which could be used
as content in the curriculum

Knowledge of how and when to intervene in and
respond to language use

Knowledge of how to provide contexts for language
development

TEACHERS' KNOWLEDGE ABOUT LANGUAGE: THEIR WORKING
THEORY OF LANGUAGE IN LEARNING

Figure 1.3 Interaction of pupils' and teachers' knowledge about
language in the classroom

2

Magic Words: Helping Young Children to Develop their Knowledge about Language

ALISON SEALEY ⸺⸺⸺⸺⸺⸺⸺⸺⸺⸺⸺⸺⸺⸺◇

A few weeks before his fifth birthday, my son asked me, 'Why do people say "Say the magic word," when it isn't "abracadabra" or anything like that? It's just "please?" Why do they?'

Like other children, my son responds to the phenomena he sees and experiences with questions, striving to make meaning of his complex, diverse, exciting world. Of course, the system he uses for engaging in communication about his experience is nearly always language. Those who witness young children's acquisition of language, with all its rules and exceptions, its variety and subtlety, cannot fail to wonder at their capacity to master this complex system.

We know that the basics of the system are acquired without formal tuition in grammar or graded vocabulary exercises. Children learn language, as Wells (1986) puts it:

> because they are predisposed to do so. How they set about the
> task is largely determined by the way they are: seekers after
> meaning who try to find the underlying principles that will
> account for the patterns that they recognise in their experiences.

Our knowledge that this is the case presents us, as teachers, with something of a dilemma. On the one hand, we are well-advised not to try to impose upon young children explicit teaching about language as a means of developing their competence. '. . . Advance abstract knowledge of the definition and function of [parts of speech such as] a pronoun will not help', as Richmond (1990) observes. 'The most important kind of knowledge about language is implicit knowledge' and 'the most important job for the adults who care for the child is to help the child's implicit knowledge develop'.

But, on the other hand, what are we to do when what the child is striving to understand is language itself, as in the example noted above? When children themselves initiate discussion about language, should we not encourage their inquisitiveness? Or is *any* explicit discussion about language necessarily so abstract and inappropriate that it can only work against the child's meaning-making process?

My own view is that there are good reasons for – and acceptable ways of – building on the inquisitive interest in language itself which even very young children exhibit. Teachers *can* help in the development of children's knowledge about language, so long as they are clear about appropriate goals and methods. This paper is an attempt to explore some of these issues.

A FRAMEWORK FOR CONSIDERING KNOWLEDGE ABOUT LANGUAGE

Because language is such an integral part of human interaction, it is difficult to summarise what 'knowledge about' it would comprise. However, there are perhaps some broad and general features of language itself which can suggest a framework into which specific examples of knowledge about language may fit.

One basic concept is that at the heart of language is meaning. Children need to develop an understanding that the very purpose of language is to convey meaning. The awareness they have from all the experience as communicators which they bring to the classroom – that language is primarily meaningful – should be enhanced and not contradicted by what happens in school. Moreover, those meanings are created and communicated by people – they are socially constructed, negotiated through human interactions. The use of language is an aspect of human behaviour.

Secondly, children's earliest experience helps to lay the foundations for the concept that language is systematic and not arbitrary. Children need to realise that language could not carry the burden of its meanings if it did not operate through its various rule-governed systems, and young children do indeed absorb many aspects of the 'rules' of their mother tongue even as they learn to talk. They may inadvertently amuse adults sometimes by over-applying such rules: 'I cutted it out' or 'I am being baby-sitted' – and they will sometimes comment explicitly on self-corrections. For example, Garton and Pratt (1989) describe a two-year-old naming parts of her body, and stopping to 'correct' herself as she used an irregular plural: 'Two footsies – no, two feetsies, *I mean*'. Unfortunately, in schools, teaching which has a rather narrow focus on language systems (such as 'grammar' or 'phonics') often without a meaningful context, may fail to contribute usefully to language in action. For one thing, such approaches to language teaching may inhibit the development of the concept of choice and diversity in language use. After all, one of the things which gives language its dynamic quality is the way in which its users deliberately break its rules in order to convey meaning in the way which they feel is most apt. Speakers can increase the impact or the humour of their utterances by flouting linguistic conventions, while writers may do so as they create poetry – or advertising slogans.

A third principal idea is that language is not monolithic, and varies enormously in accordance with a large number of factors, including purpose and function, context, place and time. Children may display an implicit awareness of some of these variations from a very early age. For example, they make use of choices from among the varieties to which they have access, as variables such as context (to which even young children, of course, are subject) demand. The range of language styles with which children will experiment may be observed as they act out any number of roles and situations in their imaginative play at home, nursery or school. And sometimes they comment explicitly on linguistic variation: 'Why did Grandma call my dress a "frock"?'; 'Rajbinder speaks a different language as well'.

A RATIONALE FOR DEVELOPING YOUNG CHILDREN'S KNOWLEDGE ABOUT LANGUAGE

When my son was struggling, in the example given at the beginning of this paper, to understand the connection between 'abracadabra' and 'please', he was, as we all do, taking for granted that some knowledge about language was shared between us. We both knew that some words really are magic, used by those who make spells and who 'magic things into' other things – or at least we both pretend that these people and events are real, if magical! But where does 'please' fit in with all that? As is the case with many of the naive and serious questions posed by young children, it was not easy to find a satisfactory answer. As I searched for one, thoughts were going through my mind along the following lines: 'Well, son, it only fits in at all if you subscribe to certain cultural conventions, and if you believe certain things about how children should view their relationships with adults, and one thing you have to realise is that different people think different things . . .'

In that sense, the question he had asked arose from a crucial aspect of language in use. As soon as we use language as our system for communicating, we become susceptible to some of its features, sometimes finding ourselves accepting the nuances and connotations of particular words, for example, without necessarily choosing those meanings, consciously, for ourselves.

Thus, when a child's individual experience of the world to date fails somehow to correspond with the notion that 'please' can really be a magic word, and he chooses to comment on that mismatch, he is initiating explicit discussion about language as part of his meaning-making. To encourage such reflection about language is part of meeting children's needs. And there will be thousands of instances like this throughout a child's life in primary school, let alone during the secondary years.

Children are entitled to opportunities for exploring the phenomenon of language and how it is used, because otherwise 'legitimised and naturalised orders of discourse [are] presented as legitimate and natural' (Fairclough, 1989). In other words, if children are not encouraged to reflect on *how* language is made to mean what it *is* being made to mean, they may come to believe that this 'element of their humanly produced and humanly changeable social environment [is] a part of their natural environment over which they have no control'. One of the first steps in learning how to control language (and thus to increase one's competence via that route) must surely be to develop an awareness that such control is possible.

In case this theoretical perspective is beginning to sound too far removed from the world of young children, let me quote another example from my own son, before considering some possibilities for the classroom.

As a child who has developed a suspicion of food which may contain unfamiliar flavours, my son decided early on to avoid anything which might be 'spicy'. One day, as I set his dinner on the table, his first reaction was, 'Is it spicy?' I replied, 'Not very spicy, no'. Just like children of this age who know quite well that 'We'll see' usually means 'No, but I'm not going to say "no" right out because I don't want an argument', my son spotted my linguistic sleight of hand. ' "Not very," ' he observed, 'means it is.' At four, he knew enough about language to be aware that it can be used to conceal, as well as to convey, meaning. Furthermore, he was by then quite capable of putting such awareness into words, in his own way.

Made explicit, by comments such as these, aspects of language and the uses to which people put it can be scrutinised. If they are never discussed, this sort of awareness of language may remain undeveloped, along with the potential for children to gain greater control over it for themselves. This view is consistent with a pedagogical approach which emphasises the potential for empowering children as learners. Such concepts form the basis of the rationale which I would offer for providing opportunities for children to explore aspects of language, at an explicit level, from the pre-school years onwards. How is this to be done in the primary classroom? Many exciting developments, often stimulated by the LINC project, are taking place around the country, and there is still much to learn. In considering some specific possibilities open to primary teachers, there are several points which might inform their plans.

RELEVANCE TO THE CHILDREN'S NEEDS AND INTERESTS

It seems highly probable that the most successful contexts for developing children's awareness of various aspects of language will be ones in which the children have a real involvement.

For example, young bilingual children have considerable personal experience on which to build their knowledge about language, and attitudes to school and learning may be affected by the school's attitude to their language, underlining the correlation between language and identity. A different dimension to such issues arises when children in an infant school express a genuine belief that the word 'Pakistani' is a swear word, shocked to hear it on the lips of a teacher. Then, it is important to explore some other aspects of what children need to know about language. The way in which this is done would depend on the specifics of the situation, but a discussion might touch on, at an appropriate level: how people may mean different things by what they say; how the meanings of words may change according to the context in which they are used; the power of words both to hurt others and to express pride, and so on.

Other occasions for teaching about language will arise from the fact that almost any aspect of the curriculum itself is learned about – at least in part – by means of language. Thus many everyday classroom experiences can provide opportunities for the development of knowledge about language.

For example, suppose that some children of lower junior school age are working in groups on a science investigation, and that in several of the groups certain children are playing very little active part in the discussions (a not uncommon scenario). The teacher may well feel that this situation is denying the children equal opportunities for participating in learning from the science curriculum. She might therefore decide to initiate some explicit consideration with all the children of the dynamics of small-group talk, including, for instance, tendencies for certain children to dominate. Since it would be very important to establish a climate in which none of the children will feel criticised or undervalued, she might start by asking the children to reflect on the different types of positive contribution which different individuals bring to science group-work. Following this, if the teacher creates an opportunity to share explicitly some perceptions about what makes for successful collaboration, this might be the first time some of the dominant children have ever realised how behaviour such as theirs affects the more reticent members of the group. Taking an investigative approach, the children might use prompt-sheets and notes (if not audio- or video-recorders) to observe closely the ways in which groups tackle shared tasks in science lessons. They might be encouraged to explore how speakers signal their intention to take a turn, for instance, and how group members can, partly by non-verbal means, help to determine who is heard and whose contribution is over-ridden. After this, the children themselves could generate some guidelines for successful group-work, reviewing these in the light of further sessions. Although such reflection would take time, this may be more than outweighed by the long-term benefits: more effective science education for all the children, and enhanced awareness of, and skills in, oral collaboration, which may be transferred to other contexts.

PROGRESSION AND DEVELOPMENT IN CHILDREN'S KNOWLEDGE ABOUT LANGUAGE

There has to be some notion of children's development in the area of knowledge about language to underpin the teacher's decisions. This is far from easy to describe, and useful research evidence is as yet very scant. Nor, despite revisions in its various stages, is the National Curriculum for English completely convincing in the 'pattern of development' it offers for knowledge about language. *English for Ages 5 to 16* (DES, 1989) lists examples of what are asserted to be 'easier' and less 'easy' features of knowledge about language, but with little supporting evidence from what children actually do. Thus it is claimed, for instance, that:

> *it is usually easier to give examples from local varieties of English (in the family or local community), than to discuss a wider range of varieties, which are more distant, geographically, socially or historically. (6.21)*

My own experience with young children makes me sceptical of the notion that children perceive their own family as a repository of 'examples of local varieties', and would suggest rather that language which *contrasts* with the familiar, being 'more distant' *is* likely to provoke comment. The notional continuum of subject matter which runs from 'easy' to 'difficult' is in itself unsatisfactory as an indicator of development.

Another perspective which is put forward on development in knowledge about language suggests that knowledge is acquired first at an implicit level, and that development would be demonstrated as children begin to acquire the skill of commenting explicitly on what functioned previously in a more intuitive way. However, it could be that opportunities to discuss explicitly ambiguities and problematic meanings, and to negotiate ways of resolving them, are perhaps at their greatest with young children, since these things arise in their own experience time and again. If we fail to respond positively to the questioning inclination of younger children, we may run the risk of inhibiting it, thereby, in the longer term, closing down aspects of their opportunities for learning.

However, perhaps a model which might be brought to bear on likely stages of progress in children's knowledge about language could be drawn from other aspects of children's language development, such as the acquisition of oral language, or progress in reading, for example. The model devised for use in ILEA's *Primary Language Record* (Barrs, 1988) suggests in particular two ways of thinking about progress in reading – from limited experience to wider experience; from dependence to independence. These axes of progression obviously have parallels in the growth of language awareness. Growing experience not only of the variety of language forms and contexts, but of the ways in which experienced language users manipulate language, should help to develop children's knowledge about language; a diminishing need for the support of others as children manage to extract meaning from a text, or to detect 'hidden' meanings from explicit messages, would also constitute signs of progress.

It is only from research based on observations of children's language behaviour (of which there is as yet very little in this specific field) that we shall learn more about how children's knowledge about language progresses. What does seem almost certain from even very limited contact with young children is that development in their knowledge about language cannot be neatly classified into 'levels' in a linear way. Furthermore, such experience suggests that not only children's competence as language users, but also their ability to reflect on their experience of language in use, begins to develop very early on. Wood (1988) suggests that '. . . most young children assume that failures of communication are necessarily the fault of whoever is listening' – as opposed, that is, to the speaker being at fault, and he wonders whether 'this assumption is the most consistent with their own, everyday experience.' He reveals, however, that in a recent piece of research carried out with nursery age children:

> *many children quickly revised this assumption when they were given* explicit *insights into other people's states of mind in response to their own attempts to instruct. They made progress in learning how to analyse and evaluate linguistic instructions.*

Could it be that, as experienced language users ourselves, we teachers and parents take for granted assumptions about young chidren's problems with and perceptions of language? Perhaps more explicit interchange with the children would enlighten both parties.

EXPLICITNESS THROUGH DIALOGUE

Open and honest negotiations between children and more experienced language users (older children, parents, teachers), which facilitate exploration of language itself, may both empower the children and enhance their competence.

A colleague reported the following incident from a reception year classroom: with help, a child wrote a caption for her picture, which together formed part of a story she wanted to tell. The sentence was, 'The hippo got stuck trying to get through the hedge and he started to laugh.' The teacher read the sentence out loud, but misconstrued the meaning because the pronoun 'he' was ambiguous. It was not the hippo, but the little boy watching who started to laugh, explained the writer. She decided, with the teacher, to draw a line linking the word 'he' to the boy in her picture. Unconventional, perhaps, but effective.

Many of the examples given so far are of language itself coming to children's attention as a result of some sort of breakdown in the flow of communication, and I have suggested that this is such a common experience for relatively inexperienced language users that it provides abundant opportunities for explicit dialogue about language.

Cracks open up in the 'making-sense' of discourse which need to be repaired in order for the communication to be sustained. But the cracks themselves can be used in the formation of the concept that meaning is problematic, partial, subjective. The greater children's awareness of this, the less susceptible they should be to the belief that meaning is self-evident, objective common-sense. They can be helped to feel that it is they who hold power over language and not vice-versa.

In order to build on such awareness as is acquired by very young children, teachers can plan for other contexts which will generate discussion about language. One fruitful strategy is simply the use of collaboration in the construction of a text. Teachers who have the opportunity to work alongside colleagues often find that, irrespective of the specific nature of a collaborative teaching session, the very act of planning along with someone else stimulates them to think more clearly about their aims and intentions. Having to share their thoughts requires a greater degree of explicitness. The same principle applies to children working together.

Of course, many assumptions can be shared, and much can remain unstated as children work towards their goal. But they will obviously find that they cannot achieve the production of their story, account, or whatever, without raising to the surface and making explicit some of the decisions which might otherwise be taken with less thought. Commentary on the language is thus an integral part of the process, serving the children's own purposes. For example, some nine- to 11-year-old children in a Birmingham school worked on a project which led them to making a short video commercial for a product they had invented. The children grappled with a means of creating a magical, fantasy atmosphere for the advertisement, which was to be for a white chocolate bar they had named a 'Unicorn Bar'. The following is a transcript of part of this discussion, and it demonstrates how dialogue about language and genre generated ideas for a new text:

T   *We want to make this atmosphere that you said. You said about a fantasy atmosphere and a magical atmosphere – how might we do that?*

C1   *Pretend there's a princess in a castle.*

T   *Yes, that's a good idea.*

C1   *And she's gonna like open the bar and she must be like romantic and that lot.*

. . .

C2   *And that could be a present to her, or something, for her birthday or something.*

C3   *Yeh.*

C2   *And she opens it and reads it like er 'New Unicorn Bar', something like that.*

T   *And then holds it up to show the camera – yeh?*

C4   *Yeh, that's a good idea.*

T   *Sounds good. That fits with all the things we've said, doesn't it?*

C2   *Magic.*

C3   *Magical, cos prince and prince . . . prince and princesses are quite magical, aren't they, cos they're in fairy stories.*

In the light of these decisions, the children went back to the slogan they had invented for Unicorn Bars:

T   *Now then, I think we should work on this er . . .*

C1   *slogan.*

T   *Slogan. The idea is – we've got 'Grab one and you'll have your wish'. Now, what we wanted to do with that was link it with this idea that when you get . . .*

C2   *Miss, I don't think it sounds magical though,*

C4   *'Catch a unicorn and he'll grant your wish'.*

T   *I agree with you. It's – that's better, isn't it? 'Catch a unicorn', it's better than 'grab' isn't it?*

All *Mmmn, yes.*

C3   *You grab (indistinct).*

C1   *'Grab''s too common, like.*

C3   *'Grab''s a bit too Brummie.*

T   *Well, I think you're right. I think we want it to sound magical, so 'Catch a unicorn' . . .*

C4   *And he'll give you a wish.*

C2   *And he'll grant your wish.*

C1   *And he'll grant your wish.*

Judging by the reactions of the rest of the class, the commercial was a great success: the other children were able to 'read' the conventions and were impressed by the quality of the video.

MODELS AND REFLECTIONS

Few would disagree that, in the words of the National Curriculum for English (DES, 1990) children 'should experience a wide range of children's literature' and 'read an increasingly wide range and variety of texts', while teachers 'should encourage pupils to read a variety of genres'. Each text provides a model for children of what texts can be like, and reflecting on the characteristics of texts, and on their own responses to them, can enhance children's knowledge about written language.

Equally, non-written 'texts' can be looked at closely (perhaps even, in an embryonic way, 'deconstructed') so as to allow children to discover the ingredients of various media of communication.

The video-making activity described above formed part of a project on language and persuasion, in which these upper-junior children considered various aspects of how language is used to persuade people – from individual conflicts of interest such as often occur in their own experience between themselves and adults (parents or teachers, for example), to the equally familiar but differently constructed persuasion by companies trying to sell their products. Before they set about making their own commercial, the children watched closely a video of familiar television advertisements, freezing certain frames and discussing how effects were created, and why. Insights gained from this experience were consolidated as the children reflected on what they had learned about this sort of text in a piece of collaborative writing. There is evidence that they brought these reflections directly to bear in the construction of their own text. This is a paragraph, taken from their writing after watching the professionally produced commercials, in which they listed some of their more negative perceptions:

> *Different people have different feelings when they see adverts. Some adverts are annoying and stupid. When you're watching a programme and it's exciting, the adverts just come and it disturbs us. It makes you lose the excitement. For example, children aren't interested in washing powders. Some of the rhymes are stupid, like 'A few more pence makes a lot more sense.' We think this is confusing.*

And from the discussion in which they were planning their own commercial:

> T   *'Catch a unicorn and he'll grant your wish' – there's no rhyme in that – can we make up a rhyme?*
> C2 *Does it have to?*
> T   *No, it doesn't have to, but it's got to be sort of catchy.*
> C3 *No, I think that's good.*
> C2 *It doesn't have to rhyme. If it rhymed, it'd be a bit out.*

Confident in their own decision, they left well alone and eschewed the rhyming slogan.

A quite different example of the importance of a discourse model is supplied by a colleague who worked with some top infant children engaged in collaborative story telling. The teachers noticed how much more confident the girls in the class were when working in pairs than when asked to retell their stories to the whole class. As well as working with all the children to improve the ethos of these sessions and encourage the girls, the teachers:

> *related personal stories to them about how* they *had felt when required to talk in different situations – for example as children at school, as teachers and sometimes in front of a large audience. They asked the children how they had felt in similar situations.*
>
> *The teachers were impressed by the children's ability to discuss such relatively abstract ideas. They felt that it was partly the teachers' modelling of appropriate language which accounted for the children's success. (Sealey and Knight, 1990)*

Models, used in the sense described here, can be supportive for children. It is not suggested that children should be presented with 'ideal types' to emulate. But models are used from the earliest stages of acquiring linguistic competence: think of nursery children 'becoming' cartoon heroes and assuming American accents as they play, for instance. Later on, if children have opportunities to look closely at texts which interest them – including those by other children – and to explore how effects are created by others, then the choices open to the children as *they* create texts are extended. Techniques employed in media education may be particularly useful for those working to develop children's knowledge about language (see, for example, Buckingham, 1990). Some of the mystique associated with unfamiliar language or forms may be dispelled as the children try out their own versions – sometimes even to the extent of parody. (There was an element of this in the 'fairy-tale princess' commercial, which subverted the potentially stereotyped nature of the theme!) It is during such processes that further understandings about authors, language and audiences may be generated.

CONCLUSION

There is as yet no consensus as to the precise nature of the development of children's awareness of language, and prescriptive advice to teachers would be unwise. What can be readily observed, however, is that children display a lively interest in language from an early age. It is that interest, along with an awareness of the fact that language is a vital and dynamic source of power, which may guide teachers in the primary phase. They are then in a strong position not only to foster their pupils' competence as language users but also to help in the development of their knowledge about language.

ACKNOWLEDGMENTS

I should like to thank a number of my colleagues in Birmingham, particularly those on the English Advisory Team, who commented on drafts of this paper and contributed some of the classroom examples.

REFERENCES

Barrs, M. *et al.* (1988) *The primary language record*. London: ILEA.

Buckingham, D. (1990) 'English and media studies: making the difference', *The English Magazine*, 23, Summer 1990.

DES (1989) *English for Ages 5 to 16*. London: HMSO.

DES (1990) *English in the National Curriculum*. London: HMSO.

Fairclough, N. (1989) *Language and Power*. London: Longman.

Garton, A. and Pratt, C. (1989) *Learning to be Literate*. Oxford: Basil Blackwell.

Richmond, J. (1990) 'What do we mean by knowledge about language?', in this volume.

Sealey, A. and Knight, C. '"We don't like talking in front of the boys": classroom talk and inequality', *Education 3 – 13* (in press).

Wells, G. (1986) *The Meaning Makers*. London: Hodder and Stoughton.

Wood, D. (1988) *How Children Think and Learn*. Oxford: Basil Blackwell.

3

Books in the Classroom and 'Knowledge about Language'

MIKE TAYLOR ⸺⸺⸺⸺⸺⸺⸺⸺⸺⸺⸺⸺⸺◇

'Knowledge about language' is very much in the air these days. There is a major funded initiative in our schools (the LINC project) with this as its focus. Linguistic terminology resonates throughout those reports which provide the framework for the National Curriculum in English, and Standard Attainment Targets for English include knowledge about language strands from level 5 onwards.

Part of the debate which surrounds such knowledge is the degree to which it needs to be made explicit in children's learning activities. In terms of a 'spiral' of language learning, most of us would accept that children's extensive knowledge about language is firstly manifested through *use* (in talking, listening, reading and writing). Later, *description* of relevant aspects of the language system can, *in context*, support children's thinking about language (when older juniors are writing a collaborative story for infants, for instance). Lastly, when pupils are capable of handling both very specific and more generalisable abstract concepts, *analysis* of 'real' language examples can, where appropriate, be profitable and 'empowering'.

The National Curriculum preserves most children and teachers in the primary school from the need to assess knowledge about language and from the inevitable pressure from publishers to 'provide' for this strand of language competence through books of programmatic activities (exercises). Nevertheless, it is common knowledge amongst those who live and work with young children that they are capable of reflecting upon language and talking about it at an early age. Young bilingual learners for instance are able to differentiate and describe features of the languages they have access to; emergent readers will point to a letter saying 'that's in my name too', or, as in the case of a five-year-old recently encouraged to write independently for the first time,' I didn't know I could write. I just listen to the sounds and make them letters'. Seven-year-olds know all about Mum's 'telephone voice'; infants writing collaboratively at the computer will share comments that refer to features from narrative structure to punctuation and spelling.

This short piece, however, restricts itself to the place of children's books in the classroom as a resource for knowledge about language. The brief analysis which follows looks firstly at how such texts support children's early reading and then, more broadly, at how they contribute to children's awareness of language and to the potential extension of their spoken and written repertoire as language users.

The evidence here is merely suggestive. It reflects one and a half hour's browsing through the kinderbox in a local children's library, looking at 20 or so books, many of which will also be in the book-corners and boxes of local primary schools. In this sense the books mentioned here chose themselves. They represent a sample of those available to myself and younger rummagers on a particular day (and not a prescribed or balanced list in terms of class, gender, culture or indeed any other feature). A list of the books will be found at the end of this article.

WHAT DO THE BOOKS TEACH CHILDREN ABOUT READING?

The ways in which writers of children's books support young readers, build upon and extend what they know about the world, and draw them into active co-authorship with the text, have been previously described by Meek (1988). Her eloquent advocacy is well known to many teachers, so a brief skeleton of her argument will suffice here.

1 As adults we can sometimes overlook the subtlety, detail and multi-levelled meaning potential of picture books. Many provide through the interaction of picture and text a rich resource for reflection upon experience, coupled with compelling introductions to such features of language as irony, ambiguity, and the subversion of known genres.

2 The 'reading' undertaken by children when they share or revisit such texts is far more than cracking the code of written surface features. They engage in a complex and rewarding relationship with the writer who, while supporting their independent reading with devices such as structural repetition and picture cues, creates space in the text for the reader's imagination to truly 'possess' the book.

3 The varieties of voice and the linguistic invention in children's books give children access to the nature and variety of written discourse – 'the different ways the language lets a writer tell and the many and different ways a reader reads'.

4 Children who have access to good story-books learn, therefore, that reading is deeply pleasurable and because of this, and
the ways it brings shape and meaning to experience, books
become a habitual source of enrichment. In this sense children
'learn to read' in a self-motivated way, refining their 'decoding' skills in the company of authors whose meanings are
compelling.

One of the books in my sample was *Where the Wild Things Are*. Savva
(1990), in her analysis of the opening page, captures the alchemy by
which the child's imagination is engaged.

> *Young children encountering the book for the first time are*
> *likely to identify with a small boy whose wolf suit looks like a*
> *'babygrow' (which has ears and claws) and who is about to land*
> *himself in great trouble. Both the illustration on the cover, and*
> *the paragraph on the inside page:*
>
> > *Max's wonderful adventure began the night he put on his*
> > *wolf suit. He stepped inside his private boat and sailed off*
> > *through night and day and in and out of weeks and almost*
> > *over a year to the place where the wild things are.*
>
> *will have set up in the reader the expectation that something*
> *extraordinary is going to happen. In the very first illustration we*
> *see that Max has constructed a den. He ties handkerchieves*
> *together to make a line and hammers this into the wall causing*
> *it to crack. He stands on books! And he hangs his teddy up by*
> *the arm. The opening sentence of the text which accompanies*
> *the illustration leaves us hanging in mid air:*
>
> > *The night Max wore his wolf suit and made mischief of one*
> > *kind . . .*
>
> *and we must turn over the page to read:*
>
> > *and another*
>
> *(This line of text is accompanied by a picture which shows Max*
> *chasing a terrier around with a fork — what might Max do with*
> *a fork if he ever catches the dog?)*
> *Again the text leaves us in suspense and we must turn*
> *the page. We are caught up in the narrative. The text and the*
> *illustrations together propel us into the story.*

WHAT DO THE BOOKS TEACH CHILDREN ABOUT LANGUAGE?

The brief analysis which follows identifies just some of the language
features shared by many of the books. (As we have seen above, their rich

potential to *readers* is reflected in the broader meanings they share in terms of values, cultural assumptions, and the vital counterpoint between illustration and words where picture meanings may reinforce, enrich or even subvert the text.)

From my very small sample, specific aspects of language which were powerfully foregrounded within the texts fell into a number categories.

The list

The chaining of items or events in the form of a list is an appealing organisational form for young children. Their own early stories in speech and writing rely on the infinite productivity of the list ('and then . . . , and then . . . ,' etc.). Similarly a list provides the young writer with a coherent way of celebrating what they know or organising their world before they have access to more sophisticated genre structures and means of internal textual cohesion (Barrs, 1987). Lists in early reading books cue into this emerging feature of children's competence (one that features strongly in oral monologue before it emerges in writing). From the young reader/listener's point of view listing may have the comfort of syntactic simplicity and familiarity, but comprehending a long list means hanging on to the subject of the sentence in one's head and keeping it in suspension until the sentence ends. Sometimes this may last a whole book as in John Burningham's *The School* where the text is revealed as follows, with each phrase under a new picture and on a fresh page.

> *When I go to school,*
> *I learn to read*
> *And to write,*
> *Sing songs,*
> *Eat my dinner,*
> *Paint pictures,*
> *Play games,*
> *Make friends,*
> *And then I go home.*

In order to understand this text the young child has to grasp intuitively that all the subsequent items relate back to the initial clause.

An almost identical format is found in Jan Ormerod's *Dad's Back* where the list assumes qualities of what Barrs terms 'celebratory psalm':

> *Dad's back*
> *with jingling keys*
> *warm gloves*
> *a cold nose*

a long long scarf
and apples in a bag

Other examples of listing in my sample included this graphic list of past tense verbs from *Mr Gumpy's Motor Car*:

They pushed and shoved and heaved and struggled and gasped
and slipped and slithered and squelched

the cumulative, alliterative list in *Grandma Goes Shopping* and a string of noun phrases from *My Brown Bear Barney*:

When I go shopping I take my mother, my little brother, my
yellow basket, my red umbrella, and my brown bear Barney.

In this book, the structure of this sentence is repeated throughout the text, thus providing another form of foregrounding.

The repeated syntactic frame

My Brown Bear Barney continues throughout with similar repetitions, 'When I play with my friend I take . . .' and so on. These frames again provide for readers/listeners a pleasurable and predictable structure to hang their linguistic processing upon, while incidently exposing through repetition important syntactic options within English.

Some books celebrate through repetition the creativity of syntax for deliberate comic effect. For instance, *John Patrick Norman McHennessey – the boy who was always late* has a string of legitimate but bizarre excuses for his tardiness, which are expressed through similarly structured convolutions of clauses in each case (my under-lining):

I am late, Sir, because on the way a crocodile came out of a
drain and got hold of my satchel and would only let go when I
threw my glove which he ate.

In John Burningham's *Where's Julius?* there is repetition throughout of the same discourse frame. Mum says 'For lunch there is . . .' (followed by a menu list). The call goes up 'Where's Julius?' The answer follows 'Julius says . . .' The consequence is signalled by 'So . . .' Once again there is the repeated use of a list (in this case the meal menu), followed by an exotic excuse appropriately codified in richly baroque and embedded syntax (my underlining)

Julius says he can't have breakfast with us today because he is
riding a camel to the top of the tomb of Neffatutam which is a
pyramid near the Nile in Egypt.

*Julius says he can't have supper with us at the moment <u>because</u>
he is throwing snowballs at the wolves from a sledge <u>in which</u>
he is crossing the frozen wastes of Novostic Krolsky <u>which</u> lies
somewhere in Russia <u>where</u> the winters are long.*

A simpler discourse structure is found in *Knock knock! Who's there?*
The beginning establishes the pattern:

Knock knock! Who's there?

*I'm a great big Gorilla
with fat furry arms
and huge white teeth.
When you let me in
I'm going to hug your breath away!*

Then I won't let you in!

Subsequently each page echoes the sequence with '*I'm a . . . with . . .
and . . . When . . . I . . .*'

Question and answer structures like this one are the basis of
many young children's books. They use a simple *turn-taking* principle
already familiar to children through spoken language. More important-
ly, perhaps, they offer a simple and engaging structure for *shared*
reading, drawing the child into active processing of pictures and written
text (as in *Where's Spot?* for instance). Question and answer as an
organisational pattern operates in a number of books in the sample
(*Jafta* and *Where's Spot?*, for instance).

Direct speech

Trying to look through the books with a child's eye I was struck by the
insistent repetition of written speech conventions (and other punctuation devices). The larger the print, the more obvious and alluring these
speckled pages became! A notable page from *Mr Gumpy's Motor Car*
which lists the animals' excuses when the car needs pushing seems to
explode with speech marks.

'Not me,' said the goat! 'I'm too old' etc . . .

Mrs Armitage on Wheels (Quentin Blake) uses direct speech plus an ever
expanding clausal structure:

*'What this bike needs,' said Mrs Armitage to herself, 'is a
really loud horn.'
'What this bike needs,' said Mrs Armitage to herself as
she cycled along 'if it's to be looked after properly, is a complete
tool kit'.*

The presence and precision of these conventions was unavoidable to the eye. Many books also separated speech by bubbles (for instance *Bet You Can't* by Penny Dale and *I Know an Old Lady who Swallowed a Fly* by Colin and Jacqui Hawkins).

Tense forms

A number of books seemed to offer a glorious celebration of the past tense. *Over the Meadow* gives present and past forms of the same verb in each verse of the song:

> *Over the meadow in the sand and the sun*
> *Lived an old mother turtle and her little turtle one*
> *Dig said the mother, We dig said the one*
> *So they dug all day in the sand and the sun.*

Subsequent verses have the following verbs: swim/swum, gnaw/gnawed, buzz/buzzed, caw/cawed, jump/jumped, back/backed and some inventions, beaver/beavered, to-who/to-whoed.

The Wind Blew by Pat Hutchins again sustains a string of past tense forms:

> *it whipped a kite into the air*
> *and kept it spinning round up there*
> *it whirled the postman's letters up*
> *as if it hadn't done enough . . . etc.*

Children listening to or reading these books again have access to powerful insights into how English works.

Phonetic/phonemic patterns

Like some of those already quoted from, my small sample included a number of rhyming books. Another strong feature of the language already noted above is use of alliteration.

Two contrasting books full of alliterative exotica and assonance were Nicola Bayley's *One Old Oxford Ox* and Allan Baile's *Drac and the Gremlins*. The latter book uses conscious parody of the language of space epics within a picture book format to play with the reader's expectations about genre (perhaps not a kinderbox book after all this one, but rich in language interest). Margaret Mahy's *17 Kings and 42 Elephants* is another strong alliterative text. Again, such books reinforce for children powerful underlying principles of the sound systems of language – what are permissible combinations of sounds (and letters) in English and in some cases other languages as well.

Figurative Language

Simile featured in a number of books as an underlying organisational principle. Notably in *Jafta* and *Big as a Skyscraper* which also uses a question–answer frame:

> *How fast are you?   Fast as a runner.*

Metaphor was also evident, most notably in *Dr Xargle's Book of Earth Hounds*. In this book, friendly aliens are being lectured by Dr Xargle about the humanoid's best friend. The rich indirectness of meaning in the book relies on pictorial as well as verbal metonomy – a flavour can be gained from the following:

> *Earth Hounds have fangs at the front and a waggler at the back. Earth Hounds have buttons for eyes, a sniffer with two holes in and a long pink flannel.*

A further richness is added to the book by the fact that the lively language and subversive illustrations are embedded in the bland genre structure of an informational text. Sharing these multi-levelled jokes with the author draws the young reader into a telling and richly satisfying intimacy.

Many of the features identified above are similar to features of spoken and written discourse identified by Deborah Tannen. In *Talking Voices* (1989) she demonstrates that conversation contains a range of sophisticated structural and rhetorical devices, all of which help to create close bonds of involvement and implicature between speaker and listener. She sees continuity between these common features of every-day conversation and literary and poetic language.

Among the critical conversational features Tannen identifies are patterns of repetition and variation operating at all 'levels' of language – phonology, morphology, words, collocations of words, and longer sequences of discourse. These combine powerfully with other fore-grounded devices such as narrative, dialogue and detailed visual imagery.

Roughly speaking these features divide into those which achieve their effects *musically* through sound patterns which 'sweep up' the listener or reader so that they move mentally to the rhythm of the writer's intention (engaging subliminally in a kind of synchronic dance), and those which create audience participation in *sense making*. In this latter case the writer helps the reader/listener to become an active participant in meaning-making through use of indirectness (telling gaps); imagery (which has to be recreated in the mind's eye) and dialogue (which can only come to life through auditory activity).

In these terms it is likely that writers of early reading books are similarly maximising the capacity of language for rich involvement to secure the active partnership of young readers/listeners and to build bridges between conversational discourse and literary language. In doing so they are both building upon what small children already know about language and foregrounding this knowledge in a manner which renders it open to conscious awareness and future use within the child's own repertoire.

> *Wells (1985a, 1985b, 1985c) and Olson (1977, 1984) believed that through listening to the language of stories being read to them, young children are learning a lot about the organisation of written language . . . Accordingly, children gradually realise that language can be used independently of the objects, people, events, actions and places it stands for, and can be further used and interpreted in other, different contexts. In other words, while being read stories initially extends children's experiences, it then allows children to begin to reflect upon these experiences as the language becomes more detached from the immediate context and children realise just how powerful language can be.*
> *(Garton and Pratt, 1989)*

IMPLICATIONS FOR THE CLASSROOM

So, what is the point of this brief analysis? Does it have any bearing upon the practical realities of the busy infant classroom? An answer might run something like this.

1   The importance of a book corner and the provision of 'real' books in the classroom is usually, and properly, justified in terms such as these. Firstly, it is a rich resource of vicarious experience through which children can reflect upon their own lives and begin to walk around in the shoes of others. Secondly, it is a meeting place between children and books where, as browsers, choosers, readers and sharers, pupils build their competence and identity as readers by engaging with books that have rich meaning for them. Along with these, I am also suggesting that we can point proudly to our book corner, confident that it is also doing another job well, that is, repeatedly exposing and reinforcing patterns of grammar and other formal properties of language.

2   The texts of children's books highlight a range of *organisational devices* which serve a number of important functions. Such devices provide a *scaffolding* for the young reader/listener. They offer the pleasure-principle of *pattern and repetition*. They create *memorable* and predictable text. They offer discourse structures (e.g. question–answer) which encourage *active participation and shared reading*.

3   As well as serving these functions, the writing also lays bare

many of the important *structural principles* of written English (grammar), e.g. phonetic/phonemic patterning, the chaining of objects or events through lists and coordination; the powerful productivity of subordinate clauses and embedding, and the ways in which the 'rules' of syntax allow certain basic elements within the sentence to be moved about (for emphasis, for instance). For example, in *Where's Julius*, 'Mum' always starts the sequence with 'For dinner today, we have . . .', a more formal register than in normal conversation with its adverbial phrase fronting the main clause (as in 'for the discerning bon viveur we have an excellent wine list and a full *à la carte* menu').

4 The potentiality within English for these kinds of structures progressively becomes part of the child's *own* grammatical repertoire. Firstly, they are borrowed and *rehearsed on the ear* as the child repeatedly processes the book as a listener or independent reader. (The fact that they are often repeated as basic organisational patterns within the text supports this process). Sooner or later they become part of children's *productive capability* as they become assimilated into their framework for novel utterances in speech and/or writing.

Katherine Perera reiterates the important link here between children's grammatical competence and reading aloud:

> *As far as reading aloud in schools is concerned, I have the impression that some teachers and headteachers are vaguely uneasy about it, feeling that perhaps it is timewasting to be reading to children who should be doing real work. Others may fear that it is old fashioned to read aloud from a class reader, for much writing on classroom practice advocates that children should be in small groups, with each group having books that match their reading ability. At first this seems a good idea but in practice it means that the poorest readers end up with stories written in simplified language that is often characterless, flat and dull. So those who need the most stimulus to their language development get the least. In fact we can be confident that in reading aloud from really fine books – books that would be too difficult for pupils to read by themselves – we are helping them to develop an ear for the language in a way that no textbook exercises can. (Perera, 1987)*

Undoubtedly, in these terms, schools with a rich and varied book provision (and by rich we refer to the different voices of authors of quality, not quantative measures) are already providing for children a major pillar of that aspect of the curriculum concerned with 'knowledge about language'.

In order to consolidate our practice in this area the immediate challenge for thinking teachers in the classroom might be sketched as follows.

Firstly we need to continue to build arguments along the lines of the one I have tried to construct to persuade parents and others who still believe that young children need grammar *teaching* and *exercises* that authors, as always, continue to do much of the job for us and that grammatical competence is extended in *real language contexts and for real purposes* (as is the case when a child is absorbed in a book or listening to a story). 'Real books' in the classroom provide not only a more viable introduction to reading than reading schemes, but also the words, cadences and structural options for shaping significant experience, which complement and extend those accessible to children from their rich experience as speakers.

Secondly we need to become more aware ourselves of the language resources and devices that successful authors of young children's books employ.

Thirdly we need to track the processes whereby those discourse features, language structures and rhetorical devices derived from, or foregrounded in reading become assimilated into children's own talking and writing. Meek's claim that there is 'a divergence in competence and understanding between young readers who have entered the reading network through the multiple meanings of polysemic texts and those who may have practised only on the reductive feature of words written to be "sounded out" or "recognised"' deserves both reassertion and re-examination at a time when concern about children's reading performance has further fuelled the 'schemes versus real books' debate. Before we bow uncritically to reading test scores as some kind of barometer of educational success, we must, among other things, establish the links between children's early reading experience and their subsequent development as talkers, writers and active interpreters of text.

ACKNOWLEDGMENTS

I should like to thank Essex Libraries for access to the children's books, and colleagues in the Eastlinc advisory team for their contributions to the thinking reflected in this paper.

CHILDREN'S BOOKS MENTIONED

Armitage, R. *Grandma Goes Shopping* (Andre Deutsch, 1984).
Baillie, A. *Drac and the Gremlins* (Viking Children's Books, 1989).
Bayley, N. (ill.) *One Old Oxford Ox* (Jonathan Cape, 1977).
Blake, Q. *Mrs Armitage on Wheels* (Jonathan Cape, 1987).
Burningham, J. *Mr Gumpy's Motor Car* (Jonathan Cape, 1973).
Burningham, J. *The School* (Jonathan Cape, 1974).

Burningham, J. *Would You Rather?* (Jonathan Cape, 1978).

Burningham, J. *Where's Julius?* (Jonathan Cape, 1987).

Burningham, J. *John Patrick Norman McHennessey – the boy who was always late* (Jonathan Cape, 1987).

Butler, D. *My Brown Bear Barney* (Hodder and Stoughton, 1985).

Dale, P. *Bet You Can't* (Walker Books, 1990).

Grindley, S. *Knock Knock. Who's There?* (Methuen, 1988).

Hawkins, C. and Hawkins, J. *I Know an Old Lady Who Swallowed a Fly* (Magnet, 1988).

Hill, E. *Where's Spot?* (Heinemann, 1980).

Hutchins, P. *The Wind Blew* (Puffin, 1978).

Lewin, H. *Jafta* (Dinosaur, 1982).

Mahy, M. *17 Kings and 42 Elephants* (Armada Books, 1989).

Morris, A. *Big as a Skyscraper* (Armada Books, 1988).

Ormerod, J. *Dad's Back* (Walker Books, 1985).

Sendak, M. *Where the Wild Things Are* (Puffin, 1970).

Willis, J. *Dr Xargle's Book of Earth Hounds* (Anderson Press, 1989).

REFERENCES

Barrs, M. (1989) 'Mapping the World' in *English in Education*. Spring 1987.

Garton, A. and Pratt, C. (1989) *Learning to be Literate*. Oxford: Basil Blackwell.

Meek, M. (1988) *How Texts Teach What Readers Learn*. Thimble Press.

Perera, K. (1987) *Understanding Language*. Sheffield: NAAE/NATE Publications.

Savva, H. (1990) Unpublished.

Tannen, D. (1989) *Talking Voices*. Cambridge: Cambridge University Press.

4

Language Study at Key Stage 3

GEORGE KEITH

THE DECLINE OF 'ENGLISH GRAMMAR'

Whenever language study and knowledge about language are discussed in the context of the English curriculum, questions about spelling, punctuation and grammar are never far from the surface. All three suffer the misfortune of being associated with the negative, the corrective, the inevitably remedial half of English teaching. The notion of actually *studying* English spelling and punctuation, as historically and intrinsically interesting phenomena in their own right, is not one that many pupils will have taken away from their school experience. Rather there is a general view that you are either lucky and you know how to spell and punctuate, or you are unlucky and you are never quite sure at any given moment. Lifelong uncertainty can generate a deeper sense of deficiency or inadequacy in some; others survive by bluffing their way through the mechanics of writing, avoiding commas and apostrophes and resorting to writing squiggles in the middle of words they are not sure how to spell.

Misspellings and mispunctuation can arouse extraordinary intolerance in some teachers, employers and self-appointed language monitors, but most English users are inclined to regard them as venial sins. Errors of grammar however are viewed more as cardinal sins and it is one or other aspect of grammatical propriety that most frequently monopolises discussions of language study and knowledge about language.

The word itself has several different strands of history, the majority of definitions shot through with beliefs and attitudes not only about the importance of grammar as knowledge about language, but also about its place in the universal scheme of mind and society. It is possible to detect in the etymology of the word (see for example the pages devoted to the word in the Oxford English Dictionary) two contrasting but related points of view. On the one hand grammar is knowledge about language in the largest possible perspective of accumulated literature and social interaction. Certainly in its origins,

grammar meant the study of Greek literature, but it also had a philo-
sophical dimension. There can be no doubt that a view of language in
terms of how time (e.g. verb tenses and adverbs), space (e.g. prepositions and adverbs) and relationships (e.g. pronouns) are mapped out
in the mind, is a matter of fundamental importance to our understanding of the ways in which we think. On the other hand 'grammar'
has also long been considered in terms of the minutiae of a language
system, or of what is sometimes referred to as 'the naming of parts' (see
Mittins, 1987). When Dionysus Thrax (first century BC) wrote his 'Art
of Grammar' the term embraced both the literary-philosophical context
and pedagogic aspects of literacy.

In the Middle Ages grammar (language study in the large as well
as the little perspective) was a part of the core curriculum along with
rhetoric and logic (*the trivium*). In the history of English education,
however, the study of language became limited to learning grammar in
its narrowest perspective, in a pedagogic style that was mainly prescriptive and proscriptive, and which concentrated on the written user of
language.

Readers who sat their O level English language examination in
the early 1960s, or before, will no doubt recognise the last days of the
grammar instruction tradition, in the following excerpt from a 1962
JMB paper:

> (a) (i) *State the part of speech of each of the underlined words
> in the sentences below.*
> (ii) *For each of the underlined words write a sentence in
> which the word appears as a different part of speech from that
> used below. After each sentence state the part of speech you
> have used.*
>> *The tears grow in an onion <u>that would water</u> this sorrow.*
>> *Because he did not work hard <u>enough</u> he failed to satisfy
>> his <u>master</u>.*
>> *The old woman's <u>only</u> friend has not been here <u>since</u>
>> Saturday.*
>
> (b) *In five of the six sentences below there is an error of
> grammar or expression. Write out the sentences, correcting the
> faulty ones as economically as possible but leaving the correct
> sentence in its present form.*
>> (i) *There is no doubt that we can reach our target if everyone
>> will do their best.*
>> (ii) *My young sister would have liked to have gone to the
>> cinema on Friday.*
>> (iii) *Accidents due to high speeds often occur on trunk roads.*
>> (iv) *I believe Jill is as skilful, if not more skilful than Jack.*
>> (v) *The tall farmer who I saw at the fair was buying sheep
>> and calves.*

(vi) You have given less trouble than any candidate in the examination.

(a) Make up seven *sentences, each at least* seven *words long, using the words underlined below as indicated. Each word may be used once only.*

    (i)   through as a preposition;
    (ii)   better as a comparative adjective:
    (iii)   talking as a gerund;
    (iv)   much as an adverb of degree;
    (v)   though as a subordinating conjunction;
    (vi)   were as a verb in the subjunctive mood;
    (vii)   litter as a collective noun.

(b) State the kind and function of each of the clauses underlined in the following sentences, and then shorten each clause into a phrase *with the same meaning.*

    (i)   When the wind blew strongly, the leaves were torn from the trees.
    (ii)   We do not know the date on which he died.
    (iii)   The sentries reported that the enemy had disappeared.

Questions such as these represent the kind of grammatical knowledge that thousands and thousands of pupils were once taught, and in which they had to satisfy examiners at the age of 16. It was also the kind of linguistic knowledge taught to many more who had no chance whatever of being entered for the O level examination or its earlier equivalent. Yet, remarkably, the tradition of English grammar teaching, which was then at least 60 or 70 years old, died quietly in the 1960s, and very few English teachers mourned its passing. It is probably true to say that it died on its feet, worn out with years of teacher effort and diminishing returns. The arrival of the Certificate of Secondary Education, the introduction of comprehensive schools, the rock 'n' roll invasion, and lax post-war morality, have all at one time or another been blamed for the demise of grammar teaching, yet there was also a growing body of research evidence in the 1960s which showed clearly that one of the strongest claims for the value of grammar teaching, namely that it had a beneficial effect on pupils' own written composition, was simply not true. It was this climate of opinion, created by critical investigation, that proved as influential as anything in changing the English curriculum of the early 1960s. A paper by Nora Robinson, for example, published in the *British Journal of Educational Psychology* in 1960 typifies the case against the grammar teaching tradition. The paper describes an enquiry into the view that a knowledge of grammar is essential for accurate and effective use of language and attempts 'to determine whether a knowledge of grammar enables pupils to write English which is accurate, logical and of good style'. Its conclusion became a widespread belief among English teachers of the 1960s:

> *In the present enquiry there is no evidence that pupils from schools where there is a higher degree of association between knowledge of grammar and ability in composition, or pupils from schools with a significantly different level of attainment in grammar, obtain, as a group, marks in composition which are significantly different from those obtained by pupils from schools with neither of these characteristics.*

In the absence of a detailed socio-cultural history of the English curriculum we must review change and developments cautiously, but it does seem that the disappearance of traditional grammar teaching from the English syllabuses of both schools and examination boards was generally welcomed by most primary and secondary teachers, even if lamented by some.

It was not just critical enquiry that changed the climate of opinion. English teachers are far more positive than that. Two new and powerful influences infused the English curriculum of the early 1960s and have developed ever since. One was a growth of interest in pupils' own creative powers as writers, which stemmed from the pioneering work of teachers like Marjorie Hourd (*The Education of the Poetic Spirit*, 1949) and reached a first flowering in celebrations like Alec Clegg's *The Excitement of Writing* (1964). The other was a growing engagement by English teachers in social issues and themes, especially those appearing in contemporary literature (e.g. text books such as Albert Rowe's *English Through Experience*, and resource books such as *Reflections* by Clement, Dixon and Stratta, or the Penguin English series, *Voices*). Both influences have encouraged growth in imaginative and social awareness, and both have created traditions of achievement to which the National Curriculum is much indebted. Other developments, such as drama and role-play, and, more recently, IT and media studies, have also made important contributions to imaginative and social learning. Additionally, we have, over the past 20 or 30 years, lived through a golden age of children's literature in which the distinction between books for children and books for adults has been completely lost in a quality of writing that can be shared with equal enjoyment by teachers and pupils.

Whither then, (or wither) knowledge about grammar?

The first note should be one of regret, not for the passing of traditional grammar teaching, but for the way in which knowledge about language has been understood for so long solely in terms of knowledge about grammar and, more particularly, in terms of a transmissive and instructional style of teaching. There is nothing especially wrong with the language knowledge exemplified in the 1962 examination paper. The terminology remains useful knowledge, if you know what you want to use it for, though the decontextualised exercises that go with it have little to recommend them. The trouble with this kind of instructional approach is that it can lead, and usually did in the classroom, to an oversimplified view of language rules and structures which does not take into account the elasticity inherent in the language system, or the complexity of the functions involved in making meanings. It is well to remember too the warning note sounded by the American linguist, Leonard Bloomfield, 'All grammars leak'. There are still English teachers in the profession who can remember the care they took when making up sentences for grammar exercises, to ensure that no sentence contained inexplicable features or deviated from familiar structures. The so called 'simplified English grammars' seemed to work best on a simplified English language.

Traditional grammar instruction also had the effect of elevating the description and analysis of sentence structures to a higher level of intellectual value in the English curriculum than it deserved, given the potential of secondary pupils to make far more significant observations about language use than being able to say whether a present participle is functioning as a gerund or not, or whether a word like 'much' is being used as an adverb of degree, or not. Anyone who can remember teaching traditional English grammar of this kind will know how long it took and how few pupils became really confident in their new knowledge. They will probably remember too how hollow is the claim that knowledge about grammar made pupils use language more logically. Grammar is a system, yes, but the system is no more 'logical' than most other creations of the mind. Hence the significance of Ferdinand de Saussure's famous example of systematicity in language, whereby we are able to say things like, 'The 6.15 left for Geneva at 6.55'. Just think of the modal shifts that have to be introduced ('would have', 'should', 'ought') in order to explain what that statement means. There is much more than simplified logic at work here.

Another regrettable effect of traditional grammar instruction was to make the teaching of English language an essentially remedial activity even for native speakers. It is almost as though children are perceived as being born with original linguistic sin, prone to error and deviation from Standard English. A sense of deficiency in language use, spoken or written, engendered in so many school children, is in no small part due to a prevailing view of grammar as correctness, prescription, and proscription. Eliza Doolittle was wiser than she knew when she said, 'I don't want to talk grammar. I want to talk like a lady'. And echoing behind Eliza's complaint is the voice of Sir Francis Bacon from another age, saying of the English language:

> . . . it wants not Grammer; for Grammer it might have, but it needs not, being so easie in itself . . . I think it was a peece of the

Tower of Babilons curse, that a man should be put to schoole to learn his mother tongue.

Many of the negative characteristics of traditional English language teaching are exemplified in the Australian State Scholarship paper shown below. For 50 years since that paper was published English language teaching throughout the world seems to have been dominated by the kinds of exercises contained in this extract. The most regrettable thing of all is not the content of the paper but the status such content has been accorded. Most teachers today, in the everyday course of giving advice, suggesting ideas and imparting bits of linguistic knowledge during English lessons, will have touched on all of the issues raised by the Queensland examiners, though participants in the National Writing Project may look askance at Question 5.

DEPARTMENT OF PUBLIC INSTRUCTION, QUEENSLAND.

EXAMINATION FOR STATE SCHOLARSHIPS.

ENGLISH.

WEDNESDAY, 16th DECEMBER, 1914 – Morning, 9·30 to 11.

NOTE FOR EXAMINEES. – In detailed analysis the special word or phrase affected by other words or phrases must be clearly stated. In parsing there must be given (*a*) the relations shown by prepositions, (*b*) the exact nature of the objects of transitive verbs, (*c*) the words, phrases, or clauses for which pronouns stand. Rules of syntax need not be quoted unless specially asked for.

(ONE HOUR AND A-HALF ALLOWED.)

1. Punctuate the following, and substitute capital for small letters where necessary: – o king they cried there is no one so mighty as you do all things obey me he asked there is nothing that dares to disobey you o king they cried will the sea obey me he asked command it o king and it will obey said one sea cried canute i command you to come no further.

2. (*a*) Give the past tense and past participle of each of the following verbs: – Eat, shear, lie (to recline), lay, hew.

(*b*) Give the prefixes and roots, with meanings, of the following words: – Innocuous, submerge, indentation, reflect, circumlocution.

3. Divide into clauses, and state the kind and relation of each clause: –

'Before the audience dispersed, the chairman again

expressed the opinion of all present that the incident to which he referred, when he first addressed the meeting, had stirred up feelings in the minds of those who witnessed it which it would be very difficult to allay, unless a satisfactory explanation were forthcoming immediately.'

4. Parse the words in italics in the following extracts: –
   (i) *Roll on*, thou deep and dark-blue *ocean* – roll!
   (ii) And o'er the antique dial-stone the creeping shadow passed,
        And all *around*, the noon-day sun a drowsy *radiance cast*.
        No sound of busy life *was heard*, save from the cloister dim
        The *tinkling* of the silver bell, or the *sisters'* holy hymn.'

5. Answer only one of the following, (*a*), (*b*), (*c*), or (*d*): –
   (*a*) Write the story of Grace Darling.
   (*b*) Compare a day in Summer with a day in Winter.
   (*c*) Relate the most exciting incident in your life.
   (*d*) Narrate your experiences in 'Camping-out'.
   NOTE. – *The composition should not cover more than about a page of foolscap.*

6. Amend the following sentences: –
   (i) No one knows who to rely upon.
   (ii) The man, whom you thought was innocent proved to be guilty.
   (iii) Will everybody please sign their names before they go?
   (iv) This is more nutritious and quite as cheap as rice.
   (v) What is the good of you going there?

The status given to this kind of 'English language', whereby prescriptive grammar became the only kind of knowledge about language worth knowing, effectively discounted or marginalised other kinds of knowledge about language, so that when traditional English language examinations disappeared there was left a knowledge vacuum in the curriculum which it has taken 20 or 30 years to begin to fill. From the introduction of 100 per cent course work at O level and Mode 3 CSE syllabuses in the 1960s, to joint certification of English language and English literature at GCSE in the 1980s, the decline of systematic study of language in the mainstream English curriculum has been inevitable even if undesired. Knowledge about language was something always tested by examination papers; what place could it have in course work? By the 1980s it had become very common for Heads of English to say that *all* their department's English teaching was 'literature based'. Primary schools, on the other hand, have tended to replace the term

'English' with 'language development', though not necessarily with the inclusion of any more knowledge about language.

The aim of this chapter is to show how since the 1960s the knowledge about language vacuum has been steadily filled with ideas and resources, many equally appropriate for use in both primary and secondary classrooms. One tangible effect of this development upon the English curriculum has been the introduction of a full English Language A level examination by the JMB in 1983, which has proved out-standingly popular with students and teachers and has been welcomed by universities, polytechnics, colleges and professional training institutions. With the arrival of LINC it is fair to say that marginal developments over the past 30 years are now highlighted.

Following a review of approaches to knowledge about language offering alternatives to traditional grammar instruction, there will be an account of how a group of English teachers under the LINC initiative have begun to apply their A level experience and resources to the requirements of the National Curriculum at Key Stage 3. Since, how-ever, this involves a quite new perspective for many teachers, which may well seem daunting to say the least, it will help to discover how that new perspective has gradually come into being. Perhaps the simplest way of apprehending it is to look at the traditional examination questions already cited, and compare them with questions set by the JMB at A level between 1987 and 1990. Note how the four sections of Paper One correspond closely with the original model of the Kingman Report (1988) and the recommendations of the Language in the National Curriculum Project.

A. Language in Society

1 Either

   (a) Some people have suggested that the language used by working-class speakers is inferior to that of middle-class speakers. Others claim that working-class and middle-class uses of language are just as good as each other.
   Discuss these conflicting attitudes to language use.
   Or
   (b) ' "He talks like us" is equivalent to saying "He is one of us." ' (Sapir, 1921). What part does language play in establishing and maintaining social groups?

2 Either

   (a) Explain some of the ways in which people talking together informally convey information about their social relationships and about the social context through their use of language. Give examples where they are appropriate.
   Or
   (b) The data which follows comes from a study of the speech

*of a group of girls and a group of boys in Reading, Berkshire.
The groups had similar social backgrounds. The first column
represents non-standard English forms used, and the second
column gives an example of each form. The figures in the
next two columns represent the percentage of non-standard
variants used by boys and girls.
Comment on the significance of these findings and discuss
some of the issues they raise.*

Non-standard forms used	Examples	Boys %	Girls %
1 Present tense -s (regular verbs)	*I walks.*	53.16	52.04
2 Present tense *does* (full verb)	That's what I does.	71.43	50.00
3 Past tense *come*	I come home yesterday.	100.00	75.33
4 *ain't* = auxiliary BE	That ain't working.	74.19	42.11
5 Negative concord	I don't want nothing.	88.33	51.85
6 Relative pronoun *what*	That record what you've got . . .	36.36	14.58
7 Demonstrative adjective *them*	Them people . . .	92.31	33.33

(J. Cheshire, 1982)

B. Language Acquisition

*1 Use the data which follows, together with examples of your
own if you wish, to show what can be learnt about children's
acquisition of language from the utterances which they
produce.*

Utterances of two- and three-year-olds

Situation	Utterance
Wanting to have some cheese weighed	*You have to scale it*
Talking about getting dressed	*Mummy trousers me*
Not wanting his mother to sweep his room	*Don't broom my mess*
Putting crackers in her soup	*I'm crackering my soup*
Wanting a bell to be rung	*Make it bell*
To mother preparing to brush her hair	*Don't hair me*

(Clark, 1982)

Interaction between Eve (24 months) and Mother (M)
Eve: *Have that?*
M: *No, you may not have it.*
Eve: *Mom, where my tapioca?*

M: *It's getting cool. You'll have it in just a minute.*
Eve: *Let me have it.*
M: *Would you like to have your lunch right now?*
Eve: *Yeah. My tapioca cool?*
M: *Yes, it's cool.*
Eve: *You gonna watch me eat my lunch?*
M: *Yeah, I'm gonna watch you eat your lunch.*
Eve: *I eating it.*
M: *I know you are.*

(Bellugi, 1970)

2 Either

(a) *Explain some of the ways in which the study of young children's language acquisition has helped us to understand how English works.*

Or

(b) *What changes in a child's use of language would you expect to happen after the 'two-word utterance' stage?*
    You can use examples from any source you want to, including your own reading and research and these utterances made by a child at two different stages of her language development:

Eve at 18 months	Eve at 27 months
More grapejuice	*This not better*
Door	*See, this one better but this not better*
Right down	*There some cream*
Mommy soup	*Put in you coffee*
Eating	*I go get a pencil 'n' write*
Mommy celery?	*Put my pencil in there*
No celery	*Don't stand on my ice-cubes!*
Oh drop a celery	*They was in the refrigerator, cooking*
Open toybox	*I put them in the refrigerator to freeze*
Oh horsie stuck	*'An I want to take off my hat*
Mommy read	*That why Jacky comed*
No mommy read	*We're going to make a make a blue*
Write	*house*
Write a pencil	*You come help us*
My pencil	*You make a blue one for me*
Mommy	*How 'bout another eggnog instead of*
Mommy head?	*cheese sandwich?*
Look at dollie	*I have a fingernail*
Head	*And you have a fingernail*
What doing,	*Just like Mommy has, and David*
Mommy?	*has, and Sara has*
Drink juice	*What is that on the table?*

(From Villiers and Villiers, 1979)

*3 Describe how young children can develop an understanding
of the meanings and uses of words in English.*

*In your answer you should refer to the data below, as
well as to examples from other sources if you wish.*

*The following information refers to the use of several
words by an unnamed male child between the ages of 1 year
9 months 11 days and 2 years 0 months 20 days.*

*At 1 year 9 months 11 days the child used the word 'tee' for a
cat (called Timmy), and for a small dog.*

At 1 year 10 months 18 days he also used 'tee' for a cow.

At 1 year 11 months 1 day he used 'goggie' for a toy dog.

*At 1 year 11 months 2 days he stopped using 'tee' for a small
dog, and referred to it instead as 'goggie'.*

At 1 year 11 months 24 days he used 'tee' for a horse.

*At 1 year 11 months 25 days he used 'hosh' for a horse, but
also called it 'tee' once more the following day. After that,
he consistently referred to it as 'hosh'.*

*At 1 year 11 months 27 days he stopped using 'tee' for a cat,
and referred to it instead as 'pushie'.*

*At 2 years 0 months 10 days he used 'hosh' to refer to a large
dog.*

*At 2 years 0 months 20 days he stopped using 'tee' for a cow,
and referred to it instead as 'moo-ka'.*

*At 2 years 0 months 20 days he used 'biggie-goggie' for a
large dog.*

(Lewis, Language, Thought and Personality, 1963)

*4 Discuss some of the ways in which ideas about the functions
of language contribute to our understanding of how children
acquire English as their first language.*

C. *Language History*

*1 (b) The passage which follows was written by William
Caxton in the fifteenth century. In it, he describes some of the
problems he encountered in trying to translate a book from
French into English.*

*By reference to the passage, comment on some of the
changes which have taken place in English spelling,
vocabulary and meanings and grammar since this passage
was written.*

Caxton on Translating
*And whan I had aduysed me in this sayd boke, I delybered
and concluded to translate it in to englysshe, And forthwyth
toke a penne & ynke, and wrote a leef or tweyne whyche I
ouersawe agayn to corecte it.*

*And wha I sawe the fayr & straunge termes therin I
doubted that it sholde not please some gentylmen whiche late
blamed me, sayeng yt in my translacyons I had ouer curyous
termes whiche coude not be vnderstande of comyn peple and
desired me to vse olde and homely termes in my translacyons,
and fayn wolde I satysfye euery man and so to doo, toke an
olde boke and redde therin and certaynly the englysshe was
so rude and brood[1] that I coude not wele vnderstande it.*

*And also my lorde abbot of westmynster ded do shewe
to me late, certayn euydences wryton in olde englysshe, for to
reduce[2] it in to our englysshe now vsid And certaynly it was
wreton in suche wyse that it was more lyke to dutche than
englysshe: I coude not reduce ne brynge it to be
vnderstonden.*

*And certaynly our langage now vsed varyeth ferre from
that whiche was vsed and spoken whan I was borne For we
englysshe men ben borne vnder the domynacyon of the mone,
whiche is neuer stedfaste but euer wauerynge wexynge one
season and waneth & dyscreaseth another season And that
comyn englysshe that is spoken in one shyre varyeth from a
nother.*

(Caxton, fifteenth century)

Glossary
[1]*broad*
[2]*translate*

2 (a) *'Time changes all things: there is no reason why language
should escape this universal law.' (Saussure, 1915)*
*Explain and comment on the implications of this
statement, and give examples where you think they are
appropriate. In your answer, you are free to agree or disagree
with the quotation or with parts of it.*

3 *Discuss some of the ways in which language change is related
to social change.*

D. *Language Varieties*

1 *The following extract is from a conversation between two
Yorkshire farm labourers, R.M. and A.M., in their fifties.
Standard punctuation is used throughout, but an
attempt has been made to represent the speakers'
pronunciations by means of the spelling.
Identify some of the distinctive lexical and
grammatical features of the regional variety of English used
in this extract.*

Yorkshire Farm Labourers

R.M. *Hello, Alf. Wheer ta for? Off a bit? I see thou'rt dolled up.*

A.M. *Nay, not far, I'm just walkin' out a bit, that's all. Tha sees I'm out o' work ageean.*

R.M. *Out of work, arta? By gow, thou'rt about as well off as me, and tha knows they say theer's nobbut a awpny[1] i't'week between t'worker and t'laiker[2] t'year end and t'laiker 'es it. If thou'rt to aks me, 'ere I am tewin[3] away t'week long for next to nowt, just keepin' body an' soul together an' niver an openin' for nowt. I were just grummlin' to misen[4] for there's bahn to be a do down at t'Wheeatsheeaf within the next week — tha'll 'av heerd on it, I expect?*

A.M. *No, I 'edn't.*

R.M. *'esn't ta?*

A.M. *No.*

R.M. *Aye, an I sud like to gooa bur a'v nooa brass. I daresay they'd let me in baht payin' but I don't like to be beholden to folk. I'll tell thi what a'v been thinkin' o' doin', but tha mun niver mention it while breeath draws up an' down thi. I were thinkin' of offerin' to do my share i' potayts. Jack Hollins has a grand lot at t'back o' t'hedge, he'd never miss a rooit or two.*

A.M. *Tha wodn't call it reight steylin', Dick, wud ta?*

R.M. *It just depends, tha sees. If we just took an odd rooit here an' there and just thinned 'em out a bit and so gev t'others a better chance to grow an' spreyd, Jack would have as many potayts together as if we'd never touched 'em. We should be takkin' them an' steylin' in a way o' speykin', but if we could do Jack a good turn we mud as weel do it.*

A.M. *I'd rayther say nowt about it. I don't think Jack likes me.*

R.M. *Doesn't ta? Aw reight, then, we'll just ger 'em an' eyt 'em an' let that fit[5] us for this time. We can do Jack a good turn some time else. An' if t'potayts is poor 'uns, we couldn't speyk a good word for 'em.*

A.M. *We'd better say nowt about 'em.*

(Wright, The Language of British Industry, 1974)

Glossary

[1] *halfpenny*
[2] *person out of work*
[3] *working*
[4] *myself*
[5] *satisfy*

2 *The first of the two passages which follow is from a journal published by the United Nations Association called* New World *(1983). It is read mainly by people interested in international relations and political and humanitarian issues. The second is from* Aircraft Illustrated *(1986), a journal read mainly by people of all ages who are interested in civil and military aircraft.*

Compare some of the ways in which language is used in these two articles to achieve their purposes.

In your answer, you should refer to vocabulary and meanings, grammar, overall structure and any other linguistic matters you think are relevant.

Passage A

Call for a ban on 'war' toys
The European Parliament wants the production and sale of 'war' toys reduced and replaced by toys which are 'constructive and develop creativity'.

Last year they passed a resolution calling on member states to ban the 'visual and verbal advertising of war toys' and Sweden, France and the Federal Republic of Germany, the world's third largest toy producer, have moved towards ultimately pegging the production of war toys.

A substantial number of individuals and organisations in the United Kingdom have expressed concern about the present state of affairs.

The European Parliament's resolution recommended in particular that the sale of replica guns and rifles which are so realistic that they might be mistaken for the real thing should be banned in order to avoid them being used by criminals.

It emphasised the danger of giving children, through war toys, a liking for weapons and expressed concern at the part the mass media was playing in 'creating a culture of war and violence'.

The resolution believed that if the production of war toys was reduced there would be a demand for other toys – particularly electronic toys and musical instruments – and asked that help should be given to manufacturers who had to install expensive new equipment and technology to make the switch.

Passage B

Revised Phantom
Matchbox's kit of the Spey-powered Phantom FG1/FGR2 has now been revised to bring the model up to the latest standard, and to improve some less desirable features.

In shape, the model was reasonably accurate, except for the front end. The original model had a radome that was too small in diameter, but this has now been changed by the adoption of a larger radome and the lower line of the front fuselage has also been revised. The electronic-countermeasures bar, a unique feature of RAF Phantoms, has now been added.

Matchbox's kit of the Spey-Phantom has a comprehensive weapons and stores fit. In the pure interceptor role the model has the four Sparrows (or Skyflashes) and four Sidewinders, with a Vulcan gun pod or long-range tank under the fuselage. Long-range tanks may be carried on integral pylons on the outer wing positions. In the strike role, bombs or rocket pods can be fitted, again with the Vulcan gun pod. A reconnaissance pod for mounting under the fuselage is also included. Of course, a mix of all these weapons, pods and tanks can be selected as required for a particular subject.

A unique feature of the Royal Navy's F-4K Phantom FG1 was the extending nose wheel strut to give a higher angle of attack for catapult launching, and the kit includes both the normal length nose undercarriage unit and the unit in the extended position.

Markings are supplied for three Spey-Phantoms. One is an FG1 from No 111 Squadron based at RAF Leuchars, Scotland, in 1983. The second is an FG1 of No 892 Squadron, RN Fleet Air Arm, based on HMS Ark Royal, during 1977. The last subject is an FGR2 of No 23 Squadron based at RAF Stanley, in the Falkland Isles, during 1983.

This is a useful revision of the only available Spey-Phantom kit in 1:72 scale.

The cost is £3.95.

English reoriented

1 Some Precursors

English classes of the 1960s are sometimes referred to as the first grammarless generation, yet throughout the 1960s action research was taking place behind the main teaching scene as it were, though very much with the needs of schoolchildren in mind. If we wish to look back a little earlier than that, we have to look at Richard Hoggart's *The Uses of Literacy* (1957), for example, to find signs of a new socio-cultural climate in English teaching, for the book proved very influential on many teachers. Without explicitly concerning himself with language, Hoggart makes reference throughout the book to a range of experiences that have since become the stuff of language study projects in primary and secondary schools, e.g. oral traditions of working class life; the language and lore of childhood; teenage talk; gender coding; the sharpness of perception expressed in dialectal forms; advertisements for correspondence courses promising culture and economic success via improved word power; myths and images in films and other popular media; the experience of 'them and uz' (recollected yet again in the 1980s by another Leeds writer, the poet Tony Harrison).

If we look at a Government publication of the 1950s, *Language: some suggestions for teachers* (1954), an embryonic Bullock Report, we can detect again the beginnings of a new climate of opinion about teaching English language. The pamphlet acknowledges a 'great revival of interest in language study at the present time' and recognises that 'even the most trifling problems of language study in the classroom raise questions that are ultimately issues of philosophy and psychology', a far cry from the simplistic notions that invariably accompanied grammar instruction as practised in the 1950s. What it has to say on relationships between language, thought and culture is still worth reading and, in its insistence on the central role of language in learning, it pre-dates the Bullock Committee's *A Language for Life* by 20 years.

More directly concerned with knowledge about language was Randolph Quirk's *The Use of English* (1962), which became a seminal work for some English teachers and influenced the best intentions behind Use of English papers which were beginning to appear as alternatives to examination papers in English literature. It stressed the notion of grammar as a descriptive activity rather than a prescriptive one; it examined notions of correctness and Standard English; it applied linguistic criticism to both literary and non-literary texts; it pointed out the range of varieties in language use; and in its well known supplement by A. C. Grimson, it set out a framework for recognising the primacy of speech and for studying the phonology of the English language. Still a valuable book and highly informative, it explains among other things why the distinction between grammatical (i.e. function) words and lexical (i.e. content) words provides a useful initial level for understanding how the English language is put together. Both primary and secondary pupils can comprehend this distinction, especially by means of word deletion activities in which selected classes of words have been removed, and apply it to their reading and writing.

2 Language in Use

Between 1967 and 1971 the Schools Council Programme in Linguistics and English Teaching, led by Michael Halliday, developed a series of initiatives which culminated in a primary programme, *Breakthrough to Literacy* (1970), and a secondary programme of language study, *Language in Use* (1971). *Language in Use* offers an approach to language study based upon a coherent view of the nature and functions of language. It consists of three sections:

1 the nature and functions of language;

2 language and individual man (including culture);
3 language and social man (including institutions).

It promotes investigative approaches to everyday uses of language and suggests guidelines for reflection and systematic further enquiry. Ahead of its time, the scheme proved difficult to assimilate into existing patterns of English teaching despite the considerable interest and respect it aroused in many teachers.

Without doubt *Language in Use* gave a new impetus to the teaching of English language and opened up new prospects. *Language Study in the Middle Years* by Ian Forsyth appeared in 1978 and Frank Skitt published a primary scheme in 1979 called *Themes for Language Learning*. Geoffrey Thornton, one of the authors of *Language in Use*, edited a series of books under the general title of 'Explorations in Language Study'. One book in the series, *Language Projects: an introduction to the study of language* (1979), by Sandra Harris and Ken Morgan, whilst describing the work of college of education students, nevertheless presents a wide range of ideas and guiding principles for investigative approaches perfectly accessible to primary and secondary pupils.

In 1978 John Keen published *Teaching English: a linguistic approach*, which embodied the investigative approach of *Language in Use*, demonstrating how pupils could be taught to use their implicit knowledge of English to solve for themselves explicit problems of spelling, word choice and sentence construction. It reiterates the importance of understanding the functions of language in any given context, if language structures are to be properly understood and used effectively, and offers a framework for investigating language functions.

A later application of the *Language in Use* approach and Hallidayan linguistics was published in Canada by James Benson and William Greaves, *The Language People Really Use* (1974). In 1984 they published in England *You and Your Language: the Kinds of English You Use* (1984). Designed for secondary use, the first volume covers styles and dialects under such headings as 'Standard and Non Standard Dialects', 'School-learned English', and 'Family-learned English'. The second volume, 'Meaning is Choice', looks at language structures.

There can be no doubt that the influence of Halliday and the approach embodied in *Language in Use* are the most impressive contributions to coherent principles and practice of language study in schools to appear since the abandonment of traditional grammar instruction. Yet it has taken a long time for those principles and practices to influence mainstream English teaching. In 15 years, investigative language study has finally gained a purchase on the 16 to 19 curriculum via A level examinations, and in 20 years, via the second Cox Report and the creation of LINC, its value has achieved the status of legal requirement in the National Curriculum for English. What needs to be emphasised now is that *Language in Use* and related approaches, with their emphasis on exploration, investigation, reflection and data collecting, demand a style of teaching that includes a willingness and a capacity to learn alongside the pupils. If in the old tradition of grammatical instruction, the teachers were the only experts, modern investigative approaches presuppose joint expertise, which calls for sharing of knowledge and experience of real, everyday language, rather than the transmission by teachers of a set of labels and closed methods of analysis. The use of terminology or an agreed metalanguage comes much more easily when there are some shared concepts derived from meaningful experiences and systematic investigation. Furthermore, it is evident from experience both in primary schools and in the JMB A level syllabus, that the functions and structures of language can be just as effectively studied by starting with the largest comprehensible units, for example, social interactions, genres, whole texts and paragraphs and working toward smaller units like clauses, words, part of words and sounds. Traditionally language study, like initial reading, has been based on a supposed gradual development of understanding, starting with the smallest elements and building upon those until comprehension of larger units is finally achieved. Learning how to move confidently between knowledge about social structures and functions of language, and knowledge about the bits and pieces of language, and to be able to see some significance in the connections between the two, is important not only for the enjoyment and comprehension of literature but also for the fullest participation in all the social and personal functions of language in everyday life.

3 Radio and Television

One of the problems of language study in schools, though it is a problem that leads to a great advantage once it has been worked through, is that both pupils and teachers are extremely dependent upon their own resources. The best data is collected from real life which means that starting points are very much concerned with method and context rather than teachers' input. This was the major problem facing teachers who wanted to introduce *Language in Use* into the English curriculum. If life itself is the textbook, *Language in Use* is a manual or guidebook for exploring the role of language in life. The BBC radio programmes, *Web of Language* (first series 1974; second series 1979), invited children in primary and middle years to explore language and life from a variety of points of view, and their popularity is as much accounted for by the resources provided as by the quality of the ideas in the programmes. There were two booklets and two audio cassettes, all of which have since been incorporated into a commercial publication.

The notion of 'a web of language' derives from the Robert Graves poem 'The Cool Web' in which language is ambivalently presented as an abstraction that lies between humans and our immediate sensations, but which also saves us from going mad. The idea of a web of words is also useful in a less dramatic way than that offered by Graves. It effectively describes the psycho-social network created by language, in which we have our being. It is a web that is at once outside us and inside our heads; it includes all our speaking, listening, reading and writing and extends across all the areas of knowledge about language, implicit and explicit, described in LINC INSET materials:

◇ language in society
◇ language acquisition and development
◇ language varieties
◇ language histories
◇ language as a system

The idea is also used by Ronald Carter and Michael N. Long in *The Web of Words* (1987), which explores literary texts by observing and reflecting upon their functional and structural linguistic features. Though intended for post-sixteen students the attention it pays to such topics as 'word families', dialogue in plays and novels, transforming one text into another for a different audience and purpose, may appropriately be directed towards National Curriculum requirements at Key Stage 3.

In the 1970s Thames Television produced a series of programmes on language for use in secondary schools. The programme covered a range of topics identified in the National Curriculum, e.g. dialectal variation; the importance of stories; language acquisition; language in society. Notably the programmes highlighted the part played by language in establishing patterns of social and individual power. An accompanying booklet has been published by Thames Television, *Language* (1979). Another theme in the programmes was the multilingual variety evident in modern Britain, and two other booklets that offer useful resources very much in the vein of the Thames Television series are *The Languages Book* by the ILEA English Centre (1981) and *Investigating Our Language* (1985) by John Richmond and Helen Savva. Both books in fact unite the themes of language and power with an approach to language study that places language firmly in a universal rather than an English context, acknowledging the growth of a multilingual British society since 1945.

Many schools have found the television series *The Story of English* (1986), made jointly by the BBC and Canadian Television, a useful resource for promoting an interest in language. Despite giving a distinctly 'imperialistic' view of English as a world language, the series covers historical aspects extremely vividly as well as informatively. One programme, for example, presents a discussion between a Breton onion seller in Wales and a native Welsh speaker. Both are able to recognise quite easily the common Celtic ancestry of their respective native languages.

More recently the BBC has produced a series of programmes for 14 to 16 year olds which is essentially socio-linguistic in outlook and presents young people talking about attitudes to accent and dialect and to varieties of registers and speech styles (*Language File*, 1990). A second series will look especially at aspects of explicit language study in the classroom.

4 Language Awareness

The Language Awareness movement, as it is sometimes called, originated out of developments in the modern languages curriculum but has attracted interest in some primary schools and secondary school English departments. In 1984 Eric Hawkins published *Awareness of Language: an introduction*, together with a series of booklets suitable for use with 10–14 year olds. The main thrust of this scheme of work is very similar to that of *Language in Use* and *Web of Language*, namely that language is a vital yet consistently underestimated feature of our personal and social lives. It covers differences between animal communication and human language, language as a system of structures and functions, varieties of language, language change, and differences between spoken and written language. Significantly, the Language Awareness approach puts language study in the context of the world's languages rather than in an English context, though *Language in Use* similarly draws attention to universal phenomena of language use. An earlier approach designed for lower secondary years which focuses on language rather than the English language, is *Language Links: the European Family of Languages* (1980) by Clive Jenkins. Its perspective is essentially historical and presents ways in which pupils may explore language change and the interconnections between languages of Indo-European origin.

The distinction between a study of language as a universal human phenomenon and the study of English Language became more marked through the 1980s. In *Language or English?* (1988) Edwards, Moorhouse and Widlake discuss the kind of language curriculum needed by bilingual students, and put forward a framework which is multicultural and multilingual. They remark that:

> the model of language we accept and the methods and
> techniques suggested for developing oracy and literacy skills are
> in many ways appropriate and beneficial to all pupils, a
> conclusion supported by many class and subjects teachers.

It is interesting that the argument for the beneficial effect of language study on language expertise appears once again, not as a justification for native grammatical instruction this time, but to illustrate the value of socio-cultural learning.

A different development in the language awareness approach has grown out of the JMB A level English Language syllabus but is specifically designed for years one to five in secondary schools. It is called the Language Awareness Project. *Language for Talking, Living and Learning* by John Keen provides photocopiable support materials with which pupils can investigate aspects of conversation, telling anecdotes, being interviewed, persuading, arguing, planning, and writing and reading in different genres. In *Language and Gender* Angela Goddard uses a similar practical approach to hidden gender messages, language stereotyping and labelling, and to different aspects of the role of language in establishing personal and social power.

The line of historical development sketched above has been essentially concerned with studying language in the context of the English curriculum. There have been other influences on some teachers, notably from the fields of psycholinguistics and sociolinguistics, which have contributed to teachers' understanding of language acquisition and the development of literacy and oracy. Throughout the 1970s and 80s a great many primary and secondary teachers undertook advanced studies in what has now come to be called Educational Linguistics, a field of enquiry in which a number of linguists have made contributions that have proved important not only in shaping views of the role of language in literacy and learning, but in opening up the content areas for the English curriculum. Jean Aitchison, Ronald Carter, Katharine Perera, Pam Czerniewska and Peter Gannon, Andrew Wilkinson, Gordon Wells, have been notably influential. One writer and broadcaster from the field of academic linguistics who has prolifically introduced knowledge about language to the widest possible public is David Crystal. His *Encyclopaedia of Language* (1987) remarkably, though justifiably, proved a best seller and is increasingly to be found in primary and secondary schools as a knowledgeable resource, accessible to both pupils and teachers. *Who Cares About English Usage?* (1984) is particularly relevant to teaching English and the debate about Standard English, and his *The English Language* (1988) gives a comprehensive overview of historical development as well as of modern controversies and approaches to the study of English language. Also helpful as a framework for considering language acquisition at Key Stage 3 is *Listen To Your Child* (1988) while his *Rediscover English Grammar* (1988) offers an accessible synopsis of grammar based on what may be regarded as the standard reference work on English grammar by Quirk, Greenbaum, Leech and Svartvik (1985).

MAPPING OUT LANGUAGE STUDY AT KEY STAGE 3

Under the LINC initiative a working party of Cheshire secondary teachers[1] undertook a review of what they had learned about language study at A level, and what they had been able to develop in the 11 to 16 age range. Their brief was to devise schemes of work, or units of study, that would effectively interpret National Curriculum programmes of study incorporating knowledge about language at Key Stage 3. It was felt that over the next two or three years teachers would welcome both a linguistic framework for schemes of work and a 'mix and match' approach that would enable them to try out interesting packages of curriculum content, investigating language along with their pupils. A number of routes may be taken through the schemes suggested below which will integrate language study within a whole English curriculum without, in the process, losing linguistic focus.

Groups within the working party devoted themselves specifically to each of the profile components of the National Curriculum in English. You will notice that Language in Society appears to have been subsumed under Speaking and Listening since it is not named anywhere else. It is not intended to suggest that there are no sociolinguistic factors involved in the reading and writing components; indeed, the contrary is true. Choice of genre and sense of audience in writing, for example, and the notion of reading as cultural practice, immediately raise ideological issues and question of power and authority which pupils are certainly aware of at implicit and instinctive levels. Language in Society in fact subsumes everything else, but experience at A level suggests that the need to establish talk as both a prime source of language and as highly sophisticated social behaviour is of considerable importance in the English curriculum, given the ideological devaluation to which talk has been subjected in our culture. It was also considered that the investigation of 'real life speaking and listening' is a social study in itself as well as a linguistic enquiry, and brings pupils into far closer contact with the social functions and social structures of language in use, than the decontextualised forms of language study to be found in the earlier tradition of grammatical instruction. Syllabuses that start off by investigating talk, unless the approach is determinedly phonetic, immediately plunge pupils and teachers into considerations of social attitudes, values and power structures.

The final section outlines aspects of language as a system, some of which may well have been considered in previous sections but which, together, make up a coherent framework for studying language as a system of structures as well as an interacting network of functions.

Speaking and Listening

1 Language and Society
This would be the most innovative area in terms of management and sustained development. It depends considerably on data collecting, accurate recording, and reflective learning. For example:

◇ using questionnaires and interviews to find out information about people's attitudes, beliefs, opinions: *vox populi* – getting people talking (will involve reflection on method of enquiry as well as on content of data)

◇ 'they don't speak our language' – enquiries into occupational dialects; jargon; officialese; slang; codes

◇ accents; Received Pronunciation; talking 'posh'; talking 'dead common'; regional stereotypes and foreign accent; stereotypes – use BBC tapes, *English with an Accent, English Dialects*

◇ 'the language of situations' (pragmatics) – having an argument; being questioned or interviewed; threatening, bullying; embarrassing situations

◇ euphemisms and taboo subjects in conversation

◇ ways people talk to each other (gender, age, social class, social power)

◇ the speech of young children as a source of knowledge about language

2 Starting Points in Literature

◇ investigating (and enjoying) reading aloud

◇ speech forms in poetry and novels (e.g. dialogue poems; conversation in stories)

◇ oral traditions in literature (e.g. ballads, legends, tales)

◇ trying to discover historical differences of pronunciation from texts (e.g. Beowulf, Chaucer, Caxton's Prologue to the Aeneid, Shakespeare) and listening to taped versions of Old, Middle and Early Modern English

3 Opportunities in Drama

◇ role play (adopting appropriate tone, manner of address, intonation, rhetorical effects)

◇ presenting scenes from Shakespeare in different ways, e.g. Hamlet's rejection of Ophelia; letter scene in *Twelfth Night*; rude mechanicals in *Midsummer Night's Dream*; casket scene in *Merchant of Venice*; witches in *Macbeth*

◇ 'rhubarb' plays, using intonation patterns only, e.g. *The Clangers*

◇ suiting gesture, facial expression, to words spoken

◇ conversation made up of one word utterances

◇ plays of Harold Pinter and Samuel Beckett

◇ taping and transcribing improvisations

◇ dramatising scenes from novels

4 Media Oriented Studies

◇ comparing soap opera dialogue, e.g. younger generation and older generation in *Neighbours* and *Home and Away* (observing and recording Australian accent)

◇ comparing speech styles of different weathermen, comedians, quiz comperes, gardening advisers
◇ describing language characteristics of news reading
◇ taping and transcribing selections from phone-in programmes, e.g. *Call Nick Ross*
◇ collecting adverts and jingles
◇ compiling short television/radio programme with, for example, newsflash interruption
◇ making tape recordings of stories
◇ language and power as demonstrated in *Cell Block H*
◇ study of American dialogue in *Cheers, Roseanne*
◇ imitating style of BBC, Argo or Listen for Pleasure cassettes e.g. *The Archers, Dick Barton, The Beiderbecke Affair, Kes*
◇ turn off sound of children's television programme and tell own story
◇ compare information provided by transcript, audio tape, video tape and combination of all three
◇ how are authority and credibility conveyed in media voices?

5 Special Topics, e.g. Humour

◇ comic verse read aloud
◇ television/radio comedians
◇ phonic ambiguity and puns
◇ effects of laughter in conversation
◇ what makes 'funny voices' funny?

Writing

1 Aims and Contexts

Primary aim is to use pupils' own writing as a source of interest in and knowledge about language.

Knowledge about language has a macroscopic dimension:

i.e. sense of audience
awareness of purpose
knowledge of topic   } BIG KAL
recognition of differences between
    writing and spoken language

It also has a microscopic dimension:

i.e. text organisation (cohesion)
sentence structure and interconnections } little kal
word choice
punctuation

Pupils constantly move between these dimensions, knowingly and unknowingly.

If reflection is an important precondition for learning about language then audience response is important feedback for learning about language through writing.

Responses can be achieved by means of:

◇ writing for different audiences
◇ working with a partner
◇ working in a small group

Asking readers to complete response cards is a valuable way of acquiring data about the language used.

A response card could ask:

◇ what is the purpose of the writing?
◇ who is it for?
◇ how far has it been successful?
◇ in what ways could it be improved?

Pupils should make their own response cards. The potential of word processors for creative learning about language should be recognised. See *Days out from Widnes* (Keith, 1990).

2 Varieties of Writing

Aware of current debates about genres for writing, the working party identified four kinds of writing which are sufficiently distinct in form and/or function, which pupils themselves recognise as different, and which feature in GCSE syllabus prescriptions for course work as well as in the National Curriculum. It was recognised that the commentary (i.e. writing about your own writing) is a relatively new genre in English syllabuses and likely to develop in a variety of ways, one of which will be reflection on the writer's own knowledge about language. The four categories considered are:

a) personal and imagined stories
b) poetry
c) persuasive writing (also given as an exemplar in non-statutory guidance for Key Stage 4)
d) writing about writing

a) Stories

◇ learning about different genres and discussing their features (see ILEA publications *Making Stories* and *Changing Stories*)
◇ use of word deletion in texts to focus on linguistic features
◇ paired or group investigations of their own individual stories to discern structural elements and to observe word choices

b) Poetry

◇ developing word games into poetry
◇ word deletion to highlight lexical choices
◇ paying attention to rhythm, syllables, punctuation (how should a text be read aloud?)

 ◇ what different sub-genres of poetry are there? (e.g. ballad, limerick, sonnet, dialogue, narrative)
 ◇ considering sounds of poetry (e.g. alliteration, onomatopoeia)

c) Persuasive writing

 ◇ importance of identifying audience and purpose
 ◇ investigating persuasion in advertising (e.g. jingles, imagery, suggestiveness, status of language user)
 ◇ considering what we can learn from talk about persuasiveness
 ◇ looking at non narrative shapes for writing arguments

d) Writing about writing

 ◇ redrafting is a prime source of knowledge about language (e.g. grammar, lexis, semantics, discourse)
 ◇ keeping a writing log encourages reflection on language use
 ◇ writing about your own linguistic achievement is an important kind of self knowledge
 ◇ writing about other pupils' writing highlights unintended effects of writing (e.g. 'Is that what was meant?')
 ◇ thinking about writing, e.g. what different kinds of writing do you do in a school day, week, or term?
 ◇ editorial work, e.g. what kinds of 'mistakes' do writers make? What comments do readers make on accuracy and presentation? Improving the text by use of word processing facilities

e) Other avenues of investigation

Investigations into other forms of writing (other genres, other functions) may be carried out as a special project. Some examples are:

 ◇ instructions
 ◇ reports and reportage
 ◇ letters
 ◇ diaries
 ◇ reviews
 ◇ playscripts
 ◇ personal notes
 ◇ scripted dialogue
 ◇ transcripts

3 Varieties of Audience

'Knowing about' audiences and about communicating with readers depends upon complex sociolinguistic relationships and it is an area where apprentice writers can on some occasions be very aptly in tune, yet on others are wildly off-key. Mapping out the network of writers and readers available to pupils is a useful first step in investigating varieties of audience, and constitutes sociolinguistic knowledge in its own right. It contributes, for example, to a better understanding of 'sufficient formality' and 'appropriate informality' and to a more confident awareness of the subtle ways in which register and tone are communicated. A level students soon recognise that these are all issues of control and power over contexts as well as over language used, and awareness of the codes, cues, unwritten rules, intuitive contacts – call them what you will – is an equally important issue for younger writers.

A range of real audiences for investigation would include: teachers, friends and classmates, other year groups, other teachers in other schools (e.g. writing exhanges), parents, newspaper editors, competition judges, public relations officers in local industries, BBC, local and national government, MPs, visitors to school plays and exhibitions, local libraries and community centres.

The concept of 'the general reader' also needs to be explored. Defined initially in terms of 'human beings interested in other human beings', pupils could explore the concept in terms of reading habits, attitudes, opportunities and preferences. An analysis of local interest magazines and newspapers makes a good starting point and could include school publications. Interviewing local newsagents on which national publications sell best, and analysing their contents, is one way of getting an insight into 'the general reader' and also of learning something about topics, tastes, and the forms, structures and styles of popular writing.

Other agencies with which pupils can interact as both investigators and writers are publishers, charities, libraries, (survey of popular fiction), local press.

Reading

1 Collecting codes, signs and signal systems (an introduction to semiotics)

Reading is interpreted here as reading media texts and the world at large as well as printed texts. It encompasses activities such as:

◇ reading uniforms, sports strip, T-shirts, fashion, personal objects
◇ reading book jackets
◇ reading signs and symbols, e.g. in town, on the road, in school
◇ reading young children's picture books including picture books for the not so young
◇ reading the messages in illustrations to books (e.g. gender, race, social class)
◇ reading behaviour, e.g. plays without words (Ronnie Barker; Eric Sykes' 'The Plank'; Rowan Atkinson's 'Mr Bean')
◇ reading sign language (this was seen as having rich potential for learning about the nature and functions of language)
◇ reading body language

◇ reading the school, e.g. the messages and images presented by the foyer, the classroom, letters from school

2 Reading imaginative literature

This is an area that is almost overwhelmingly rich in resources and data. The working party concentrated on features of language that could be investigated both creatively and analytically.

◇ nouns and naming, e.g. *The Wizard of Earthsea*
◇ lexical deviance and standard syntax, e.g. *Jabberwocky*
◇ archaic language of Beowulf, Langland, Sir Gawain, Chaucer
◇ riddles, nursery rhymes, litanies, old songs, proverbs, e.g. *The Hobbit*
◇ what makes a poem a poem?
◇ myths, ancient and modern, creation myths from different cultures, contemporary myths, e.g. *The Iron Man*, comic book characters
◇ the structures and content of fairy stories, e.g. rewriting *The Three Billy Goats Gruff* or *Cinderella*
◇ invented words, e.g. *Bottersnikes and Gumbles*; word play
◇ stereotypes and formulae, e.g. Enid Blyton, Willard Price
◇ the language of science fiction
◇ the sounds and rhythms of stories and poems (reading aloud)
◇ exploring metaphor and ambiguity both in literature and in everyday uses of language
◇ exploring use of dialect in literature, e.g. Dickens, Hardy; local dialect poets and storytellers

3 Moving between genres

The notion of investigating varieties of texts was introduced at A level as a valuable approach to finding out more about language forms and functions. It now serves as a helpful preface to learning something about different genres of writing. The method most recommended is set out below:

a) Collection of data
Pupils should collect as many different kinds of texts as they can (at least 13), though teachers can successfully initiate the activity by collecting the texts themselves. An alternative is to ask a class to empty its bags and pockets. It is important that the texts should be available for spreading out on a table top. Primary pupils have been known to empty waste papers baskets. Texts may vary from bus tickets to copies of *David Copperfield*.

b) The sort and talk stage
Small groups should agree on principles of classification and compare them with those of other groups. Each category of text should be given a title.

c) Testing the model
Pupils should see how other texts fit into their model and whether
expansion or refinement is necessary.
d) Reconstructions
It is often possible to recreate a person's life from texts or to
construct the contexts in which texts are produced and received.
e) Transformations
Texts may be transformed in a variety of ways, e.g. an AA guide
to the geography of a favourite novel or play; turning a pocketful
of texts into a poem; combining texts such as a travel diary
interspersed with postcards sent home.
f) Making new texts
Personal letters in dialect; invented letters that have a story
behind them, followed by writing the story; using the format of a
particular report for pupils' own report on a topic they have
chosen; intertextual writing.

Investigating the system

From time to time there will be opportunities to explore the English
language as a system. Worthwhile topics at Key Stage 3 would be:

1 understanding how speech is produced;
2 understanding how grammar grows in young children;
3 understanding morphology, i.e. the systems of prefixes and
   suffixes in the English language;
4 charting a history of changes in English;
5 classifying how new words are created in English;
6 exploring different word classes and their functions in texts;
7 compiling dictionaries or glossaries of key words in school
   subjects;
8 exploring the origins of selected fields of words, e.g. food and
   cooking; music; technology; sport; fashion and design; everyday objects;
9 observing the stylistic and pragmatic effects of modal verbs,
   the passive voice, the placement of modifiers; the use of
   alternative lexical choices; use of pronouns;
10 comparing alphabets of the world and making translations of
    selected words and phrases;
11 conducting a languages survey of the school and the
    community;
12 inventing codes, symbols and mini-languages.

The suggestions above for schemes of work place knowledge
about language firmly in the mainstream of children's development as
language users. *English for Ages 5 to 16* expresses strongly a belief in the
wisdom of such a course:

We believe that knowledge about language should be an
integral part of work in English, not a separate body of
knowledge to be added on to the traditional English curriculum.
(6:2)

ENGLISH NOW AND IN PROSPECT

In spite of the political tensions and compromises embedded in the
National Curriculum or possibly because of them, English as a traditional school subject has undergone a national stocktaking which may
be turned to teachers' advantage. The redressing of the balance between
the privileged status of 'literature' and the Cinderella status of 'language' has long been overdue. There exists now an impressive body of
ideas and resources, outlined in the first section of this chapter. It was
simply an accident of history that explicit study of language came back
into the English examination curriculum, post-16, rather than in the
years five to 16. But the experience gained has been valuable and has
enabled one representative group of teachers to find room quite com-
fortably in the existing curriculum for more informed and investigative
approaches to language. All requirements in programmes of study for
all three profile components can be encompassed in the framework
suggested, though it is important to recognise that the scheme described
here is just one formulation of the theoretical and practical approaches
recommended by LINC. There will no doubt be many others in the next
two or three years.

The Language in the National Curriculum project represents a
culmination point of threads of innovative work done over the years in
all phases of education: infants and junior school projects; secondary,
leading to A level; undergraduate and PGCE courses; and teachers' own
studies and researches into areas of educational linguistics for Diplomas
and MEd degrees. It is time now to celebrate knowledge about language, not lament its inclusion in the English curriculum, or fear
imagined consequences.

One very welcome consequence of incorporating into the English
Curriculum the kind of language study described in Cox II and embodied in the schemes of work of the previous section, is a new respect
for the data of everyday language use. Language study is a scientific
enquiry as well as a human interest, and the satisfactions to be derived
from it stand alongside the satisfactions to be derived from works of
imaginative literature. Far from threatening the continued existence of
English in the curriculum, the inclusion of empirically based language
study (how language is *really* used) could make English a point in the
secondary curriculum where science and art could reunite as disciplines
and endeavours leading towards greater human understanding.

It is interesting finally to compare a piece of work that might be
undertaken by third-year secondary pupils with the kind of schoolwork

that lies behind the examination questions at the beginning of this chapter:

Topic: The language of unscripted commentary

◇ Data: tape recording of radio sports, fashion or public events running commentary. Pupils should work in pairs and choose own event, then select one or two minutes of interesting material.

◇ Method: transcribe accurately what the commentator said. Pupils will need to decide on punctuation conventions, e.g. dashes for pauses.

An example from a cricket commentary is given below:

> . . . *and the score goes up to thirty-four for two, Edrich twenty-two and Cowdrey out this morning, caught Burge, bowled Hawke, ten – and England now, of course, metaphorically on the back foot – and the batsmen still to come (which many of you will no doubt be counting up) and some Englishmen may be glad that, now, that Jack Flavell was left out in favour of a batsman – Parfitt next, then Sharpe, then Parkes, then Titmus, Trueman, Gifford, Coldwell – now a little fussing about someone behind the sight-screen, before McKenzie bowls to Barrington – Barrington giving a look round the field, a slightly closer field for him, three slips, gully and not a leg-slip but a backward short leg, only just backward of square – six men close – McKenzie comes in, bowls, and Barrington makes a most ungraceful little jab there to a ball that goes through to Grant . . .*

◇ Observations: about the differences between the transcript and the spoken words; about specialist terminology; about the functions of radio commentaries.

◇ Activity: write the passage for readers. How would it be reorganised? re-phrased?
Write a short glossary of the cricket terms for non-experts.

◇ Further reflections: what differences are there between the implicit grammar of speech and the explicit grammar of writing?
Tape record a short sequence from another commentary and compare the words used, the grammatical features, and the style of spoken delivery.

An activity of this kind leads pupils to consider much deeper questions about grammar than parsing or clause analysis exercises will allow. It is concerned with the generative sources of grammar in speech and writing, and investigates the language used in terms of overall purposes and social contexts, as well as in terms of structures and specific linguistic features. It also meets requirements of programmes of study at Key Stage 3:

Extracted from *English 5–16* (the Cox Report)

Speaking and Listening

4 Help to develop in pupils speaking and listening their grasp of sequence . . .
  . . . emphasise the importance of clear diction and audibility.
5 . . . making use of audio and video recordings as appropriate.
8 . . . talking about stories, poems, playscripts and *other texts* . . .
9 Teaching about language through speaking and listening . . . should focus on regional and social variations in accents and dialects
  . . . the range of purposes which spoken language serves . . .
  . . . the forms and functions of spoken Standard English.
18 Pupils should consider language appropriate to situation, topic and purpose.

Reading

17 Pupils should be taught how to handle, and be given experience in using, a range of information texts in a variety of media.
23 Pupils should be taught how to respond to the way information is structured and presented . . .
  Pupils should discuss . . . differences in the use and meanings of words . . .
27 Pupils should discuss . . . the effects, in context, of different types of vocabulary . . . grammatical features . . .

Writing

22 . . . pupils' development as writers should be marked by . . . increasing conscious control over the structure and organisation of different types of text
  . . . an increasing proficiency in rereading . . .
  . . . an ability to reflect on and talk about language . . .
  . . . a widening knowledge of some of the main differences between speech and writing
  . . . a developing understanding of the range of purposes which language serves . . .
24 . . . pupils should be made aware of the following range of functions . . .
  . . . reporting . . .
  . . . narrating . . .
  . . . describing . . .
  . . . reconstructing . . .
28 Teaching should bring out the fact that as speech typically takes place in a situation where both speaker and listener are present . . .

whereas writing generally requires greater verbal explicitness. Pupils should be helped to recognise that because writers are not able to use the voice to emphasise key points in a sentence, they have to use a wide range of grammatical structures . . .

30 . . . pupils should come to understand that, at its most characteristic, speech is . . . spontaneous and informal which means topics . . . emerged in an unplanned and unstructured way; in contrast, writing needs a more tightly planned structure . . .

Activities of this kind promote reflection on implicit knowledge about language use which, through investigation, leads not only to more explicit understanding, but also to more proficient use of language. There are many more; some will not be unfamiliar to English teachers though perhaps their full linguistic potential has not always been recognised. There is no doubt that the application of ideas about the nature and functions of language to the teaching of English has already become a powerful groundswell. It is not something introduced by the Kingman and the Cox Committees. Influenced in its early days by the work of Michael Halliday, its value has received generous recognition in *English for Ages 5 to 16* and has already entered the 11 to 16 curriculum of schools offering English Language at A level. For those pioneering teachers the risks of learning alongside their students and of reorienting their approach to English were daunting. The overwhelming response to experience, however, is a conviction that their teaching has received a new lease of life. LINC, in its interpretation of programmes of study for knowledge about language offers a similar new lease of life.

REFERENCES

Aitchison, J. (1978) *Teach Yourself Linguistics* (2nd edn). EUP.

Aitchison, J. (1981) *Language Change: Progress or Decay?*. London: Fontana.

Aitchison, J. (1983) *The Articulate Mammal* (2nd edn). Milton Keynes: Open University Press.

Aitchison, J. (1987) *Words in the Mind*. Oxford: Blackwell.

Bacon, Sir F. (1605) *The Advancement of Learning*.

BBC (1990) *Language File*. TV series produced by Paul Ashton.

BBC *Web of Language*. First series 1974, second series 1979. Published by Oxford University Press under same title, 1980.

Benson, J. and Greaves, W. (1984) *You and Your Language: the Kinds of English You Use*. Oxford: Pergamon.

Carter, R. (ed.) (1982) *Linguistics and the Teacher*. London: Routledge.

Carter, R. and Long, M. N. (1987) *The Web of Words*. Cambridge: Cambridge University Press.

Clegg, A. (1964) *The Excitement of Writing*. London: Chatto and Windus.

Crystal, D. (1987) *The Cambridge Encyclopaedia of Language*. Cambridge: Cambridge University Press.

Crystal, D. (1984) *Who Cares About English Usage?*. Harmondsworth: Penguin.

Crystal, D. (1988) *The English Language*. Harmondsworth: Penguin.

Crystal, D. (1988) *Listen To Your Child*. Harmondsworth: Penguin.

Crystal, D. (1988) *Rediscover English Grammar*. London: Longman.

Czerniewska, P. and Gannon, P. (1980) *Using Linguistics*. London: Edward Arnold.

DES (1975) *A Language for Life* (The Bullock Report). London: HMSO.

DES (1988) *Report of the Committee of Inquiry into the Teaching of the English Language* (the Kingman Report). London: HMSO.

DES (1989) *English for Ages 5 to 16*. London: HMSO.

Doughty, P., Pearce, J. and Thornton, G. (1971) *Language in Use*. London: Longman.

Edwards, C., Moorhouse, J. and Widlake, S. (1988) *Language or English?* in Jones, M. and West, A. (eds) *Learning Me Your Language*. Stanley Thomas Publishers.

Forsyth, I. (1978) *Language Study in the Middle Years*. London: Longman.

Goddard, A. (1989) *Language and Gender*. London: Framework Press.

Harris, S. and Morgan K. (1979) *Language Projects: an introduction to the Study of Language*. Leeds: E. J. Arnold.

Hawkins, E. (1984) *Awareness of Language: an introduction*. Cambridge: Cambridge University Press.

Hoggart, R. (1957) *The Uses of Literacy*. Harmondsworth: Penguin.

Hourd, M. (1949) *The Education of the Poetic Spirit*. Oxford: Heinemann.

ILEA English Centre (1981) *The Language Book*. London: ILEA.

Jenkins, C. (1980) *Language Links: the European Family of Languages*. London: Harrap.

Keen, J. (1978) *Teaching English: a linguistic approach*. London: Methuen.

Keen, J. (1989) *Language for Talking, Living and Learning*. London: Framework Press.

Keith, B. (1990) *Days out from Widnes* in *Writing and Micros*. London: Nelson.

McCrum, R., Cran, W. and MacNeil, R. (1986) *The Story of English*. BBC Publications.

Ministry of Education (1954) *Language: Some Suggestions for Teachers in Primary, Secondary and Further Education*. London: HMSO.

Mittins, W. (1987) *The Naming of Parts*, Sheffield: NATE.

Perera, K. (1984) *Children's Writing and Reading*. Oxford: Blackwell.

Quirk, R. (1962) *The Use of English*. London: Longman.

Quirk, R., Greenbaum, S., Leech, G. and Svartvik, J. (1985) *A Comprehensive Grammar of the English Language*. London: Longman.

Richmond, D. J. and Savva, H. (1985) *Investigating our Language*. London: Edward Arnold.

Robinson, N. (1960) 'The relation between knowledge of English grammar and ability in English composition', *British Journal of Educational Psychology*, 30, pp. 184–186.

Schools Council (1970) *Breakthrough to Literacy*. London: Longman.

Skitt, F. (1979) *Themes for Language Learning*. London: A & C Black.

Thames Television (1979) *Language*. Thames in association with Hutchinson.
Wells, G. (1981) *Learning Through Interaction: the study of language development*. Cambridge: Cambridge University Press.
Wilkinson, A., *The Foundation of Language*. Oxford: Oxford University Press.

NOTES

1   Noreen Cooke (Knutsford HS), Gill Cope (Frodsham HS), Maggie Earl (Holmes Chapel HS), Jan Hodgson (Penketh HS), John Huddart (Tarporley HS), Mary Jay (Sir John Dean's Sixth Form College), Michael Jones (Senior English Adviser), Sue Knowles (Wilmslow HS), Robert Lever (Norton Priory HS), David Marriott (Widnes Sixth Form College), Phil Mitchell (Queens Park HS), Ann Pownall (Primary Advisory Teacher), Martin Rostron (Priestley Sixth Form College), Alison Whelan (Knutsford HS), David White (Secondary Advisory Teacher).

5

The New Grammar Teaching

RONALD CARTER ——————————————————◇

INTRODUCTION

This paper explores some recent developments in the study and teaching of English grammar. I argue that the entirely justifiable grounds for the rejection of old-style grammar teaching should not be allowed to prevent appraisal of new-style grammar teaching. New-style grammar is functionally oriented, related to the study of texts and responsive to social purposes. It provides a basis for developing in pupils an awareness of and knowledge about language which can be both rich and motivating as well as relevant to the main parameters of the English curriculum.

WHAT WAS GRAMMAR TEACHING?

The following example from an O level GCE paper (1961) demonstrates clearly what kind of grammatical knowledge was required from school children and what view of the learning process was enshrined in the English curriculum at that time.

> *Leaving childhood behind, I soon lost this desire to possess a goldfish. It is difficult to persuade oneself that a goldfish is happy and as soon as we have begun to doubt that some poor creature enjoys living with us we can take no pleasure in its company.*
>
> *Using a new line to each, select* one *example from the above passage of each of the following:*
>   *(i)   an infinitive used as the direct object of a verb*
>   *(ii) an infinitive used in apposition to a pronoun*
>   *(iii) a gerund*
>   *(iv) a present participle*
>   *(v)   a past participle*
>   *(vi) an adjective used predicatively (i.e. as a complement)*
>   *(vii) a possessive adjective*
>   *(viii) a demonstrative adjective*

(xi) *a reflexive pronoun:*
 (x) *an adverb of time*
(xi) *an adverb of degree*
(xii) *a preposition*
(xiii) *a subordinating conjunction*

The main test here is of a pupil's ability to identify grammatical forms as a set of discrete items and to label them. Learning how to do this would have involved innummerable practice exercises and a commitment to memory of certain facts including an accompanying metalanguage. It is also not unlikely that this information would have been quickly forgotten after the examination, no matter how intensive the drilling exercises or transmissive the teaching strategies. Although it is argued below that such evidence should not invalidate a connection between learning about grammar and language competence, the research findings based on this kind of grammar teaching draw bleak conclusions for the effects of such grammar study on pupils' own use of language[1]. In fact, the learning process probably did not involve, on the part of pupils, actual productive *use* of the forms they were learning to identify and label. The kinds of texts used are also, it should be noted, always remote from actual use and normally drawn from those lesser late Victorian prose writers with the most otiose styles.

Lest we should imagine that such exercises belong to a distant past here is an example of an exercise from a currently best selling series of textbooks for the junior school:

> *Underline the correct alternative to complete the sentences.*
>
> *Haven't you (any/no) shoes my size?*
> *There are (any/no) shoes your size.*
> *There is (anything/nothing) left.*
> *We haven't (anything/nothing) left.*
> *There were (any/none) of the books I wanted.*
> *They didn't have (any/none) of the books I wanted.*
> *Isn't there (anyone/no one) here to help?*
> *There is (anyone/no one) here to help.*

The exercises illustrate the central role of drilling 'correct' forms, of learning grammar by heart as if it were a set of unchanging facts about English. The exercises are furthermore constructed on a deficiency pedagogy. Pupils lack the necessary knowledge and the gaps should therefore be filled. It is, of course, no accident that gap-filling is one of the main teaching and testing devices associated with such exercises with the teachers fulfilling the role of a kind of linguistic dentist, polishing here and there, straightening out, removing decay, filling gaps and occasionally undertaking a necessary extraction. The deficiency view here is that pupils lack the right language and that such deficiencies or gaps have to be made good. It should be noted too, that the exercise is a test of whether pupils avoid double negatives. Double negation (e.g. we haven't *nothing* left) is a taboo grammatical construction in books of this kind, although it is a standard feature of many modern dialects of English.

The exercise here is drawn from a textbook bought in large numbers by parents wishing to help their children with English. For the majority of parents this *is* an English lesson and it is the kind of English which many parents are prepared to pay for. It is also exactly what is meant by 'grammar' when used by politicians, employers, secretaries of state for Education and Prince Charles. For such people improving one's grammar is equivalent to a kind of linguistic etiquette. Knowing how to distinguish a count from an uncount noun or that a sentence should not be ended with a preposition is rather like knowing which spoon to choose to eat (or is it drink?) your soup *with* (with which to eat your soup). There is a clear social and institutional relevance to grammar which cannot be discounted and we will return to this later in this paper.

However, one further rather more insidious connection between social forces and old-style grammar teaching needs to be deconstructed at this stage. It comes out clearly in the equation, made regularly by some politicians and public figures, between lack of attention to grammar and a general decline in standards of behaviour and social discipline. In particular, the drilling of grammatical forms is seen to impart discipline and character. There is a clear connection made in such thinking between grammatical order and the social order where it is only one small step from splitting infinitives to splitting heads open on football terraces. (This might also give some pause to those who debate whether or not English is a 'discipline'.) It is no coincidence, of course, that in grammatical exercises the word drill is a metaphoric extension from the parade-ground and from an armed-services view of the individual. In the army the individual is disciplined to assume a common and uniform identity, to move in step with an homogeneous whole, subjugating the personal to the larger requirements of the nation state, having defiencies corrected, acquiring 'character' and backbone, being knocked into shape to speak, as it were, one language. The metaphor also serves to clarify the intimate connection found by many in authority between English and being English between, to quote the title of a fascinating recent book on this question, *English and Englishness*.[2]

Other main contemporary complaints about grammar teaching and English teaching (for the two are indistinguishable to many people) are based on a view of language as static, as an unchanging order. Changes in grammatical usage, therefore, come to be regarded as equivalent to a 'decay' or breakdown in our institutions. For some, and even more illogically, such changes are equivalent to slovenliness of thought. Evidence that language is a dynamic process and is, of its very nature, subject to perpetual change is inadmissible. The fact that there has been a 'complaint' tradition, which in the history of grammar study and teaching dates back to the early seventeenth century, is discounted.[3]

It does not, of course, help either clear thinking or principled discussion when the word grammar is itself misunderstood. Teachers, in particular, need to know that many people use the term 'grammar' *not* to mean the syntactic ordering of language within the clause but rather as a hold-all word for spelling, punctuation, standard accent, formal as opposed to slang expressions, as well as for grammatical features in their own right.

Many of the above views are, of course, misconceptions, but in their dismissal of such misconceptions many teachers have been drawn into what I would argue is an equally unsatisfactory counter position. Their position is usually founded on the following main assumptions:

1 Teaching grammar or about grammar would necessarily in-volve a return to old-style grammar teaching with the im-position of rules regulating the individual's creativity with language.
2 Learning about grammar does not lead to enhanced language competence and should not therefore be undertaken.
3 Only the more academically advanced students can discuss patterns of grammar explicitly. If we do this, we foster a kind of cultural elitism.
4 Issues of language must enter our consciousness in the way that our mother tongue is first acquired, implicitly, obliquely and unconsciously.

The recommendations of the Kingman and the Cox Committees do not include a return to old-style, traditional grammar teaching as the core of English. Both reports, however, make recommendations for explicit teaching about language to occupy more space on the English curriculum. It is not suggested that such knowledge about language (henceforth KAL) should be separately tested and it is stressed that it should be integrated within existing domains such as reading, writing, speaking, listening, literary and media studies. There is also a clear recognition that there is more to language than grammar; grammar is, after all, only one level and one set of patterns in language organisation. However, grammar study *is* recommended as part of KAL. What are the implications of this? To what extent is a new grammar study emerging and how different is it from the old?

Grammar and ideology

The 'syllabus' for KAL, as specified in the Cox Report, represents a clear rejection of the old-style instrumentalist conception of grammar. KAL involves approaches to language which stress its endless variety of

forms and functions and requires a methodology which is not transmissive and teacher-centred but investigative and project-based. Instead of factual information to be learned probably by rote and with a
focus on linguistic form in isolation from context or from broader social
functions, the Cox Report underwrites a KAL which is attentive to the
ways langauge is used across varieties of spoken and written modes, in
literary and non-literary contexts and as an expression of social attitudes especially in relation to central ideological functions such as
Standard English. Although claims to improve performance in the *use*
of language which might result from such explicit attention to language
are sensibly played down in the Cox Report, there is much of demonstr-
able value for pupils in being better informed about the uses of
language, including their own use, and in learning not simply to look
through language, to the content of a message but rather to *see through*
language and be empowered better to understand and explain the ways
in which messages are mediated or shaped, very often in the interests of
preserving a particular viewpoint or of reinforcing existing ideologies.
An example of the differences between old-style and new-style grammar can be provided by an examination of the following headlines
taken from British national newspapers in 1984 at a time when a
national coal strike led to a not inconsiderable polarisation of political
positions. The three headlines are taken from (1) the *Guardian* (2) the
Daily Express and (3) the *Morning Star*:

1 NCB *chief fit after incident at pit*
2 *Coal Supremo felled in pit fury*
3 *MacGregor scraps pit visit in face of angry demo*

There are several features of language which merit comment here. These
include: the characteristic conventions of newspaper headlines such as
omission of articles; the deletion of a main finite verb; abbreviations
(*demo*) and alliterative patterning (*pit/fit*; *felled/fury*); the formality
differences signalled by lexical choices e.g. *incident/demo* and by
naming devices: *Coal Supremo*; *MacGregor*; *NCB chief*. And so on.
Also relevant here would be features not immediately recognised when
the headlines are laid out as above. These are such features as typo-
graphy, the placement of the main caption in relation to pictures as well
as to other headlines. Of some significance in this connection, for
example, are the styles of sub-headlines which in some newspaper styles
support the main caption.

But analysis of language in and for itself does little to reveal the
contrasts between these headlines in terms of ideology. The relationship
here between language and ideology is not a transparent one; it is
signalled with some subtlety and works to subject the reader to a
particular interpretation of events. In the case of headline (3), for
example, MacGregor is placed in the role of main actor in the clause and

is made responsible (*scraps visit*) himself for the act of cancellation (*scraps* is a transitive verb). There is no reference to his physical position or disposition. By contrast headline (2) represents MacGregor as acted upon (*coal supremo felled*) and underlines the lack of 'agency' by use of a passive verb, markedly emotive lexis (*felled/fury*) and, in contrast with (3), an intransitive verb *felled*. Headline (1) seeks to be altogether more neutral by use of the word *incident* and the use of a complement structure (*NCB chief (is) fit*) avoids a passive/active distinction with its necessary assignment of agency. In other words, each headline inserts a different view of events. In (3) there is no suggestion that those taking part in the demonstration are directly responsible for action by MacGregor whereas in (2) MacGregor is the object of an action which we assume is initiated by the fury of the miners at the pit. In the opposition between coal supremo and miners the headline subjects the reader to a position which is limited by a preordained interpretation of events. In (1) there is no overt taking of sides, although in the case of such struggles neutrality signals greater allegiance to those social and political forces which seek to maintain a status quo. In all three headlines there is a relationship between stylistic choice, text structure and the ideological construction of a particular reading position. In each case different grammatical and other choices encode markedly different ideologies.

This kind of language study is not a mere naming of grammatical parts for their own sake (see the example on page 104). The aim is to develop tools for talking and writing about language which encourage a critical awareness and, beyond that, a powerful capacity to analyse particular linguistic forms as they are used within a broad conception of culture. There is a metalanguage but it is introduced as needed, in context. It is not taught for its own sake but to provide an economic and precise way of discussing particular functions and purposes.

COX, GRAMMAR AND VIEWS OF ENGLISH

The Cox Working Party outlines five main views of English teaching:

   ◇ a personal growth view
   ◇ an adult needs view
   ◇ a cross curricular view
   ◇ a cultural heritage view
   ◇ a cultural analysis view

The committee points out that such views are not mutually exclusive and that such 'views' cannot be easily developed in isolation from each other. Indeed, grammar teaching and study can be shown to underlie each of these main views. The examples taken from the above headlines are a clear example of grammar being explicitly treated for purposes of cultural analysis and for developing an associated critical language awareness.

Personal growth and adult needs

One way in which *personal growth* and *adult needs* views can be developed is to compare the different grammars we hold. Such grammars are both *dialectal* grammars and *diatypic* grammars. Dialect grammars are the differential grammars we possess according to the regional and social groups into which we are born; diatypic grammars are the grammatical styles we all use along a continuum from spoken to written English. In the case of both sets of grammars choices from the different systems depend on context, audience, purpose and, especially in the case of dialect, what view we have of ourselves, our own individual and social identities, or indeed the view we have of others, our degree of identification with the person or persons we are talking to. For example, double negatives are a natural and normal part of most dialects of English except the dialect of Standard English which, for arbitrary historical reasons, does not allow double or multiple negation. Teaching explicitly about such dialect grammars can be done in such a way as to show respect for personal dialects, argue against the popular media view that double negatives are illogical (in support of which there is only prejudice not evidence), yet demonstrate that for many adult writing and speaking purposes double negatives are not normally appropriate. For example, letters of application for jobs will not normally advantage the writer if double negatives are used. Such teaching of grammar is a long way from the corrective yes/no grammar exercises of old-style grammarians tellingly illustrated by the exercise to 'correct' possible double negation in the example on page 105.

Grammatical differences between the diatypes of speech and writing can be discussed in a similarly explicit, flexible and supportive manner, and with due attention to the social functions of grammar within a broad view of language as a social semiotic. There is space here for just two examples:

EXAMPLE A

1 The extension of fishing limits by Iceland and other countries *has meant Fleetwood's traditional grounds have been closed.*

2 Iceland and other countries *have extended their fishing limits and this has meant Fleetwood's traditional grounds have been closed.*

3 Better, more mechanised farming with increasing efficiency by farm managers *has aggravated unemployment.*

4 Farming *has improved and become more mechanised and* farm managers *have also improved their efficiency. This has . . .*

EXAMPLE B

1 Paraded through the streets, *he is said to have shown defiance in the face of death.*

2 When he was paraded through the streets, *he is said to have shown defiance in the face of death.*

> (*Examples adapted from Perera, 1984, see also Perera, this volume*)

The examples A1 and A3 exhibit grammatical features more normally used in written texts. The particular feature in these cases is the expanded noun phrase; examples A2 and A4, for example, are not markedly expanded and are more characteristically used in spoken texts. Similarly, example B1 is a sentence fronted by a non-finite subordinate clause, a feature more normally found in writing; the straightforward subordinate clause of time in example B2 is likely to be how we would say the same sentence.

Sensitive teaching will allow no absolute preferences here, for such analysis can easily result in a prescriptive stance. Instead, discussion of the respective grammars will illustrate different functional tendencies with the structures in A1, A3, and B1 being more characteristic of writing than of speech. Such teaching will also underline that, in appropriating more writerly styles, children need to be encouraged to produce certain structures more regularly than others. An adult needs view of English teaching embraces such an orientation. We might also note that increasing use of expanded noun phrases is a feature of the suggested National Curriculum writing attainment target at level 4 while the use of non-finite subordinate clauses is a feature of the suggested writing attainment target at level 9. Only the most insensitive of grammar teaching and study would, however, seek an automatic or mechanical connection between individual forms and specific levels of attainment. The key words here are tendencies and orientations towards particular uses and functions of grammar.

Teaching 'explicitly' also needs glossing for it can readily suggest a transmission of facts about grammatical functions which may only be a short step from drilling knowledge of grammatical forms. Teaching explicitly about grammar here is quite obviously a matter of teacher judgement and sensitive intervention. The intention should be that such knowledge forms an incremental part of writing development and be mainly discussed with pupils in the context of their own *use* of language. In most cases it is pedagogically and strategically preferable for the teacher to generate tasks in which competence *precedes* reflections on language and in which reflection is itself *prior to* discursive analysis of particular grammatical properties. Indeed, less formal, more individualised and expressive functions of grammar should be integrated with more formal and public uses of grammar in an essentially investigative and exploratory manner. In this way, a personal growth 'view' and an adult needs 'view' can be perceived to be neither mutually exclusive nor incompatible.

Speech and writing are also systems which are open to cultural analysis. There are a number of possible topics for investigation within this 'view' of English, such as: the social prestige of writing; the associations of the words 'literate' and 'illiterate'; differences and distinctions between societies with predominantly literate or oral cultures; the power of the spoken language in the history of language change; the effects produced on hearers by texts which are written to be spoken and those which are spoken 'unrehearsed'; the ideological factors inherent in the fact that grammars of English are currently based on written, not spoken language data – which conditions our view of what grammar is. Such exploration underlines that pedagogic and curricular approaches supporting separate 'views' of English can be usefully combined and integrated.

Cross-curricular views

The knowledge about grammar which might be fostered by a cross-curricular view of English teaching will probably include a knowledge of the grammar of texts. Such a knowledge of grammar is again functional. It takes us beyond the operation of grammar within clauses to the functions of grammar in the creation of particular types of text or *genres*. It is a knowledge of grammar which allows recognition of the typical configurations of language which societies assign to culturally significant texts, such as narrative, report, argument, instruction, explanation and so on.

Much of the recent work on the patterns of grammar within curricular genres has taken place in Australia under the influence of Michael Halliday and such work is now properly characterised as one of the most important and influential movements within language and education. Here are two texts by 11-year-old children, which have been analysed by one of Halliday's associates (see Christie, 1986). Before we examine the grammars of these texts we might ask what are the functions of some very basic linguistic categories?

1 What is the difference between the use of singular and plural nouns in subject position?
2 What are the different functions produced by the different tenses (present v. simple past)?
3 What kinds of conjunctions characterise the two texts? What are their respective textual functions?

1 *A long time ago there was a kangaroo who did not have a tail*
   and all the animals laughed at him and that made him sad.
   How did he get it back? he got it back by dipping his tail into

> *lolly-pop siarp (syrup). The animals started to like him and then thay played with him. Would you like it? I would not because it would be most annoing.*
>
> *The End*
>
> 2 *Sharks have special sense organs that can sense things up to 1 mile away. The shark uses fins to balance itself and it has to keep swimming or else it will sink. The shark's teeth are razor sharp and although you can only see two layers of teeth there are many in the jaw. Usually smaller fish follow the sharks around in hope of gathering up scraps that the shark may leave.*

Firstly, there is a distinct difference between *sharks* and *a kangaroo*. Most obviously, *a kangaroo* is individuated as a unique entity created for the specific purposes of this text while the pluralised *sharks* or the reference to *the shark* indicates a general property, somehow representative of all sharks. Secondly, the generality and representativeness of the shark is underlined by the present tense (e.g. *sharks have*; *the shark uses*; *the shark may leave*). The simple present tense is pervasive in this text. It functions to represent not so much presentness as permanence. Thus, it is not unlike the function of the sentence, 'Oil *floats* on water', which serves to encode a general truth rather than the particularity of a present action. In the description of *the shark* the present tense functions to create a state of affairs; in the 'kangaroo text' the simple past tense serves to record a particular and unique action. Thirdly, the two texts are marked by a different use of conjunctions which is in turn characteristic of the different text types. The first text is marked by conjunctions such as *and* and *then* which indicate a temporal sequence; in the second text, on the other hand, the conjunctions such as *although*, *in (the) hope of* structure a relationship between propositions and actions which is descriptive or argumentative rather than chronological. All of the grammatical features recorded under the above headings conspire to make the first text *chronological* and the second *non-chronological*. Once again, distinctions between these genres are central to National Curriculum attainment targets and programmes of study for writing:

Level 4

>   (ii) *Write stories which have an opening, a setting, characters, a series of events and a resolution; produce other kinds of chronologically organised writing . . .*
> (iii) *Organise non-chronological writing in orderly ways.*

Although there is, of course, more to the organisation of different genres than grammar, grammar plays a central part in structuring the text, functioning in each case not as a discrete item but as an organising component. We should also note that the grammatical items discussed here are basic or core items; neither their identification nor use in relation to the texts can be said to be in any way difficult. It is unnecessarily defensive always to claim that grammar is difficult or elitist or only for the very brightest children.

The cultural heritage view

An inspection of grammar in relation to texts which occupy a place within the cultural heritage is on one level less problematic. It is less problematic because teachers will generally be more familiar with handling uses of language within such contexts. The tradition of practical criticism and of the close reading of texts embraces the expressive uses of grammar in poems, short stories and in extracts from longer fiction. In general, however, such treatment has not been markedly explicit or analytical in discussion of the part played by grammar in the creation of meaning. The following is a very brief example of how attention to a single basic grammatical feature can support understanding of creative uses of language:

> The car ploughed uphill through the long squalid straggle of Tevershall, the blackened brick dwellings, the black slate roofs glistening their sharp edges, the mud black with coal-dust, the pavements wet and black. It was as if dismalness had soaked through and through everything. The utter negation of natural beauty, the utter negation of the gladness of life, the utter absence of the instinct for shapely beauty which every bird and beast has, the utter death of the human intuitive faculty was appalling. The stacks of soap in the grocers' shops, the rhubarb and lemons in the greengrocers! the awful hats in the milliners! and went by ugly, ugly, ugly, followed by the plaster-and-guilt horror of the cinema with its wet picture announcements, 'A Woman's Love!', and the new big Primitive chapel, primitive enough in its stark brick and big panes of greenish and raspberry glass in the windows. The Wesleyian chapel, higher up, was of blackened brick and stood behind iron railings and blackened shrubs. The Congregational chapel, which thought itself superior, was built of rusticated sandstone and had a steeple, but not a very high one. Just beyond were the new school buildings, expensive pink brick, and gravelled playground inside iron railings, all very imposing, and mixing the suggestion of a chapel and a prison. (From Lady Chatterley's Lover by D. H. Lawrence)

There are several ways in which responses to this text can be developed. It would, of course, be inappropriate to put grammar under the microscope from the beginning but, given an appropriate pedagogic sequence, one initial question about grammar would be to focus on the noun phrases in the first sentence and to ask what is the function of the repetition in its various forms of the word *black*.

The question prompts many different answers depending on the purpose of the lesson and the place of this text within that lesson. Observations will be likely to centre on the way in which the repetition functions to emphasise an ambiance of unremitting gloom in Tevershall. But a more concentrated focus will reveal that not only is the word *black* repeated but it is also repeated in different grammatical categories:

◇ *blackened* brick – past participle
◇ *black*, slate roofs – adjective
◇ *black* with coal dust – post-modifier
◇ the pavements wet and *black* – complement

Black here occupies, as it were, every grammatical position available. It pervades every possible grammatical structure in the same way as it penetrates every interstice of the town of Tevershall.

The role of grammar here is to provide analytical categories not for their own sake but in support of making intuitions more precise. With a knowledge of noun-phrase organisation in English the teacher and students can, if required, penetrate further into the text and in the process make their literary insights both more accountable as well as more retrievable for others. The knowledge is also transferable to other texts and can provoke interesting discussion of why some writers (e.g. Hemingway) use only the most elemental of noun phrases with only minimal adjectival pre- and post-modification. The analytical categories can, when presented sensitively, also provide a framework which is generative and creative of different meanings in different texts. Analysis of grammar is likely to fail in this context if it narrows interpretive opportunities or suggests automatic correlations between forms and meanings; instead the aim is for fuller grammatical understanding to create fuller interpretive opportunities (for further examples see papers in Carter (ed.), 1982).

Before leaving the question of grammar study in relation to texts accepted as part of the cultural heritage, we can note that Lawrence is one of the few canonical authors to treat dialects and dialect grammars as an expressive resource in the construction of both character and context in his novels and short stories. The opposition in speech styles in a story such as *Odour of Chrysanthemums*, for example, between Elizabeth Bates, who is the main character and who uses the dialect of standard English, and the other characters in the community who use a local Nottinghamshire dialect, is on one level at least a social and cultural opposition. Contrasting grammars are a signal part of Lawrence's exploration of alternative worlds and styles of living; once again grammar is also a central component in the expression of social meaning. Such approaches also provide a basis for integrating language and literary studies – areas of the English curriculum in schools which may have been kept separate for too long.

Grammar and cultural analysis

One final example must serve now to underline the main points in this paper so far: that grammar cannot be seen in isolation; that grammar needs to be located in use and in its creation of contextual meanings; that grammar is a social domain within which marked social and ideological patterns are created; that grammar study can play a central part within the English curriculum. The example is drawn from a recent study of *Language and Power* by Norman Fairclough and involves some (again) very basic grammatical analysis of the uses of language in an interview given by the British prime minister, Margaret Thatcher.[4]

> *government should be very strong to do those things which only government can do it has to be strong to have defence because the kind of Britain I see would always defend its freedom and always be a reliable ally so you've got to be strong to your own people and other countries have got to know that you stand by your word then you turn to internal security and yes you HAVE got to be strong on law and order and do the things that only governments can do but there it's part government and part people because you CAN'T have law and order observed unless it's in partnership with people then you have to be strong to uphold the value of the currency and only governments can do that by sound finance and then you have to create the framework for a good education system and social security and at that point you have to say over to people people are inventive creative and so you expect PEOPLE to create thriving industries thriving services yes you expect people each and everyone from whatever their background to have a chance to rise to whatever level their own abilities can take them yes you expect people of all sorts of background and almost whatever their income level to be able to have a chance of owning some property tremendously important the ownership of property of a house gives you some independence gives you a stake in the future. (Interview with Michael Charlton, December 17, 1985)*

There is much that could be said concerning language and language use in this extract but of relevance to our discussion here is the deployment of two very basic categories of grammar: the use of pronouns and the use of the simple present tense. In the case of the latter feature the effects are not dissimilar from those discussed above. Here sentences such as:

> *a house* gives *you some independence* . . .
> *you* have to be *strong to uphold the value of currency* . . .
> *you* expect *people to create thriving industries* . . .

frame a discourse which encodes an unchanging order within which some central 'eternal' truths prevail. The present tense serves to create a view of Britain and of people in Britain as operating according to values which are certain, non-negotiable and permanent. The use of the pronoun *you* occurs as follows:

> you've *got to be strong to your own people*
> you *have to create the framework for a good education system*
> you *have to say over to people*

You operates here similarly to an indefinite pronoun. It lacks, however, the marked social connotations of *one* in the same context and serves instead to register a sense of solidarity and commonality of experience which subtly and deceptively links the speaker with 'people', allowing her to present her views and values as if they were theirs.

Discussion of this interview extract brings us back to the importance of encouraging pupils to *see through* language (see Carter and Nash, 1990). The metaphor of seeing through is important here for the aim is to take pupils beyond a stage where language is a transparent medium through which content is seen. A more lasting and generative capacity is provided if pupils recognise the ways in which grammar mediates points of view and encodes ideologies. Pupils are thus empowered to see through the ways in which language can be used to incapacitate, to distort or hide a true state of affairs, to subtly conceal rather than openly reveal. What can result is a critical language awareness of the relationship between language, ideology and social and cultural power – a relationship in which grammar plays a not insignificant part and for an awareness of which its study can be especially enabling.

KNOWLEDGE ABOUT GRAMMAR: SOME ISSUES

The new grammar teaching presents a number of pedagogic challenges for both teachers and pupils. Foremost among these is a challenge to present grammar in the classroom in ways which avoid the worst excesses of formalism without losing sight of the fact that grammar is systematically organised. A further major challenge is to find ways of teaching grammar which are sensitive to a continuum of implicit to explicit knowledge and which recognise that appropriate and strategic interventions by the teacher are crucial to the process of making implicit knowledge explicit. Additionally, there is much work to be done to

explore in what ways knowledge about grammar might inform processes of language development. It is not tenable to claim that there is no
connection between explicit grammar study and enhanced language
performance in spite of research evidence (largely pre-1970s) dis-
avowing such a connection, not least because such research (see Note 1)
investigated grammar teaching based on 'old-style' descriptive
frameworks and methodologies. A new approach to grammar brings
with it further questions for classroom practice and classroom-based
research, about which it is essential for us to retain an open mind.

This paper has not sought to examine pedagogies for grammar
but it may be useful to posit here a number of principles which can serve
to underlie hypotheses about the teaching of grammar. Such hypotheses
need to be subsequently tested:

1 Competence precedes reflection

From an early age children possess considerable degrees of implicit
knowledge about grammar; for example seven-year-old children are
able to recognise grammatical deviation and to make grammatically
correct judgements of sentences from a list (see Garton and Pratt, 1989:
esp. ch. 7). Lyons (1988, 1989, reprinted in this volume) demonstrates
the extent of implicit grammatical knowledge which a nine-year-old
child brings to a writing task. It is vital to recognise and value such
knowledge and to build upon it. As argued above, the general (though
not exclusive) pedagogic principle that a competence in using the
language precedes effective reflection on language should be upheld.

2 Develop existing knowledge about grammar

Research into early language development also underlines how children
draw on implicit knowledge to help them in decoding word meaning, in
detecting and monitoring problems of comprehension, and in structuring different types of written text (see Garton and Pratt, 1989: ch. 6).
Although limited, there is evidence to support the view that reflective-
ness on language occurs naturally and without prompting. Such overt
awareness manifests itself in a number of ways: from a reflective and
obviously pleasurable repetition of particular patterns of words and
structures to explicit explanations of the 'points' of language use which
are in some ways odd or playful or creative, such as jokes or puns or
particular ambiguities. (See note 5 for brief discussion of the complex
grammatical knowledge required to process a children's joke or an
ambiguous headline.) Teachers have commented on the enhanced sense
of control such conscious recognition of language use can confer.
Accordingly, an important principle across primary and secondary
contexts is that the process of making such knowledge explicit should
not be imposed or engineered but rather fostered and supported as
naturally as possible, as needed in specific contexts and in ways which
reinforce the process as one of positive achievement with language.
There can be no return to decontextualised exercises or gap-fillings or to
the deficiency pedagogies in which such procedures are grounded.

Much might be learned here from studies of the relationship between raised language consciousness and second language development (Faerch, 1985; Rutherford, 1987).

3 Support knowledge about grammar in relation to texts

Strategies should be developed which prevent too great a degree of self-consciousness about language (which can be inhibiting) but which, in the upper-secondary years especially, also enhance understanding of the systematic nature of grammatical organisation and its uses. One primary principle which this paper has tried to illustrate is that of, wherever possible, exploring grammar in relation to extended, preferably complete spoken or written *texts*. An examination of grammar in texts means that grammatical form is not an exclusive focus, for grammar is necessarily seen only as part of a more complex social and textual environment and as realizing specific functions in a purposeful context. A study of grammar in texts is a study of grammar *in use*.

4 There is more to KAL than performance through language

It is vital to continue to promote effective language use through processes which support intuitive and implicit responses to using language. We should also recognise that pupils *do* demonstrate increasing knowledge about language simply by *using* language and working with it. However, such procedures are a necessary but not sufficient condition for knowledge about language and about grammar as a component of language (see Mallett, 1988). An important principle is: however well we perform at any activity or any exercise of our human capacities we can only benefit from stepping periodically into a more reflective or analytic frame from within which our competence can be more systematically reviewed.

CONCLUSIONS

I have attempted in this paper to draw a line between old-style grammar teaching and a counter-position of no grammar at all. Old-style grammar teaching has been shown to be reactionary, pedagogically and methodologically arid and conceptually ill-founded. But the removal of formal grammar from the language classroom has denied children opportunities to explore a remarkable human phenomenon and to display their own considerable resources of implicit knowledge; it has also disempowered them from exercising the kind of conscious control and conscious choice over language which enables them both to *see through* language in a systematic way and to use language more discriminatingly.

The proposed changes to English in the National Curriculum involve a shift towards a more language-centred curriculum. The recommendations are bound to leave a number of questions unanswered. Some of these questions are fundamental and will, as I have indicated, require urgent exploration. But the curriculum for English nationally will undoubtedly require more explicit attention to the medium of language and to the role of grammar within that wider framework of language study. I have tried to indicate briefly how knowledge about grammar might be related to each of the five main views of English teaching developed and supported by the Cox Committee.

In this context, a return to grammar is to be welcomed. But it will need to be a new-style grammar teaching, not an old-style grammar teaching. It is unlikely that the return to grammar will restore the kinds of codes and values old-style grammar is believed by many people to symbolise if not to uphold. But it will mean that language in the classroom is not to be encountered wholly by unconscious, implicit and indirect means. Grammar is a fundamental human meaning-making activity which can be investigated as a fascinating phenomenon and explored from the powerful basis of considerable resources of existing knowledge possessed by the very youngest of children. In this respect, a study of grammar should always be rooted in children's positive achievements, that is, in what children can already *do* with grammar. Knowing more about how grammar *works* is to understand more about how grammar is used and misused. Knowing more about grammar can impart greater choice and control over grammar as an expressive and interpretive medium. Knowing more about grammar, as part of KAL, is to be empowered to respond to and to use grammar as central to the creation of textual meanings.

NOTES

1   See, for example, research undertaken by or reported in Elley *et al.* (1975); Braddock *et al.* (1963); Robinson (1960); Harris (1960); Macauley (1947). The following quotation from Braddock *et al.* is representative:

> *In view of the widespread agreement of research studies based upon many types of students and teachers, the conclusion can be stated in strong and unqualified terms: the teaching of formal grammar has a negligible or, because it usually displaces the same instruction and practice in actual composition, even a harmful effect on the improvement of writing.*

Such conclusions do not, of course, invalidate the new grammar teaching which uses a) different models and descriptive frameworks for grammar b) different methodologies. See Walmsley (1984).

2   See Brian Doyle, *English and Englishness*, New Accents Series (Doyle, 1989).

3   See Milroy and Milroy (1985) for a detailed account.

4   See Fairclough (1989: ch. 7).

5   See, for example, the following:

Q. How do you make a Swiss Roll?

A. Push him down a mountain.

(Swiss is a modifier of the noun roll; the answer (A) depends on a knowledge that Swiss can also be a proper noun (designating a nationality) and that roll also operates as a verb of motion.)

GIANT WAVES DOWN QUEEN ELIZABETH'S FUNNEL
(There are several possible explanations of this headline. Most depend on GIANT being both a noun and an adjective and on WAVES being a noun and a verb of action.)

REFERENCES

Braddock, R. *et al.* (1963) *Research in Written Composition.* Champaign, Illinois: NCTE pp. 37–8.

Carter, R. (ed.) (1982) *Language and Literature: An Introductory Reader in Stylistics.* London: George Allen and Unwin.

Carter, R. and Nash, W. (1990) *Seeing Through Language: A Guide to Styles of English Writing.* Oxford: Blackwell.

Christie, F. (1986) 'Writing in Schools: Generic Structures as Ways of Meaning' in Couture, B. (ed.) *Functional Approaches to Writing.* London: Francis Pinter, pp. 221–39.

Doyle, B. (1989) *English and Englishness.* London: Routledge.

Elley, W. B. *et al.* (1975) 'The role of grammar in a secondary school English curriculum', *New Zealand Journal of Educational Research* 10, 1, pp. 26–42.

Faerch, C. (1985) 'Meta-talk in FL classroom discourse', *Studies in Second Language Acquisition* 7, 2, pp. 184–99.

Fairclough, N. (1989) *Language and Power.* London: Longman.

Garton, A. and Pratt, C. (1989) *Learning to be Literate.* Oxford: Basil Blackwell.

Harris, R. J. (1960) *An Experimental Inquiry into the Functions and Value of Formal Grammar in the teaching of English with special reference to the teaching of correct written English to children aged twelve to fourteen.* Unpublished PhD Thesis. University of London.

Lyons, H. (1988) 'Needing to Know About Language: A Case Study of a Nine-year-old's Usage', *Language and Education* 2, 3, pp. 175–88.

Lyons, H. (1989) 'What Katy Knows About Language', *English in Education* 23, 2, pp. 38–49 (and this volume).

Macauley, W. J. (1947) 'The difficulty of grammar', *British Journal of Educational Psychology* 17, pp. 153–62.

Mallett, M. (1988) 'From "human sense" to "metalinguistic awareness"', *English in Education* 22, 3, pp. 40–45.

Milroy, J. and Milroy, L. (1985) *Authority in Language.* London: Routledge.

Perera, K. (1984) *Children's Writing and Reading.* Oxford: Blackwell.

Robinson, N. (1960) 'The relation between knowledge of English grammar and ability in English composition', *British Journal of Educational Psychology* 30, pp. 184–6.

Rutherford, W. (1987) *Second Language Grammar: Learning and Teaching.* London: Longman.

Walmsley, J. (1984) *The uselessness of 'Formal Grammar'?.* CLIE Working Paper, No. 2.

6

Critical Language Awareness in Action

ROZ IVANIČ ⸺⸺⸺⸺⸺⸺⸺⸺⸺⸺⸺⸺⸺⸺⸺⸺⸺⸺◇

Learning about language went out of fashion in the 1970s. If you mentioned grammar in an English class, you were apologetic about it to colleagues, saying you knew you shouldn't. If you studied applied linguistics, you found that research had proved that exposure is more valuable than instruction. If you read articles about language teaching, you found that you should be using 'the communicative approach'. Classrooms were full of simulations, or empty: learners were out on the streets, communicating for real.

Recently, however, the idea of learning about language has got back on the agenda under a new name: 'language awareness'. Is this the same thing in disguise? If not, what is it? I think the answer depends on your view of language and on your view of the purposes and processes of language learning. I will explain what I mean in three stages. Firstly I will outline two prevalent views of language and language varieties in recent years, and what sort of language awareness is associated with them. Secondly I will describe what we mean by a critical view of language and critical language awareness, advocating this as the most relevant for bilingual learners. Thirdly I will suggest how critical language awareness can help bilingual adults become active, self-assured communicators. Having established what critical language awareness is, and what use it can be for language learners, I will end with a checklist of objectives for learners and teachers who want to incorporate critical language awareness in their work.

Throughout this article I will be drawing on ideas developed by my colleagues in the Centre for Language in Social Life, particularly Romy Clark, Norman Fairclough and Marilyn Martin-Jones. Many of these ideas are elaborated in greater detail in a paper entitled 'Critical Language Awareness' (Clark *et al.*, 1987).

NON-CRITICAL VIEWS OF THE NATURE OF LANGUAGE

In this section I will describe two prevalent views of language and of language varieties in recent years, and the sort of language awareness work associated with them.

Until the early 1970s the study of language was the study of patterns. Both linguists and language learners were interested in the abstract systems of sounds and structures in the language they were studying. Language learners had to understand those patterns and then reproduce them correctly. For example, lessons focused around patterns such as 'The interrogative' (see example 1).

EXAMPLE 1

THE INTERROGATIVE FORM

1 *When forming the interrogative put the auxiliary in front of the subject.*
2 *If there is no auxiliary use the 'dummy operator' DO with the correct tense and concord.*
3 *If speaking, use a rising intonation at the end of the sentence.*
4 *If writing, put a ? at the end of the sentence.*

The single criterion for success was accuracy. With a view of language as an abstract system, as a set of patterns which are either correctly or incorrectly formed, 'language awareness' was nothing more than a 'grammar grind'. It was formal, boring, often incomprehensible and unrelated to language use. Nevertheless teachers persisted in teaching knowledge about language of this sort because it was what they had learnt, and they knew of no alternatives. Many people still think of 'language awareness' in this way. I believe that language awareness work of this sort will be as sterile and unconducive to acquisition as it always was.

The view of language as pattern made one very important and positive contribution to the way people think about language varieties. One pattern is not linguistically superior to another: all language systems are equal. Chinese languages are not intrinsically superior to European languages; English is not intrinsically superior to Hopi; Urdu is not intrinsically superior to Gujurati. Some linguists and language teachers extended this egalitarian view to include varieties within one language; others treated the 'standard' variety as the correct pattern, and treated other varieties – usually called 'dialects' – as deviations from the norm.

In the 1970s many linguists and language teachers adopted a very different view of language. In this view, language is not thought of as a pattern, but rather as a purposeful process: the noun 'language' turns into a verb: 'We are languaging'. We only 'language' in order to get something done: to express some ideas and/or to have some inter-personal effect, such as persuading. From this perspective, language functions are far more interesting and important than language patterns. For example, lessons focus around topics such as 'Requesting'. The interrogative form mentioned above as a key item on the 'language as pattern' syllabus would appear as one of the ways of making a request (see example 2).

EXAMPLE 2

REQUESTS

Requests are polite commands. Here are some of the ways of requesting something:
1 *If you are asking something which will not be any trouble, use a command with the word 'please':*
   e.g. 'Send it by second class post, please.'
2 *If you are asking anything which could be an effort, use a question, usually with the word 'can':*
   e.g. 'Can you open the window?'
3 *If you need to be extra polite, or if the thing you are asking for will cause a lot of trouble, add words such as 'possibly':*
   e.g. 'Could you possibly lend me £5?'

Context is essential to this view of language. 'Languaging' depends on who is speaking or writing, to whom, where, and for what purpose. These considerations led to the notion of 'register': differences in the context demand different uses of language. English in the corner shop is different from English in science lessons. With this view of language, accuracy is far less important: fluency and appropriacy are the main criteria for successful language use. Dell Hymes, the father of 'communicative competence', argued that: 'Rules of appropriateness beyond grammar govern speech . . .' (Hymes, 1974). The words 'appropriate', 'appropriately', 'appropriateness', 'appropriacy' are alarmingly frequent in language syllabuses, assessment schemes and language awareness materials in current use. 'Appropriacy' sounds more liberal and flexible than 'accuracy', but I believe it is just as much of a straitjacket for the bilingual trying to add English to her repertoire.

While this view of language as purposeful process seems in many ways to be an advance on 'language as pattern', it has had an unfortunate spin-off in thinking about language varieties. The notion of appropriacy is extended to prescribing which language or which variety of language is appropriate for particular purposes. The term 'diglossia' has been coined to refer to the way in which bilingual or multilingual people use different languages in different contexts. For example, a child in Haringey may use Turkish at home, Arabic in the Mosque, Black British English in the playground, and 'standard' English in the classroom. Textbooks teach that one variety of English is appropriate for plays and nursery rhymes, while another variety of English is appropriate for business letters and academic writing. The dominant conventions of appropriacy are treated as natural and necessary.

To some extent these two views of language are treated as alternatives. Linguists and language teachers often identify themselves as either 'language as pattern' proponents or 'language as purposeful process' proponents. Those who espouse 'language as purposeful process' exclusively also believe that the only route to communicative competence is via exposure and purposeful language use. For them, language awareness is totally irrelevant to language learning. That's why knowledge about language went out of fashion for a decade from about 1970 to 1980.

In fact, both views are equally right and important: language is indeed a complex system of patterns, and these are the resources on which we draw in the process of purposeful communication. This relationship is represented by layers 1 and 2 in Figure 6.1. Recently linguists and teachers have been trying to achieve a mixture, if not an integration of these two views.

Most current language awareness materials reflect this mixture. An example is the 'Awareness of Language' series (Hawkins (ed.), 1985), with the accompanying book explaining the rationale for language awareness work of this type (Hawkins, 1984). They have sections on language patterns, on language functions and on differences between registers according to context. They present varieties of English and the languages of the world as part of the 'rich tapestry of language', asserting that they are all equal, but not addressing the fact that they do not have equal status. I believe that language awareness based on this view of language is potentially harmful. It unintentionally legitimises the conventions of appropriacy, and it can help to entrench prejudices rather than defusing them.

A CRITICAL VIEW OF THE NATURE OF LANGUAGE

In this section I will try to explain what I mean by a *critical* view in contrast to the others. This view is represented by Figure 6.1. (This diagram is based on one which is presented and explained in much greater detail in Fairclough, 1989.)

Linguists and teachers who adopt a critical view of language don't disregard language as pattern and language as purposeful process, but they consider that these views are inadequate without the critical dimension. Instead of a 'normative' view of language use as conforming to conventions of appropriacy, they propose a 'creative' view of language as constructing and sustaining identity. The essential ingredient of a critical view is layer 3 in Figure 6.1. Language is shaped by social forces. Powerful social groups determine how things, and particularly

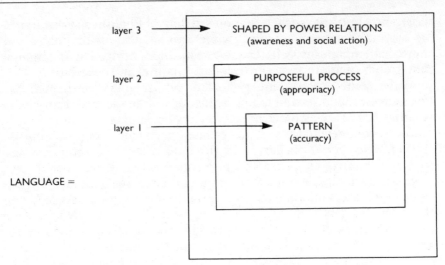

Figure 6.1 A critical view of language

people, should be described. Power relations affect how people speak to each other. Historically, the communicative practices of dominant groups have come to be accepted as correct, appropriate, the norm; this has effectively excluded most people from many realms of action. For example, people who don't use language in an academic way don't decide what counts as knowledge; people who don't use language in a legal way don't make laws. This amounts to a totally different view of 'accuracy' and particularly of 'appropriacy'. Instead of saying that certain ways of using language are correct and appropriate in certain contexts, the critical view of language emphasises the fact that prestigious social groups have established these conventions: they are not 'natural' or necessarily the way they are.

The critical approach also recognises that language can help to shape social practice. For example, referring to adults as 'boys' or 'girls' reinforces or sometimes creates the idea that they are socially inferior. A more positive example of this is the one mentioned by Morgan Dalphinis in a recent issue of *Language Issues*: by using the word 'bilingual' to refer to anyone who operates in two or more languages, regardless of proficiency, we can affect the image of the people we are talking about.

An important element in a critical view of language is the concept of change. Language is not fixed, but dynamic, constantly adjusting to social pressures, for better or worse. The positive side of this is that people do have power to change the way language is used. A good example of this is the change in conventions for academic writing in the last ten years. It used to be considered incorrect, or at any rate inappropriate, to use the pronouns 'I' and 'you' in journals. Everything had to be couched in technical, impersonal, so-called objective language. Many writers disapproved of this, because they were sceptical of objectivity and because they recognised that this highly specialised style of writing doesn't really contribute to the quality of the ideas, and excludes people who aren't familiar with it. Gradually over the last ten years some writers have introduced a more personal, direct style, hoping to erode the conventional notion of what is appropriate. This is an area in which I am a language learner myself – trying to write articles for journals in accessible language.

Teachers who adopt a critical view of language pay attention to form and function, but not without also discussing the way in which power relations affect language. For example, bilingual adults need to know not only how to form questions and how they function as polite requests, but also about who has the right to ask and why (see example 3). There are more examples of this approach in the articles by Ira Shor and Mike Baynham in *Language Issues* Vol. 2, No. 1.

EXAMPLE 3

WHO HAS THE RIGHT TO ASK QUESTIONS?

(A) At the doctor's
When you last went to the doctor, did s/he ask any questions?
What were they?
Did you ask any questions?
What were they?
Did you want to know anything more?
If so, why didn't you ask?

Discuss your answers as a group.

There is also a critical view of language variety. This view takes account of the way in which power relations determine the status of languages and language varieties. Instead of just asserting that all varieties are equal, critical linguists and language teachers identify why some are more prestigious than others. Instead of seeing 'Standard English' as the best variety, it might be more useful to call it 'standard-ised' English and learn about the process of standardisation. Instead of accepting that monolingual fluency in English is everyone's ideal, a critical view of language values a bilingual repertoire and identifies the social forces which don't value bilingualism.

With a critical view of language, accuracy and appropriacy are not things to be learned, but things to be questioned and understood. Learners will want to know what the conventions are, but not be drilled into reproducing them. Instead, they want to be in a position to choose confidently when and if to conform to them. The criteria for success in layer 3 are awareness and social action. This means that a good language user is not just an accurate reproducer of the patterns, nor someone who conforms to conventions of appropriacy. Rather, the good language user understands how language is shaped by social forces and in turn affects other people, and acts accordingly. The contents of *Language Issues* suggest that many members of NATECLA operate consciously or subconsciously with a critical view of language: it seems the only one appropriate to bilingual adults and to people with antiracist aims. And a critical view of the nature of language entails bringing critical language awareness onto the learning agenda.

Critical language awareness involves talking about everything represented in the diagram on page 126. The way it differs from other types of language awareness is that it includes, in fact emphasises, layer 3 of the diagram. Returning to the rhetorical question in the introduction, I believe that language awareness informed by a critical view of the nature of language is very far from being a return to 'the grammar grind' associated with language as pattern. The content is not patterns but the social and historical processes which affect language. The aim is not accuracy or appropriacy but socially responsible language use. Critical language awareness is not an optional extra but an integral part of developing resources for communication. In the next section I will try to explain the relationship between awareness and action in more detail.

WHAT'S THE USE OF CRITICAL LANGUAGE AWARENESS?

Critical language awareness is an essential prerequisite to language use in three ways. Firstly, people find it hard to learn a 'different' language without knowing how they feel about it in relation to the language they use already. Secondly, once people realise that there is a difference between 'person-respecting' and offensive language, they will want to know what the differences are and make their choices accordingly. Thirdly, once people know that rules of accuracy and appropriacy are not fixed but subject to social influences, they will want to choose between conforming to them, reproducing the conventions as they are, or challenging them, helping to break new ground. In this section I will elaborate on each of these three aspects of critical language awareness in use.

People usually come to English lessons with extremely ambivalent feelings about English, or about written English and standardised English. One half of them is saying that English is good, they like it, they want it, and they want to reject everything else because it doesn't get them anywhere. The other half of them is saying they hate it, because it rejects their identity and excludes them. This love–hate relationship with English is a conflict which can't be resolved: it is two sides of the same coin. But if it isn't resolved, and especially if it is working insidiously at a subconscious level, it keeps interfering with learning.

This was vividly illustrated for me one year when I taught a group of women mainly from an Afro-Caribbean language background. At the beginning of the year we read some stories which included some

Creole and London Jamaican features. They said they thought this was bad English, that when their parents spoke Creole or Patois at home they didn't join in and they were British now. They varied enormously in their success with written English and didn't make a lot of progress. In retrospect I think that an unconscious hate of standardised English was probably stopping them from acquiring it, even though they kept assuring me that they wanted to. Later in the year when they knew me better and we had talked a lot more, I invited Roxy Harris, the director of the ILEA Afro-Caribbean Language and Literacy Project, to talk about Afro-Caribbean language issues. By the end of this lesson some of the women in the group were saying they were proud of their families' languages and didn't want to lose them. After that we were able to talk about written, standardised English as a means to an end (O level GCE in those days), and not as an elusive ideal. When discussing their writing we were able to discuss Creole inter-language features with interest and pleasure, not as something evil to be eradicated. Examples like this convince me that it is essential to discuss how people feel about the languages and language varieties they use and about the one they are learning. By understanding any conflicts in values they can control them and free themselves to learn the prestige language or the prestige variety (if they have to) more dispassionately.

Critical language awareness also makes people aware of how language can be patronising, demeaning, disrespectful, offensive, exclusive, or the opposite. Critical linguists are trying to find a term for what they consider good language use. One suggestion is 'Popular English' (Progressive Literacy Group, 1986); I currently use the term 'person-respecting language'. This aspect of critical language awareness starts from people's experience of being labelled, patronised or excluded. However, if the discussion were to stop at awareness, it would be demoralising and pessimistic. It must be tied to the intention to 'do as you would be done by': to examine and develop your own language use on 'person-respecting' principles. This, of course, is a language development objective for everyone: not just bilingual adults but all people, including teachers.

People sometimes object to this suggestion on the grounds that attitudes need changing and then language will look after itself. I think this is an oversimplification, as a recent experience illustrates. A student preparing for her final 'Language and Education' exam came to consult me. She said she wanted to prepare to answer a question on anti-racist issues in language. I assumed she was going to ask me to go over the lecture or recommend more reading, but instead she said: 'I want to be sure how to refer to people. I want to check which terms black people find offensive, and which they prefer.' Here was a case of someone whose attitudes were clear but needed advice on person-respecting language. I also believe that person-respecting language can improve attitudes, that it is one of the responsibilities of education to promote it.

Critical language awareness is a first step towards person-respecting language use.

Thirdly, critical language awareness can give language learners the self-assurance to make choices in how they use language. Self-assurance involves understanding social situations, knowing what the options are for action, and knowing the consequences. This is often taught in courses under the titles of 'Confidence Training', 'Assertiveness Training', 'Assertion Training' or 'Personal and Social Development'. I prefer the term 'self-assurance', because it doesn't emphasise pushing yourself forward. Critical language awareness doesn't insist on complying with 'rules of appropriacy', but it doesn't insist on opposition either. It simply puts people in control.

Often bilingual people will choose to conform to the conventions, because opposing them is too demanding. For example, most bilingual people will try very hard to use standard English in a job interview, will conform to the convention that the interviewers will decide on the topics for discussion, and will not complain if the interviewer says 'We will expect you to work a bit harder at your English'. It is not in their interest to be oppositional in such a situation: they won't get the job! Any good communicative language teaching will teach them how to conform to the conventions. Critical language awareness additionally helps people to conform with open eyes, to recognise the compromise they are making, to identify their feelings about it, and to maintain an independent self-image.

However, in many situations bilingual people can weigh up the advantages and disadvantages of challenging the conventions, and may sometimes feel confident and safe enough to challenge. They may not accept it when someone doesn't attempt to pronounce their name properly; they may request certain information in a language other than English; they may codeswitch with monolingual friends without feeling guilty; they may use non-standardised forms of English in writing and demand that they are recognised as acceptable. These are brave social actions, because they are likely to be dismissed as self-important, inflexible, rude, wrong. But if bilingual people don't try, just occasionally, to contribute to change, it may never happen.

Many people, especially bilingual learners themselves, object to work of this sort because they say bilingual people just need competence in standardised English, and they don't want to waste time discussing it. Members of minority groups don't need anyone to tell them about the way social practices, including language, exclude them from power. Members of dominant groups may need critical language awareness, but that's another matter. I think this view is misguided for two reasons. Firstly, however critically aware bilingual adults are, it is important that this awareness is brought into the classroom. It is important that everyone knows what everyone thinks about language values and language use. If they are not discussed, the learners might assume, rightly or wrongly, that the teacher advocates the status quo – or vice versa. Secondly, each individual in a class has many identities. For example, a man who speaks Urdu may be subject to oppression on grounds of race, language, employment, and class. On the other hand, he may behave as a member of a dominant group on the grounds of gender, literacy, religion, sexuality and age. So people may be treating him with disrespect at work, but he may be treating his wife and children with disrespect at home. I doubt that there is any group in any educational establishment which could be uniformly described as totally oppressed on all counts. Respect is an issue for everyone.

CONCLUSION

I was asked to write about language awareness. I have tried to answer the questions: awareness of *what?* and awareness – *what for?* There are other things to consider too, for example *how* to develop critical language awareness. I've only hinted at this, because it seems to be well covered by other articles in *Language Issues*. There are also many suggestions in publications on language awareness by the ILEA Afro-Caribbean Language and Literacy Project (1984–88).

As a way of summarising what I mean by Critical Language Awareness in Action, here is a checklist I developed for use in workshops with teachers. Checklists are commonplace in language learning these days. They usually itemise communicative activities which learners can tick off as they prove they are competent in them. This is a checklist of a rather different type, probably not so easy to tick off. However, I hope it will act as a useful guide to recognising and developing critical language awareness in your work.

A checklist of critical objectives for language learning

A Critical awareness of the relationship between language and power

1 Recognise how people with power choose the language which is used to describe people, things, and events.
2 Understand how many types of language, especially written language, have been shaped by more prestigious social groups, and seem to exclude others. That is what makes them hard to understand, hard to use confidently, or hard to write.
3 Understand how the relative status of people involved affects the way we use a language. (For example, a doctor speaks differently from a patient.)
4 Recognise that when power relations change, language changes too – both historically and between individuals.
5 Understand how language use can either reproduce or challenge existing power relations.

B Critical awareness of language variety

6 Recognise the nature of prejudice about minority languages, other languages of the world, and varieties of English.

7 Understand why some languages or language varieties are valued more highly than others.

8 Understand how devaluing languages or language varieties devalues their users.

9 Value your spoken language.

10 Recognise that speakers of languages and varieties other than standardised English are experts.

C Turning awareness into action

11 Recognise how language can either be offensive or show respect – and choose your language accordingly.

12 Recognise what possibilities for change exist in current circumstances, and what the constraints are.

13 Learn how to decide whether to challenge existing language practice in particular circumstances.

14 Learn how to oppose conventional language practice if you want to.

NOTE

This article is based on presentations and workshops I have done with Romy Clark, Norman Fairclough or Marilyn Martin-Jones in the year 1987–88 at the British Association of Applied Linguistics (BAAL) Conference in Nottingham, Oxfordshire LEA Conference on Language Awareness, ILEA Language and Literacy Unit ESL Conference, and the London Language in Inner City Schools Conference.

REFERENCES

Clark, R., Fairclough, N., Ivanič, R. and Martin-Jones, M. (1987) 'Critical Language Awareness', *Centre for Language in Social Life Working Papers Series No 1,* University of Lancaster: Department of Linguistics.

Fairclough, N. (1989) *Language and Power.* London: Longman.

Hawkins, E. (1984) *Awareness of Language: An Introduction.* Cambridge: Cambridge University Press.

Hawkins, E. (ed.) (1985) *Awareness of Language* series. Cambridge: Cambridge University Press.

Hymes, D. (1974) *Foundations in Sociolinguistics: An Ethnographic Approach.* Pennsylvania: University of Pennsylvania Press.

ILEA Afro-Caribbean Language and Literacy Project publications (1984–88). List of titles available from ILEA Language and Literacy Unit, 1 Gerridge Street, London SE1 7QT.

Progressive Literacy Group (1986) *Writing on our Side*, Vancouver, BC.

Part 2

Language and the Curriculum

The Development of Initial Literacy

YETTA GOODMAN

When I first began to study how first graders learn to read, I discovered that even those children who had taken tests which predicted they were not good risks for learning to read provided evidence that they had all kinds of knowledge about written language. All were aware of the alphabetic nature of English print. They knew that the print in books and on other objects in the environment communicated written language messages. They knew how to handle books – which way was up, how and when to turn pages, and which aspects of the print were significant for reading and which were not. They knew that print was read from left to right most of the time. They were already predicting and confirming, using graphophonic, syntactic, and semantic cues with varying degrees of proficiency. They used pencils to write, observed the writing of others, and knew that what they had written could be read. It slowly became obvious to me that children's discoveries about literacy in a literate society such as ours must begin much earlier than at school age. Becoming increasingly aware of the significance of social context and with a developmental view of learning, I hypothesised that children develop notions about literacy in the same way that they develop other significant learnings: that is, children discover and invent literacy as they participate actively in a literate society. I believe that *all* children in our highly literate society become literate, even when they are part of a group within that society that values literacy in ways different from the majority.

In this chapter, I explore the kinds of learnings that all children develop as they become literate, the kinds of personal as well as environmental factors that play a role in literacy development, and the kinds of written language principles young children develop as they interact with their environment (Goodman, 1980). These explorations are based on research I have been doing with two- to six-year-olds since 1973 (Goodman and Altwerger, 1981) and on the research of others who have greatly influenced my work.

GENERALISATIONS ABOUT LITERACY

Building on the work of Halliday (1975), K. Goodman and I extended to literacy learning the idea that learning language is learning how to mean. The child learns how to mean through written as well as spoken language. Initially, as children interact with the literacy events and implements in their culture, they grow curious and form hypotheses about their functions and purposes. They discover, as they are immersed in using written language and watching others use it, that *written language makes sense*. It communicates or says something. As this generalisation begins to develop, children also become concerned with the organisation of written language in terms of *how it makes sense*. They begin to find stability and order in the form of written language in the everyday context of its functional use. As these two generalisations are developing, children discover that *they can make sense through written language* as they use it themselves. They develop control or ownership of the strategies of comprehension and composition similar to those they have used in oral language, making allowances for the different constraints of written language forms and functions. They become more intuitively aware of the transactions among the reader, the writer, and the written text. These three overarching generalisations are driven by and, in turn, drive the development of the roots of literacy as children continue to experience written language.

THE ROOTS OF LITERACY

Although it may seem obvious, it is important to remember that children's development of literacy grows out of their experiences, and the views and attitudes toward literacy that they encounter as they interact with social groups (the family, the local community, and other socio-economic classes, races, or ethnic groups). The soil in which the roots of literacy grow has significant impact on each child's development (Goodman, 1980). The ingredients in this soil include the amount of functional literacy that children encounter in the environment and the quality of those encounters; the attitudes and values about literacy expressed by other members in the social group; children's intuitive awareness of the symbolic nature of oral language, art, music, and dance; and children's own oral language.

Literacy can be said to have three major roots, each with smaller branches within it. These roots are:

the functions and forms that the literacy events serve;
the use of oral language about written language, which is part of the literacy event and reflects society's values and attitudes toward literacy;
conscious awareness about literacy, including its functions, forms, and context.

Functions and Forms of Literacy

Children develop both reading and writing as they participate in meaningful literacy events. They develop control over functions and forms of reading. They respond to names, logotypes, and directions that usually occur as one- or two-word items embedded in conventional environmental settings. Their responses show understanding of the symbols' meanings even when the item is not read according to its conventional alphabetic form. For example, a stop sign may be referred to as 'stop', 'don't go', or 'brake car' but, for the child, the meaning is the same. In learning to read environmental print, there seems to be little difference among social class groups.

The ability to read connected discourse, which includes books, newspapers, magazines, and letters, also develops through children's participation in literacy events. In this area, though, there are differences in responses among social classes. Although economically poor children develop ideas about connected discourse and know a good deal about how to handle books, middle-class children seem to develop greater flexibility and adult conventional knowledge about this type of reading. There are wide individual differences within all groups, but all the children who have been studied have some knowledge of book-handling before they come to school.

The functions and forms of productive writing also are developing in all the children we have studied before schooling. They know what purpose writing implements serve and, at a young age, they respond in different ways to 'draw a boy' and 'write boy.' As with reading of connected discourse, productive writing varies a great deal from one household to another.

Using oral language about written language

Children and other members of society talk about the literacy events in which they participate. Words such as *read, write, pencil, story, letter,* and *book* all relate to concepts that are expressed orally during a literacy event. At 14 months of age, Alice brought her mother a book and said, 'Read me, read me.' Eduardo, aged 3½ years, pointed to a large *M* on a bulletin board and asked his dad, 'Does that say McDonald's?' Children as young as three years begin to use *say* as a metaphor for *read*. 'What does this say?' and 'this says my name' are common expressions used by three- and four-year-old children in response to written language.

Children talk not only about written language that relates directly to the literacy event itself, but also about literacy experiences in relation to schooling, job-hunting, books read, or bible use. These interactions all influence children's developing attitudes and values about literacy, including belief in their ability to learn to read and write. Some children as young as three years express the fear that learning to read or write will be very hard and can only be learned in school, whereas others are confident that they read already and that no one has to teach them because, as one youngster put it, 'the words just fall into my mouth.' These attitudes seem to be related to social class differences. Middle-class children tend to respond more confidently to learning to read than do lower-class children.

Conscious knowledge about literacy

At the same time that children use written language functionally to read and write and to talk about those experiences, they become aware of written language as an object for study and discussion. This conscious awareness – being analytic about the functions and forms of written language – develops in concert with the use of written language. It has been called, by some researchers, *linguistic* or *metalinguistic awareness*. Although I do not reject these labels, I believe it is important to distinguish a conscious or overt knowledge about language from intuitive awareness that children demonstrate when they use language. Reading, writing, or using oral language in the context of reading and writing is not necessarily conscious knowledge. The child is using linguistic knowledge intuitively just as he or she does when speaking or listening. Likewise, calling written forms by linguistic labels may not demonstrate conscious linguistic knowledge, since the child may at this point know the names of the forms and functions of literacy without consciously analysing them. Children can appropriately call a dog by its name long before they can explain that it always has four legs and barks and why it is more like a cat than like an elephant or a fish.

There is evidence that children do begin early to develop conscious knowledge about the forms and functions of written language. Quincy, aged four years, says as he looks at the word *Ivory* on a card which has had its logotype shape retained: 'It says soap, but you know if you put a dot up here (he points to the *i*) that's in my name, and if you put a line down here (he points to the *o*) that's in my name, and this . . . this . . . (he is pointing to the *y*) this is. (Then he points to each finger on his left hand with one of the fingers on his right hand as he continues his analysis.) This is a *q-u-i-n-c-y* . . . That's a *y*.' Quincy is an example of the many children who develop conscious knowledge about written language before they receive formal instruction in school.

PRINCIPLES OF LITERACY DEVELOPMENT

Thus children have many experiences with written language as they grow. For some children, these experiences begin when they are as young as six months old, as mothers and some fathers read to their children, enveloping the child and the book together into an emotionally satisfying literacy event. Other children generate written language in other kinds of literacy events (for example, looking for a particular gas station that sells at the lowest price; finding letters or words on highway signs during a family game in the car; or watching for a particular written symbol on television because, when that symbol appears, the child will be allowed to stay up late).

As children participate in literacy events, actively reading and writing, they develop three major principles about written language: the *relational* or *semiotic principles* are the understandings that children have about the ways that meaning is represented in written language, the ways that oral language is represented in written language, and the ways that both oral and written language interrelate to represent meaning. The *functional principles* are the understandings that children have about the reasons and purposes for written language. The *linguistic principles* are the understandings children have about how written language is organised and displayed so that communication can occur, considering the orthographic, graphophonic, syntactic, semantic, and pragmatic systems of language.

During early development, children may construct principles which they later have to discard. Some of these principles may actually interfere with the development of others for a period of time. The principles will overlap and interact, and the children will have to sort out which principles are most significant to meaning and which are not very useful; which operate differently given the constraints on each; and finally, which may be important in the understanding of other symbol systems the child is developing. These principles cannot be taught through traditional structured reading programmes. They emerge for all children, but because of the idiosyncratic nature of the use of written language, the times and ways in which these principles emerge will vary extensively.

Relational principles

Children learn to relate written language to meaning and, where necessary, to oral language. They develop the knowledge that some unit of written language represents some unit of meaning. Although this relationship may include words or letters, it also includes propositions, ideas, concepts, images, signs, symbols, and icons. Many children also know that their drawings represent ideas or things in the real world. They know the picture of a dog is not the dog itself but represents a dog. By the time most children enter school, they are aware that written language represents meaning. The developing writer and reader comes to know the relationships between writing, the object being represented, oral language, and the orthography.

These relational principles can be observed in a number of ways. Ferreiro and Teberosky (1982) suggest that children first believe that written language is a particular way of representing objects. It is not a drawing but acts like a drawing as the children respond to it. Children believe that print related to a picture says the name of the items represented in the picture, not that it is an oral language equivalent to the print. According to this theory, for children at a particular level of understanding, print that reads 'the boy plays ball' says 'boy' and 'ball', although the children may interpret the picture as 'the boy is playing ball'. Children later develop the idea that there is an equivalence between oral and written language, first treating it as syllabic and finally as alphabetic.

My own research with children in English provides support for these conclusions drawn from research with children in Spanish and French. When told to write his name, three-year-old Josh wrote what appeared to be a small – Ɔ . As he did this he said, 'This is a boy.' Then, without any further probing, he wrote a much larger character – Ɔ – which resembled the first in form, and he said, 'This is a dad.' Finally, at the bottom of the paper, he made the same character even larger – Ꝺ – adding a second character which looked like an O superimposed over the first, and said, 'This is the boy and the dad together.'

Josh's father's name is Joseph. Although the child was using characters that resembled the first two letters of both his and his father's names, these characters did not represent sounds for him; they represented 'the boy' and 'the dad'. The child was able to represent his meanings in written language, and these meanings signified something in the child's personal experience. After a period of time of using size, shape, and number to invent written language forms, children develop alphabetic principles to relate oral and written language.

Children also show their developing awareness of the relationship between the length of the written string and the oral string. As they read or write, children will elongate their oral response to match their reading or writing. Eric, four years old, read 'cee-ree-ull,' stretching out the sound until he was finished pointing to the words *Kellogg's Raisin Bran*. As Mary wrote her name, she continued voicing the sounds of her name until she was finished writing it. Observation of children pointing with their fingers while an adult reads to them or of children's oral production as they watch an adult take dictation provides evidence of this developing principle.

Additional evidence of the development of the relational principle has been provided by researchers who have shown that children know written stories are represented in books following a particular story format (Doake, 1981; Haussler, 1982). They will repeat almost verbatim a whole story that has been read to them often, showing that they know how to represent the story form as well as its meaning.

Functional principles

The degree to which literacy events are meaningful and purposeful to the child and the value those events have for the child will influence the development of functional principles. In homes where parents are college students, computer programmers, or authors, children will discover functional principles different from those developed by children whose parents read only the Bible daily or whose parents use writing selectively for shopping lists, filling out forms, and taking phone messages. Negative or positive statements made by adults about schooling and the ability to read and write, and the difficulty with or pleasure derived from reading and writing as shown by adults will also influence how children come to understand the functions of literacy.

Specific functional principles that children develop early include ownership and labelling, extension of memory, sharing information about self and others, invitations and expressions of gratitude, representation of real and imagined events (such as narratives), and control of behavior and information. For example, children will produce their own name as a label or recognise their name in appropriate settings. When children respond to printed items embedded in context, they tend to use nouns for naming items and imperative phrases for direction-giving signs in the environment. Stores and names of products and games usually are called by related names, whereas stop signs and school crossing signs elicit responses such as 'don't go' or 'watch out for kids.' We have samples of children's notes, written a year or two before they enter school, which express a concern, a message, or an invitation for their parents or siblings. These are real uses of spontaneously produced written language.

In addition, the play in which children participate prior to schooling, both at home and in child care centers, demonstrates the development of functional principles. As children pretend to be mothers, gas station attendants, store clerks, doctors, or teachers, they use reading or writing appropriate to those occupations. The impact of home minicomputers and the new computer age in general on the functional principles of literacy that children develop can only be speculated about at this time, but that this understanding of literacy will appear in the play and real use of written language by children between the ages of two and six is unquestionable.

Linguistic principles

Linguistic principles help young children solve the problems of

1 how the written language system is organised;
2 how the organisation of written language changes, depending on its function and its relationship to other symbol systems;
3 what the units of written language are, depending on its functional and relational uses;
4 which features of written language are most significant in which settings;
5 the stability of the organisational system (that is, which rules are most reliable and which are not very useful).

The evidence shows that children hypothesise about all the linguistic cueing systems needed for written language. The orthographic system, including directionality, spelling, punctuation, and form variations, as well as the graphophonic system, is new to children. The phonologic, syntactic, semantic, and pragmatic systems are developed through oral language use, and children exhibit a growing awareness of how these systems operate differently under the constraints of written language.

Children's early scribbling resembles the writing system used conventionally by adults in a society, but the writing of children in an Arabic literate culture will look different from the writing of children in an English literate culture. Samples of children's writing demonstrate that written language can be represented by single characters as well as in a scriptlike form. Punctuation, spacing, and directionality are used inventively at first and later, more conventionally.

Children seem to work through some of the same problems that the adult inventors of written language historically have had to solve, such as which way to display letters and how to organise the writing into units. Aesthetic issues are evident in children's work as they balance their art with their writing. Children explore these problems, discovering solutions that may be more appropriate for orthographic systems other than their own. For example, Roxanne, a six-year-old, wrote a story with no spaces between her words, but she made the final letter in each word backwards when possible and underlined the last letter when it was not possible to reverse it. In Hebrew, some of the final letters of words are marked so that they look different from the same letter in medial or initial positions. When Roxanne was asked why she had done this, she said, 'So you can read it better.'

The work of Charles Read (1975) and others has provided insights into the ways in which children invent a spelling system based on their knowledge of phonology. Their spelling becomes more and more conventionalised, regardless of instruction.

Punctuation is another convention that children begin to develop as they write. Bissex (1980) reports that her son used the exclamation mark before any other form of punctuation. Other children discover the use of the period, sometimes overgeneralising its use as a word boundary market before they control the use of space to separate words. At age six years, Jennifer used dialogue in her first-grade writing, but it was not until she was seven years old that punctuation related to dialogue appeared in her stories:

January, Grade 1
. . . The mastr yald at hem you onle have two galns of hone he tot to the flor He sed tri to gev me som mor natr. [The master yelled at him, 'You only have two gallons of honey.' He talked to the flower. He said, 'Try to give me some more nectar.']

March, Grade 2
*. . . 'So he said I will go to the camping stor, and I will ask what
I need to go on my trip.' . . . So he 'said Im going camping'*

Children provide evidence that they know about syntactic
aspects of written language as well as the semantic and pragmatic
aspects. For example, children develop control over the principle that
some morphemic endings remain the same regardless of their phonologic composition. At age four to six years, children spell words such as
walked, jumped and *kissed* with the letter *t* at the end. (See Jennifer's
spelling of *talked*.) Later, they realise that *ed* is the most common
graphic representation of past tense in English. Some young readers
overgeneralise this rule, reading or writing *walkted* for *walked*. Two
first graders, in spontaneous writing, showed additional evidence of
experimenting with morphemic issues. Carol, writing a letter to her
grandparents, spelled the ordinal numbers as 'firSt,' 'fourSt,' 'sixSt,' as
she was relating what grades she and her brothers were in. However,
when she read the letter aloud, she produced the conventional oral
English forms. Michael wrote to a friend about his 'sidiren' and
'bidren,' but when he read his letter aloud, he read the words *sisters* and
brothers. Could his morphemic endings have been overgeneralisations
from the spelling of *children*?

Miscue analysis, which compares readers' observed responses to the listeners' expected responses, has provided evidence that
children control syntax as they read. Miscues result in syntactically and
semantically acceptable sentences, and substitution miscues are most
often the same part of speech as the expected response. When children
even as young as three years are reading or writing narrative stories,
they usually begin with 'once upon a time.' We have never collected a
child's letter that began with this traditional story starter. Rather, most
letters open with 'Dear _____,' 'how are you?' or the like.

There may be certain hierarchical sequences in the development
of specific principles of language. For example, it seems that children
develop a syllabic principle about written language before notions
about alphabetic principles emerge. Also, children do not seem to
represent the preconsonantal nasal when they begin to invent spelling in
English, although it appears later in their development of literacy skills.

LEARNING TO BECOME LITERATE

The development of written language is very complicated. The generalisations about and the roots and developing principles of literacy all
interact as children develop control over making sense through written
language. With this knowledge, children enter school where, too often,
they are placed in a rigid instructional setting that ignores and is
incompatible with what they already know. No published instructional
program has ever provided the generalisations and concepts that people

must develop to learn to read and write. A highly structured instructional system that focuses on mastery of one rule or skill before another loses sight of the complexity of learning written language. It oversimplifies what children really do learn and focuses some insecure children on insignificant and often erroneous principles about language.

In further research, each aspect of written language must be studied in greater depth and over longer periods of time. The focus should be on single subjects and on groups of children from widely different backgrounds who are reading and writing spontaneously. We must have more evidence of how capable the human toddler is of solving his or her personal needs for written language.

School is an important setting for literacy learning. There, the learning of literacy skills can be an exciting and stimulating experience; however, it can also be discouraging and inhibiting. Teaching children literacy through functional use has been advocated for more than 80 years (Iredell, 1898; Huey, 1908). Although there still is much that researchers and teachers must learn about literacy learning and teaching, we currently have the scientific foundation for helping teachers make learning to read and write an exciting literacy curriculum for all children.

REFERENCES

Bissex, G. L. (1980) *Gnys at Work: A child learns to read and write*. Cambridge: Harvard University Press.

Doake, D. (1981) *Book Experience and Emergent Reading in Pre-school Children*. Ph.D. dissertation. University of Alberta.

Ferreiro, E. and Teberosky, A. (1982) *Literacy Before Schooling*. Exeter, NH: Heinemann.

Goodman, Y. (1980) 'The roots of literacy' in Douglass, M. (ed.) *Claremont Reading Conference*: Claremont Graduate School.

Goodman, Y. and Altwerger, B. (1981) 'Print awareness in pre-school children'. Occasional Paper no. 4, College of Education, University of Arizona.

Halliday, M. A. K. (1975) *Learning How to Mean*. London: Edward Arnold.

Haussler, M. (1982) *A Psycholinguistic Description of Beginning Reader Development*. Ph.D. dissertation, University of Arizona.

Huey, E. B. (1908) *The Psychology and Pedagogy of Reading*. New York: Macmillan.

Iredell, H. (1898) 'Eleanor learns to read'. *Education*, pp. 233–38.

Read, C. (1975) 'Children's categorization of speech sounds in English'. NCTE Research Report no. 17.

8

What Do We Know about Reading that Helps Us Teach?

MARGARET MEEK

The short answer is: a great deal: more every month, in fact. But we are still uncertain how to turn what we learn into what we do in classrooms. The move from research and theory to the implementation of the results as practice has always been, at best, indirect. But now that teachers are to undertake detailed assessments of children's reading at all levels of attainment, we are anxiously looking for how we can turn what we are learning about reading into evidence of pupils' progress.

So the question of 'what counts as being able to read' is more important than ever. We have to take care that, in reformulating, re-editing or revising our views on reading and our ways of teaching that we don't merely swing from one good idea or one interesting operation to another. We need principled reasons for the ways we teach reading, and, in education these are bound to come from more than one source. Some insights have survived the test of time. There is renewed evidence in every generation that experienced readers are more con-fident than inexperienced ones because thay have read more books with contentment and success. Huey, now much cited as a source of reading wisdom, was virtually ignored from 1906 until nearly 1970 because his insights didn't 'fit' the current teaching modes. The teaching of reading has a history of which we, as learners and teachers, are a part. Whatever we take from the latest research report makes a different kind of difference to each one of us. My belief, that the pleasures and profits of reading are worth the effort that each new text demands of me, influences my concern to let beginner readers discover the power and the excitement of reading, not simply its usefulness as a skill for information retrieval. I judge my success in helping children to learn by their exploratory approach to texts, by their inclination to take risks in discovering how texts mean.

Others who recognise that 'many children find learning to read extremely difficult, despite the great deal of time and effort expended by their teachers' (Perera, 1984) are perhaps more realistic. But in what follows I am sticking to my conviction that committed readers and writers help children to read and write because they know what these processes are good for. Nothing that I have read in books or articles or seen in the classrooms in the last ten years has unsettled this idea. Children need positive invitations to read, demonstrations, information, explanations that fit their understandings and texts that engage them if they are to learn what reading is all about. If they are having difficulties, they need more of these not less. Without the insights that accompany success they do not want to go on.

SOCIAL & LINGUISTIC COMPLEXITIES

Two axioms give us a framework for sorting out some of our perplexities. The first is: reading cannot be properly understood or learned if separated, in theory or in practice, from the other language processes that are part of being literate in a literate society: speaking, listening and writing. The second is: although adults treat reading and writing as the activities of individuals, children learn to read, at home and at school, in ways that are distinctly social. Until they are confident about what the Cox Report calls 'all types of writing' which call for their 'reading, understanding and response' most children learn to read in the company of other people, both adults and peers. What parents, teachers and children tell each other about reading and writing can be as powerful in its effects as anything written in academic studies, journalistic debates or as the latest cure for dyslexia. As Shirley Brice Heath and Michael Cole make plain there is always a powerful context for what children are doing with language. Thus where and how children learn to read, and continue to practice as readers, is always part of the reading process as they engage in it. If they are at their most stretched in a reading clinic rather than for their own diversion on a rainy day, we must see that their view of reading is locked into concerns with health or sickness rather than with a chosen pleasure. My own raw untreated evidence comes from bilingual children who ask their classroom peers for help because they will understand the explanation. It comes from teachers who see how even young children can instruct newcomers to the reception class in 'how we do reading here.' To be born into a literate society is to encounter language in print in the world at large before learning to read it in school. In the last decade researchers have concerned themselves with how children 'awaken' to literacy by looking at the ambient, public or embedded language of public signs, messages and instructions. We hold this language in common, and, as Margaret Donaldson says, 'the setting supports understanding'. This is also the part of early reading that is most like the interactions of learning to talk. If you have seen the BBC Horizon film called *How do you read?*, you'll remember the incident when Frank Smith and three-year-old Matthew go to buy cards in a department store and Matthew tells Frank where the cards are because he can read the sign. No serious researchers now discount such understanding but neither do they discount that, *by itself*, knowledge and experience of sign writing, from Macdonald's golden arches to the ubiquitous Coke will guarantee reading success in every child.

Deciphering 'Lloyd's Bank' from the top of a bus stuck in traffic is a useful diversion for parents and children, and a significant recognition for an adult illiterate. But the interpretive background for making meaning is derived from a number of other occurrences of the same sign. Teachers count on language in the world to encourage children's interaction with written language. They then go on to extend the learner's base for this significant understanding to other places, including classroom writing and books. Similarly, encouraged by Shirley Brice Heath and others, we now look for, or try to discover, the repeated, familiar literacy events in the early years that children spend at home, so that we may turn their understanding of these to reading at school. The diversity of research evidence that comes from this move is sometimes daunting. When we compare the detailed observation Barbara Tizard and Martin Hughes made of working class girls talking, reading and playing with their mothers, with Gordon Wells' assertions that being read to before school is the core of success in early literacy we realise that research generalisations have to be modified by some cross-cultural differences. Our only near certainty and it is powerful enough – seems to be that for some children learning to read is not only a different culture but a different language.

A teacher who knows what her pupils' homes and lives are like, who reads in the way their parents read has much less to learn about teaching reading than one who meets children whose lives at home are a complete mystery to her. Evelyn Gregory reports the case of a Chinese boy who, given a book to take home before he could read it at all, confused his parents when he asked them to help him to read it. Where this family came from, a book was a reward for being able to read, not the encouragement to do so. So they had little confidence in their child's teacher. It was diminished even more when the boy brought home its drawings, which, for his parents, were evidence of neither reading nor writing. The upshot of all this is a recurrent question; do we know what we need to know about the literacy competencies that children bring with them to school, and how, or in what contexts, are our reading instructions being interpreted? We must now pass from intuitive guessing to genuine knowledge in this area. For too long we have assumed that we know about children's reading 'background', when often we have been wide of the mark.

IMPLICIT/EXPLICIT KNOWLEDGE

When we read to children at home we demonstrate 'how reading goes'. We let the apprentice follow by looking at the lines of print while we 'turn' the page. We try to make the cohesion of the text produce a coherent meaning that the listener will understand. We match most of the words on the page with what we say, recognising that there is a difference between what words say and what they mean. The reading completed, we may talk about the content of the story or the account, relishing parts of it, or looking at the match of pictures and text. If we expect our young apprentice to join in, he or she will be guided by what we say. Children know that in close contacts, they can do these things without risk. Most parents and teachers have learned, from popular journalism, television and book promotions, that early reading should be enjoyed by both partners in the enterprise. At school children next discover reading as a classroom activity explicitly organised for a large group.

Some children adapt easily to this change, others latch onto the important words of the teacher's instructions. So for some time they may be confused, trying to fit what they already know about what reading is like to what they are expected to do in class. They get new expectations of 'schooled' literacy, and what counts as reading in this class becomes a set of classroom rituals rather than interactions with the texts. When parents enquire about reading lessons they are often confused by children's account of events. They are worried in case children don't get a chance to demonstrate how well they read at home. Real trouble begins if the parents expect the children to have direct access to a selection of books and instead they come home with a tin full of words written on pieces of cards which they are supposed to 'test'. Misunderstandings about reading procedures are easily sorted out. More difficult for the teacher to cope with is the parents' initial enthusiasm for new texts in classrooms followed by a worrying insistence that children aren't 'getting the words right' at sight. In the new partnership teachers will have to be quite explicit to parents about the relationship of language to learning, the nature of children's implicit, contextualised understandings, and the way they are related to both the social interactions in the classroom and the understanding of words on a page of text. As the NATE document says, 'Children can learn to use their language for a wider range of purposes with a wider range of people'. As we plan this growth we also have to show, especially in reading how children's implicit understanding of language becomes explicit, how they *know* what the words mean, or, better still, what the book is *about*.

RECORD KEEPING

We are learning to do this by devising new ways of keeping records and thus making the incremental learning visible. By using tools like the *Primary Language Record* teachers can demonstrate to parents how their judgements match what children say and do. In this more diversified form of assessment children's growth in reading competencies loses much of its competitive element as the narrow indication given by a mark on a scale is replaced by descriptions and analysis of children's actual interactions with print. A classroom is the place where children become a community of readers and writers. Successful reading depends on its becoming purposeful, understood, modelled, discussed in terms of the text which pupils both choose and share. Where there is a rich diet of reading matter of all kinds children's implicit and explicit knowledge of language grow by leaps and bounds. They are encouraged to take risks safely, by returning to texts they know well for reassurance that their skills have not deserted them, as well as reaching out to texts of greater complexity to increase their repertoire of dealing with different generic kinds and so proceed to reading independence.

The classrooms I now see are more than places where children learn to read. With their messages of genuine impact, their wide variety of books, children's written work in many languages, they are genuine literacy workshops for children whose 'stages' may be different, but who are profiting from insight applicable to all. One of the most significant insights comes from Bruner's discussion of narrative in *Actual Minds, Possible Words*. It makes plain that narrative is not simply a process of storytelling to be set against telling the observed truth, or 'the facts'. Instead it is a way of considering possibilities, of making worlds. When we discuss children's reactions to what they have read, or encourage them to write, we discover the powerful nature of the alternative worlds of their imagination.

The evidence collected for adults who read a great deal has convinced them that when they are 'lost in a book', both children and adults experience a change of consciousness. But not all adults and not all children know this experience. But we do know that reading and writing give human beings the world twice. Vygotsky expressed the idea:

> *Every function in the child's cultural development appears twice: first on the social level and later on the individual level; first between people (interpsychological) and then inside the child (intrapsychological).*

When one child helps another to read, both benefit; the pupil-learner discovers how reading goes, the pupil-teacher has to know what she or he knows about reading in order to explain it. The real teacher discovers where they both will go next.

SPECIFIC UNDERSTANDINGS

No teacher in her senses believes or suggests that children learning to read needn't pay attention to the words on the page. If we, as competent readers, aren't reading under the guidance of the text, we aren't really reading. Yet the absolutely fixed utterance of a text aloud (I can't bear to write 'decoding' because presumably the reader already knows the language of the text) is no guarantee that the reader understands the sense of the text. So we have to be clear that meaning is what counts. A reader who is puzzled by the words but knows that they make sense is in a better state than one who believes that reading consists of 'recognising' words as they stand, that meaning is not what counts. Young readers know they can read when they tackle a whole book on their own; first if it is a book they are familiar with, they discover that the words stay the same every time they begin the story again. Later they recognise how the author does it and seem to see through the words to the meaning. That is what Enid Blyton has taught generations of girls and some boys to understand because she always plays the game by the rules. There's no going forward to reading without some of this awareness of the 'recurrence of features', the generic nature of writing in a culture. A story isn't the only way to learn this. For the young a Mother Goose Anthology is every bit as good. They learn to see what they memorise. I learned it from a hymn book. Getting the words right is only a step to reading, not reading in itself. The next move is to interpret or interrogate the text so as to go on to ask, 'Do I believe that?' or 'Do I like these people?' or 'How do we know that?' This usually comes when the reader discovers a change in the way something is said. When they know for example how a narrative works, readers are free to inspect unexpected words and phrases in the next story they read. They can also tolerate uncertainty of not knowing all the words. In contrast reading information books involves the reader in adjustments of the picture of the world that exists for him or her *outside* the text.

Now let's look at how it is possible for teachers to be bamboozled by expertise. I don't mean that reading experts set out to deliberately confuse teachers, but the effect is often to take away whatever confidence we have in our own explanation of events we see, and in our own understanding of what might help children with specific difficulties.

In 1977 in *The Cool Web* my colleagues and I reprinted a chapter from Chukovsky's *From Two to Five* to indicate how rhymes and children's play with language were part of their more explicit understandings of what language is and as such, a vital contribution to the pattern of children's reading. This same evidence crops up again in Bryant and Bradley's (1985 – reprinted 1985, 1986, 1987) *Children's Reading Problems* as one way to improve children's phonological skills as a remedy for reading 'backwardness'. The authors say that children learn from nursery rhymes 'a great deal about the phonological structure of language' and 'parents can go a long way towards removing the problem of reading difficulties by encouraging their children to play with sounds in the years before school.' Anne M. Bussis and her colleagues, in their exhaustive longitudinal study of children learning to read called *Enquiry into Meaning*, pick up the Opies' evidence and continue:

Our data indicates that children also recognise and anticipate rhythmic structures in written language when they read texts that possess this literary quality . . . Although children's understanding of literary styles and rhythms seemed to play a significant role in their negotiations of text, we know of only one article in the reading research literature that treats such knowledge as an important consideration for young readers.

The article wasn't that of Bradley and Bryant. Now I don't want to claim that my colleagues and I saw the possibilities of children's nursery rhymes for the understanding of phonology before others. Instead I am suggesting that we were enthusiastic about rhymes, those amazing bits of popular culture that have survived over ages as children's literature, things made with words as proverbs, iterative tales, memorable words that somehow don't disappear. If we take them as a way of preventing reading difficulties, the magic vanishes. They become part of a treatment, a therapy, and die. Please teach children nursery rhymes, and the phonology will come, noticed with fun.

Reading research breeds its own brand of evidence. The consequent problem is that reading specialists are bound to ignore the evidence that arises spontaneously in classrooms because it isn't generalisable. Yet in classrooms and other places where children read is precisely where the evidence is. Most of what teachers learn from research has long been part of their understanding. Only lately has it come to be appreciated.

THE INFLUENCE OF ETHNOGRAPHY

As a simple explanation of ethnography I use Clifford Goertz's term 'a thick description'. That's what the teaching of reading needs because it is visibly a different kind of activity for all teachers and readers yet it has common features. After a long series of arguments about method we are coming to see that in a record of what a reader, a teacher and a parent do is embedded their different views of the task of learning to do it and all the contextual features of this learning and teaching. In keeping the record the teacher has to begin by interpreting her own 'common' sense about reading, writing, speaking and listening and re-ordering it as a reorganised body of considered thought on the subject. The teacher then begins to behave like an expert who has privileged access to children's evidence. When she records, interprets and categorises the evidence, she becomes expert. As a result of this kind of recording, different as it is from the results of reading tests, we have begun to understand that what we see children do and say are important parts of our understanding of what they do when they read. We have, I think, taken two steps at most towards understanding what we know and to making this local knowledge more generally available.

First we have begun to record what parents, teachers and children say about reading; how they do it together, what they like, what they find difficult and at the same time what they know about language as a system, and what they do with it. Then we have come to see that children's engagement with texts is a wide spectrum of language competence, involving narrative, rhythm, memorable language ('And it was still hot!') and the intertext of jokes and books within books (Each Peach Pear Plum). Here is one incident for the record. See if you can count how many aspects of language and reading awareness are embedded in Veronica Smith's anecdote. Then ask, will the child's reading go forward or backward from here?

Mrs Smith visited, in their reception class in the infant school, some children who had been progressing well in the nursery before their move to 'real school'. She asked them if they read the same books in their new class as they had in the nursery. One child said, 'The Very Hungry Caterpillar' and added 'but I can't read it in school'. Remembering that the child had been both fluent and pleased when reading this picture book in its entirety, Mrs Smith suggested that they might read it together again. The child read to her with skill and competence, the cumulative tale of how the caterpillar ate a variety of food on each day of the week except Saturday and Sunday and in doing so made a hole in each page. 'There you see you read it,' said Mrs Smith. 'But I can't read it in school,' persisted the child. 'Why not?' said Mrs Smith. 'Well,' said the child, with that patience they show when talking to the slow witted. I can do the eatings on Monday, Wednesday and Thursday but not on the other days because the teacher has not put them on a card yet.'

I am not concerned to blame the teacher: we all have short records of believing that we have to learn from children. Yet I am pinning my hopes on the possibility that, once we have learned that expertise is not confined to experts and that children, especially those experiencing difficulty, are the ultimate test of our teaching, we may take the most unprecedented step of listening to children's views of the task of learning to read. So far they have persuaded me that we have even more to learn.

REFERENCES

Barrs, M. et al. (1989) Primary Language Record: handbook for teachers. London: ILEA.

Bruner, J. (1986) Actual Minds, Possible Words. London: Harvard University Press.

Bryant, P. and Bradley, L. (1985) Children's Reading Problems: psychology and education. Oxford: Oxford University Press.

Bussis, A. M., Chittenden, E. A., Amarell, M. and Klausner, E. Inquiry into Meaning; an investigation of learning to read. Hillsdale Lawrence Erlbuam Associates.

Cole, M. and Griffin, P. (1986) 'A Sociohistorical Approach to Remediation' in De Castell, S., Luke, A. and Egan, K. *Literacy, Society and Schooling.* Cambridge: Cambridge University Press.

Chukovsky, K. (1963) *From Two to Five.* California: University of California Press.

Donaldson, M. (1988) *Sense and Sensibility: some thoughts on the teaching of literacy.* Reading and Language Centre, University of Reading.

Goertz, C. (1983) *Local Knowledge: further essays in interpretive anthropology.* New York: Basic Books.

Heath, S. B. (1983) *Ways With Words.* Cambridge: Cambridge University Press.

Meek, M., Warlow, A. and Barton, G. (1977) *The Cool Web: the pattern of children's reading.* London: Bodley Head.

NATE (1988) *Learning to be Literate in a Democratic Society.* Sheffield: NATE.

Perera, K. (1984) *Children's Writing and Reading: analysing classroom language.* Oxford: Basil Blackwell.

Tizard, B and Hughes, M. *Young Children Learning.* London: Fontana.

Vygotsky, L. S. (1978) *Mind in Society.* Harvard: Harvard University Press.

Reader, Writer, Text

NICK JONES ⸺⸺⸺⸺⸺⸺⸺⸺⸺⸺⸺⸺⸺⸺⸺⸺◇

*Everything can be known about a reading public, back to the
economics of printing and publishing and the effects of an
educational system, but what is read by that public is the
neutralised abstraction 'books', or at best its catalogued
categories. Meanwhile, but elsewhere, everything can be known
about the books, back to their authors, to traditions and
influences, and to periods, but these are finished objects before
they go out into the dimension where 'sociology' is thought to
be relevant: the reading public, the history of publishing. It is
this division, now ratified by confident disciplines, which a
sociology of culture has to overcome and supersede, insisting on
what is always a whole and connected social material process.
(Raymond Williams)*

This attempt to 'map' the process of reading arose out of the early,
exploratory stages of the LINC project, in response to the question:
how might we interpret the notion of 'knowledge about language' in
relation to the field of reading? Both Kingman and Cox argued strongly
for the encouragement of pleasure in reading, and for a significant
breadth of reading experience. Both gave an especial weight, for
secondary pupils in particular, to the study of literature – what Kingman called 'the powerful and splendid history of the best that has been
thought and said in our language'. It was not in the remit of either
committee, however, to establish the kind of framework for thinking
about the reading process *as a whole*, which might help to answer that
initial question. Nor, as a profession, do we possess for reading the kind
of shared vocabulary of concepts and approaches which the National
Writing Project has been able in its own field both to absorb and to
generate.

The purpose of this paper, therefore, is to offer for discussion a
condensed but systematic account of reading/writing as a cultural
practice. For the teacher, the paper maps ground to be considered both
in the adoption of strategies for approaching individual texts, and in the
context of broader, whole-school policies for reading development.

The paper takes the form of a set of diagrams and a related
commentary. The diagrams and the commentary together form an
incremental sequence, which looks in turn at different aspects of the

reading process. Each section is keyed to a quotation from the Cox report – not in a spirit of biblical citation, but in order to locate the argument clearly within the context of present legislation.

Diagrams are by their nature reductive – especially other people's. This in itself, however, is a kind of invitation. The most useful diagrams, it might be argued, are those which provoke the most vigorous mental scribbling, the most ingenious acts of defacement. By the same token, the definitions which accompany the figures should be taken in the context of the argument about writers, texts and readings which the model itself proposes. These are the working definitions of a situated reader, frozen at the point of utterance. Defrost at room temperature, and use your own recipes.

SECTION 1

Reading is much more than the decoding of black marks upon a page: it is a quest for meaning and one which requires the reader to be an active participant. (Cox 16.2)

A common presumption of the relationship between writer, reader and text is that represented by Figure 9.1, in which the reader is seen as the passive receiver, or consumer, of the text which the writer produces. Or, by extension, the writer is seen as transmitting information – an

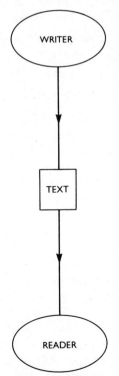

Figure 9.1 Reading and writing as one-way process

instruction, an opinion, a story – by encoding it within a text, from which a reader who shares that code (written Standard English, for example) may subsequently retrieve it.

This individualised, 'one-way' account does not, however, answer to the multiplicity and complexity of actual reading experience, and we might usefully extend and rework this model in a number of ways. To begin with, we need to comprehend the *transactional* or interanimative nature of reading relations: that what the reader *brings to* the text is as significant as what he or she *takes from* it. The arrows go both ways. Secondly, we need to incorporate a sense of the differing *contexts* in which the act of writing and the act of reading separately occur.

SECTION 2

> *The full development of both reading and writing . . . requires a broad definition of text. (Cox 17.22)*

Text

We can define a *text* as any deliberate selection or combination of words, sounds or images in a stable form.

While our major concern, as teachers of reading, is with printed verbal texts, the contemporary significance of video and other predominantly visual media, including illustrated books, means that these too must come within our definition; spontaneous spoken language

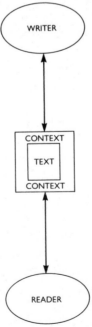

Figure 9.2 Reading and writing as two-way process

becomes 'a text' once it has been recorded and presented as such; at the boundary of our concerns we might regard clothing as 'textual' in a comparable way (cf. 'dress codes'). For this reason, you may prefer to replace the term 'writer' by a more general term, such as 'composer'.

Texts are material objects, which carry within them the particular histories of their composition, and consequent possibilities of meaning. The term *text* therefore implies both a reader and a writer. In its origin the word means *something woven*, which implies a purposeful working upon the available resources of meaning. The *realisation* of this meaning, and the completion of the work, is nonetheless dependent upon the reader. It may be helpful to distinguish the *text* – the material object – from the *work* in this sense.

Reading texts does not of course exhaust the possibilities of reading. A meteorologist, for example, 'reads' natural signs; a detective 'reads' the accidental traces of human activity.

Context

All texts are read within a *context* which conditions the reader's expectations, and the interpretations which then appear possible; the context is indeed one part of the meaning that is communicated. The context will be different for different readers, or for the same reader at different times. The reading context is to this extent beyond the control of the writer – who will nonetheless have written with certain ideal or possible contexts in mind. The marketing of books, as of other media products, is one of the more conspicuous and systematic aspects of this contextualising process, and a reminder that there are *intentions* intermediate between those of writer and reader.

This double sense of the context of reading – the broad context assumed by the writer, and the particular context in which each reading occurs – is one aspect of its transactional or negotiated nature.

SECTION 3

> *Learning to read involves recognising that writing is made.*
> *(Cox 16.13)*

Composition

One part of the story of a text is the history of the choices made during its composition. A writer's *intentions* are always implicit within this process, whether or not they are overtly signalled within the text, or deducible from it. It is impossible to read anything without making some assumption as to the writer's tone and purpose.

These intentions encompass the writer's sense (which may be no more than speculative) of the context in which the text will be received, including the envisaged readership, occasion, and purpose, and the means of publication.

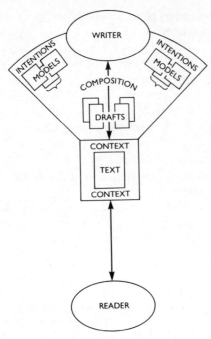

Figure 9.3 Writing in context

Somewhere in the writer's mind, though not always in the forefront, is the multiplicity of remembered *models* which makes it possible for writers to conceive of texts of this or of that kind. These might range from standard proforma for simple writing tasks, to creative syntheses of otherwise quite disparate material. The various conventions for addressing or invoking an audience are one part of this discursive repertoire.

In the act of composition, the writer works interactively upon the text as it emerges, often in the form of successive drafts. It is a common experience of writing that only through this process of trial and reflection does the writer gain a clear sense of what it is he or she is working to produce. The process of drafting therefore requires a constant shifting or oscillation of role from *writer* to *reader*; in the classroom or the workplace, that process may involve the active collaboration of other readers, and other writers.

Each of these aspects of composition underlines the extent to which the production of writing occurs within, and is dependent upon, a cradle of cultural relations.

SECTION 4

Children should know about the processes by which meanings are conveyed, and about the ways in which print and other media carry values. (Cox 2.25)

Culture of production

The form a text takes during composition is dependent upon *the means of the production of meaning* available to this or that writer within a given culture. It is regulated by what is economically and technically feasible, and by the relative degree of access to material resources. It is also dependent upon a writer's access to language, to the locked or unlocked storehouse of grammatical and rhetorical resources through which meanings are made. Both are aspects of the social *history* of that culture. Because language is always social, its forms and conventions are inscribed with the variable patterning of privilege or proscription, the *ideological* values which have been attached to certain modes of expression, or to certain categories of writing. Except in the most rigid of communities, these values do not go uncontested; new thoughts become thinkable as conventions emerge or recede. The definition of 'Literature' is a recurrent example.

The writer

Within this culture of production, the *writer* occupies a position of tenuous independence. The alternative term, *author*, suggests a tradition of thinking that locates too simply the authority of the text,

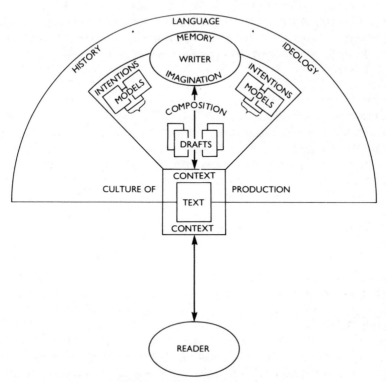

Figure 9.4 Culture of production

casting 'the' author as the solitary originator of meaning. Many texts are anonymous. Many are written by one hand but 'authorised' by another. Very often the writing process itself will be collaborative, as in most media products. What a writer does is not *determined* by the culture, but is always conditioned by it. At one end of the scale, a writer may be employed by a particular set of commercial or political interests, or subjected to the constraints of a narrowly conceived assessment test. At the other, he or she may be writing a difficult love letter. The task is equally embedded in the available possibilities of the language.

Figure 9.4 denotes the 'individuality' of the writer in two ways. *Memory* is the sedimented knowledge of our participation in a common history. Shifting and unreliable, it nonetheless constitutes the uniqueness of the subject. *Competence* is one aspect of memory: that part of the repertoire of written forms and conventions that we have grasped and organised as our own. *Imagination* is the capacity of the human mind to elude conventions, to think in metaphor, to fuse and to reconnect the elements of language and experience. It is imagination that renews and transforms the resources of a culture.

SECTION 5

> *Reading takes pupils beyond first-hand experience: it enables them to project themselves into unfamiliar environments, times and cultures . . . Reading is also one of the means by which we interact with the society in which we live.* (Cox 16.3/7)

Culture of reception

The sense which a reader makes of a given text depends upon the extent of the overlap or correspondence between the culture in which the text was produced, and the culture in which it is encountered. It may be that writer and reader inhabit almost entirely the same 'cultural sphere', sharing the same dialect, the same history, the same values and conventions. Within the writing community of the classroom, for example, this will often be the case – though it would be an unusual classroom if this were *always* the case. At the same time, in the 'imaginary museum', or perhaps department store, of the late twentieth century, the reader/viewer is afforded an often dizzying choice of codes and allegiances. In such a culture, the meanings which may attach to an object or a work are inevitably complicated; perceptions may range from a comfortable familiarity of signs and assumptions, to a sense of dislocation and bewilderment. Most difficult for the teacher, perhaps, are those cases in which an apparent continuity of language obscures real differences of usage or association. The historic and continuing promiscuity of the forms of English, both within and beyond the United Kingdom, is evidently a factor.

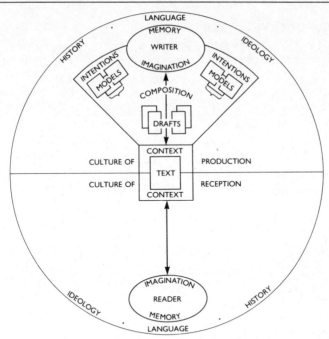

Figure 9.5 Cultures of production and reception

Reader

Like the writer, the reader both depends upon and can transfigure the cultural patterns by which a text is underwritten. The social nature of codes ensures the possibility of meaning; the particularity of memory, the unique fusion of images and evaluations with which each reader accompanies the text, ensures its indeterminacy.

A reader's *competence* is not singular, and cannot be measured by a single indicator. It derives from all the uses of language that he or she has heard or read or practised. It will vary, for example, according to the reader's familiarity with a chosen genre, or with the degree of attentiveness which a text compels. Difficulty does not inhere in texts, but in the match between texts and readers; it is to that extent unpredictable. By the same token, the imagination of the reader may quite outstrip that of the text's originator, creating works in the mind of an unforeseen resonance and complexity. (In an important sense, the *quality* of a reading is unknowable outside the memory of the reader; it can be postulated only upon the basis of the talk or the writing that follows from it.)

SECTION 6

> *The development of a methodology that is based upon informed concepts of reading and response rather than upon conventional, narrowly conceived ideas of comprehension and criticism is now the priority. (Cox 7.22, quoting M. Benton)*

Reading context

The process of reading, as shown in Figure 9.6, is a reverse image of the process of writing: writing culminates in the text, and reading departs from it – or, more accurately, from *the text in its context*.

The *context* of a reading, unlike that projected by the writer, is always localised and specific, and functions as a kind of *frame*, or co-ordinate. It tells the reader what to expect, what resources may need to be drawn upon. The reader's *sense* of context is therefore a mental construct, and open to influence by the agencies of mediation. Expectations are shaped in ways which are both publicly and privately coded: by differences in editions; by differences in the mode of reproduction; by the various means through which a text can be recommended, prescribed or promoted; by associated brand-loyalties or cultural aspirations.

Such perceptions are clearly bound up with the reader's own sense of his or her *identity* as a reader, particularly at the outset. Is this a book *whose reader I wish to become*? Is this advertisement/menu/parking ticket for the likes of me?

Textuality

The attentive reader inhabits the language of the text, examines the

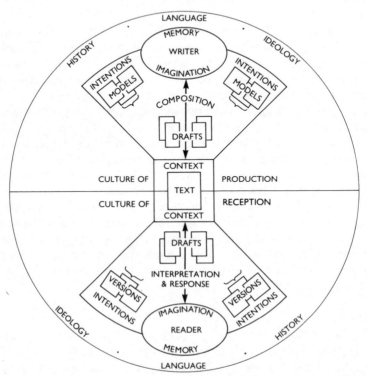

Figure 9.6 Reading in context

writer at work (or at play) within it. In this way, readers learn both to
admire and to distrust writers; the reader who engages less closely with
the machinery of the text is the less moved by it.

Readers learn to identify the tokens of particular genres, and the
patterns of discourse by which texts are organised – the logic of an
argument, the progress of a narrative, the implications of a cinematic
montage.

In their deployment of these resources, texts direct the behaviour
of readers in varying ways. The more 'open' a text, the more it
encourages the play of memory or of intellect, and liberates or enlarges
response. (This is one possible definition of 'literature'.) The more
'closed' a text – the workshop manual, the political interview – the more
it aspires to close down interpretation, and to constrain response.
Closed texts require obedient readers. Good readers, however, decide
when to submit to the authority of texts, and when to take liberties.

Interpretation and response

In the figure under discussion (Figure 9.6), the process of composition is
mirrored by that of *interpretation and response*. This is one among
many possible formulations: it is notable that there is a range of
explanatory terms in educational use which point to aspects of reading
(of which 'comprehension' and 'criticism', quoted above, are two of
the commonest), and that its layered complexity is everywhere
acknowledged.

The term *interpretation* insists upon the *active* nature of all
reading. Readers make sense of texts only by drawing upon a knowledge which lies outside the text, and by selecting, however provision-
ally, from among a range of possible interpretative frames and
conventions. However habitual this process may sometimes seem, it is
never merely automatic.

At the same time, the linking of interpretation with *response* is an
acknowledgment that all readings are evaluative, and ideological. What
does this text mean, or not mean, *to me*? Does it give me pleasure? Does
it earn my approval? The term *response* also points to the pragmatic
force of reading, its power to prompt changes of thought or action.

This coupling of interpretation and response does not however
imply successive operations: the one is always and already implicit
within the other. *Interpretation* might therefore be read in the musical
sense: the 'score' of the text is realised in a performance – whether
voiced or silent – which is both a decoding *and* a response.

Draft reading

Since reading is always a process of bringing meaning to a text, of
collaborating *with* the text and its writer, it may be helpful to think of it
in terms of the kind of 'drafting' with which we more readily associate
the act of composition. First impressions may need correcting. The

picture on the cover may turn out to have been a cheat. The reader's private forecasts as to the development of a plot or an argument may need to be adapted or abandoned. In schools, this process of debate and refinement is often collective; but even the solitary reader experiences the 'dialogic' nature of reading, matching and rematching the patterns of the language to his or her own 'knowledge of the world'.

The development of this personal encyclopedia of reference and probability will be especially marked over time, and must be part of any notion of maturation in reading or in language understanding. The School Rules that inhibit the intake year may be read differently by those with greater experience of the system in practice – as might the 'formula' of a formula novel.

As with composition, draft reading is a two-way process. The attentive reader 'discomposes' the text, ruffling the surface of the language, examining the pattern of its assumptions. At the same time, the reader too may be discomposed, his or her sensibilities reordered by the disturbance of memory which certain *modes of reading* tend to produce.

Modes of reading

Because this account seeks to represent the processes common to all reading, it has focused upon the multiplicity of texts rather than upon the differences between them. The variousness of texts, however, invites a corresponding variety of *modes* of reading, and it is part of the process of interpretation and response to decide *what kind of reading* the text requires or deserves. Ought it to be read twice, for example? This is a matter both of insight and of disposition. Readers are offered positions by texts which they can accept or refuse. Readers too have *intentions*, and there may be many reasons for wanting to read 'against the grain' of a text as the reader perceives it.

One commonly made distinction is that between 'reading for pleasure' (or 'aesthetic' reading) and 'reading for information'. Though such distinctions are never absolute, the variability of intention is real enough, and so is the range of appropriate reading strategies.

Similarly, 'aesthetic' reading itself encompasses both the kind of reading which 'gets into' a book and travels with it, intent only upon arrival; and the kind which circles and contemplates until a meaning emerges. These differing responses are not purely a matter of text-type – the difference between a novel and a poem, for example. The same texts can be read in different ways, and for different combinations of pleasure and information.

Versions

For all the above reasons, different readers come to different *versions* of the texts they consider, as may the same reader on a different occasion. In this way, readers develop their capacity for understanding. Under-

standing is not an activity, keyed to the reading of separate texts. It is a
residue of feelings and insights which may be enriched or eroded by
further reading and reflection. Fully to understand a text is to understand something of the culture in which it was produced or reproduced;
how it comes to mean what it means; and who means it.

SECTION 7

*As children read more, write more, discuss what they have read
and move through the range of writing in English, they amass a
store of images from half-remembered poems, of lines from
plays, of phrases, rhythms and ideas. Such a reception of
language allows the individual greater possibilities of
production of language. (Cox 7.8, quoting Kingman 2.23)*

Intertextuality

The term *intertext* is used to describe the associative networks of textual
memory from which our sense of a culture is woven. It is not bound to
particular cultures. Readers of print and of television across the world
share many of the same stories, the same slogans, the same photographs. They need not, however, share the meanings they make of them.
The intertext is not to be conceived as a body of material objects, as in a
library. It is constituted only in the collective subjectivity of readers, in
the fragmentary *versions* of texts which readers carry with them.

Each reader therefore constructs for him- or herself this network
of interrelatedness. The nature of the observed connections will vary
from generic resemblances between texts which may be commonly
perceived, to chance personal associations. As individual memories are
erased or overlaid, the patterns to which they contributed may be
weakened, or may be reinforced by new readings.

The concept of the intertext encircles all the elements of this
model. Much of what we know derives from it, in particular our literary
competence. A reader's active sense of the forms and the conventions of
language is derived less from formulated statements (such as this one)
than from a complex diffusion of examples that suggest other examples.
This draws attention to the double-sidedness of writing and reading:
writers derive their *models* from the intertext, whether by unconscious
influence or by conscious imitation; what they then construct is re-
turned to it in the form of the textual *versions* which other readers
fashion in response.

The concept of the intertext might be compared to that of *literary
tradition*. The difference is that traditions are selective, and are defined
or contested by the judgements of public bodies – publishing houses,
reviewing panels, examination boards, universities. The intertext, on
the other hand, is subjective, and all-embracing. Since it is constituted
only in the memories of readers, it cannot be institutionalised; it has no
authority.

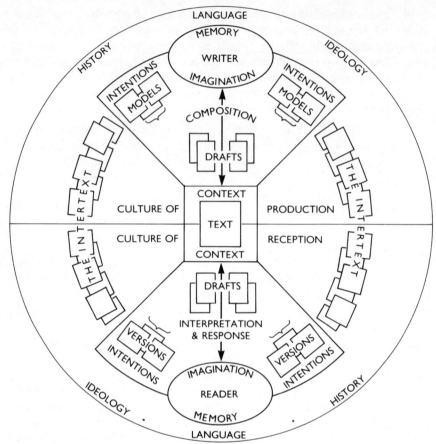

Figure 9.7 Reader writer text

CONCLUSION

Reading for meanings

The 'meaning' of a work is not to be found solely in the text itself, nor in the intentions of its producer, nor in the inventiveness of individual readers. Meanings are made in contexts, through the conjugation of readers and texts.

It follows that there are no single, authentic meanings – but nor is there an infinite possibility. The text is neither a transparent window nor a mirror. It focuses, blinkers, refracts and is sometimes opaque to the eye of the reader.

Meanings also depend upon the vantage points of those who make them. They accrue and are scraped off, are haggled over and revalued. The poet's juvenilia are included in an appendix to the *Collected Works*; *Instructions to Servants* reappear on tea-towels in the gift shops of stately homes.

In one sense, but a very limited sense, he [the writer] knows better what his poems 'mean' than anyone else; he may know the history of their composition, the material which has gone in and come out in an unrecognisable form, and he knows what he was trying to do and what he was meaning to mean. But what a poem means is as much what it means to others as what it means to the author; and indeed, in the course of time a poet may become merely a reader in respect to his own works, forgetting his original meaning, or without forgetting, merely changing. (T. S. Eliot, The Use of Poetry and the Use of Criticism *(1933))*

Good readers come to know the instability of meaning, by knowing what bears upon the process by which meanings are made.

ACKNOWLEDGMENT

An earlier version of 'Reader, Writer, Text' appears in Peter Dougill (ed.) (1990) *Developing English*, Open University Press.

A NOTE ON SOURCES

This paper draws loosely upon three broad areas of critical thinking. One is the area of aesthetic theory known as reader-response, including particularly the work of Wolfgang Iser (*The Act of Reading*, Johns Hopkins University Press, 1978), and Louise Rosenblatt (*The Reader, the Text, the Poem*, University of Southern Illinois, 1978). The second is best represented by Raymond Williams' lucid analysis of literature as social production, *Marxism and Literature* (Oxford University Press, 1977). The third influence is the semiotic tradition exemplified by the work of Roland Barthes (*Mythologies*, Palladin, 1972; *Image-Music-Text*, Fontana, 1977; *The Pleasure of the Text*, Hill and Wang, 1975) and Umberto Eco (*The Role of the Reader*, Hutchinson, 1981). The epigraph is from Williams, 1977, p. 140.

10

What Katy Knows about Language

HEATHER LYONS ⎯⎯⎯⎯⎯⎯⎯⎯⎯⎯⎯⎯⎯⎯⎯⎯⎯⎯ ◇

As a result of the Kingman enquiry into the teaching of English language (DES, 1988b) the question of just what children need to know about language has once again come to exercise all those of us concerned to help them develop as confident and fluent writers. I want to give an account, which I hope may be instructive, of what one nine-year-old knows about written language. Ever since I was her teacher for a term (the term in which she had her ninth birthday) Katy, along with a number of other children in her class, has been writing to me. Whenever she writes, I write back. The letters are written in an exercise book and each time Katy or I receive it the whole correspondence can be re-read. Looking again at the twelve letters that Katy wrote to me over the first nine months of our correspondence, I have been struck by how much she knows about language. She knows about the requirements of written as against spoken language (in particular about writing for an absent reader); she knows about English syntax; she has a knowledge – if as yet incomplete – of English orthography. In accordance with new National Curriculum requirements in English, these are all matters in which teachers of seven- to 11-year-olds are to instruct their pupils, (National Curriculum Council, March 1989). In the programmes of study for seven- to 11-year-olds we read:

> *Children should discuss their writing, its pattern and structure, using appropriate terminology when the teacher judges it to be necessary. (ibid., p. 48)*

Examples are given of aspects of children's writing that may need such discussion. These include the structure of written texts, the sentence grammar of English, the spelling and writing system and the sounds of English.

In what follows I propose to describe and illustrate what Katy knows *already* under each of these headings, drawing on her first 12 letters. In conclusion I shall consider what Katy's case may have to tell us about what needs to be done and how we might respond as teachers preparing to implement the National Curriculum.

THE STRUCTURE OF WRITTEN TEXTS

Once children become capable of producing texts that extend beyond a single short sentence, they most commonly write narrative. Their sense of story can help to structure the telling of some homely episode, or to place in sequence imagined events of a kind met with in the storybook. Katy is quite at home with this way of structuring what she writes. The stories she wrote for me while I was her teacher were something to be looked forward to. But what about the structure of texts which cannot be told as stories? How does Katy cope in her letters with this? In her first letter to me, she writes:

> *On Christmas Day my auntie and uncle came over and brought over a lot of presents too . . . First I'll tell you what my auntie and uncle look like. My auntie has got: dark red, maroon hair quite long. She wears glasses when she reads or plays a game . . . and often never wears trousers. My uncle is very tall and when I sit on his shoulder I can touch the ceiling. He has black hair (not much) and he can play the piano by sound because he cannot read music.*

Here what she has to say appears as a catalogue of descriptive items. This simple listing of information is superseded in later letters by a more sophisticated method of textual organisation. For instance, in her twelfth letter she writes:

> *I will go to Santa Claus even though I don't believe in that stuff and could bet it was Mr Evans. I always used to wonder how there could be a Father Christmas in the Butts, one in Littlewoods and one in the North Pole, I found out when I heard my dad's heavy feet and saw him put the presents in my room. How did you find out there was no father Christmas? I have nearly got most of my Christmas presents.*

What seems to be happening here is an exploration of ways to organise information without resorting to such structures as a simple chronology of events. Opinions are expressed and questions are asked by means of description of events and stating of knowledge; the whole passage conveys this nine-year-old's scepticism about Father Christmas in an easy, flowing prose. Only the last sentence jars slightly; it has the air of the tacked-on afterthought characteristic of more immature attempts at non-narrative writing.

Besides these examples of Katy's developing command of non-narrative writing, a systematic scrutiny of all 12 letters reveals a further important aspect of her knowledge of the structure of written texts. Katy knows that she is writing to communicate to someone who isn't there. She knows that writing is different from speaking in this respect, because writing creates shared meanings less readily than speech. This means that a greater degree of explicitness is needed if what she has to say is to be understood by her reader. This understanding is especially evident at the start of a letter, or where there is a change of subject. A change of subject is frequently signalled by placing it in relation to what has gone before or what is to follow. This may occur either immediately in the text or in the time scale covered by the letters.

> *Going back to Christmas . . . (Letter 1)*
> *Anyway, lets get back to the point. First I'll tell you . . . (Letter 1)*
> *When it was our turn to show our topices, this is how it went. Well, we all filed into the classroom as usual . . . (Letter 2)*
> *Now I'll tell you about how my mum and dad got divorced. Well, it all happened in Oct 1984 . . . (Letter 3)*
> *Here are my favourite authors as follows . . . (Letter 8)*
> *If you turn to the back of the book you will see I have stuck in a picture of myself . . . (Letter 9)*

Another feature of Katy's letter-writing which demonstrates her awareness of her reader is her use of the aside. This has an air of deliberateness about it, and has the effect of drawing the reader into some kind of complicity with Katy as the writer.

> *Going back to Christmas on Christmas day my auntie and uncle came over and they brought over a lot of presants too.* My sister thinks they have got no taste or colour at all. *(Letter 1)*
> *I wasn't very pleased when Mr. Brooks said to me that I went rambling on in my stories, just because I had done seven pages.* I personely myself think that you can't explain yourself just in one page. *(Letter 2)*

The next example from the seventh letter shows for the first time a confident use of parenthesis to mark the aside.

> *I am glad to say I felt fine in the holidays* (probably because I had a rest from Brooksy). *(Letter 3)*

LETTER-WRITING

What does Katy know about the specific requirements of letter-writing as a form of written language? Clearly she knows that forms of greeting and signing off must occur, and that the form adopted can vary. Her form of address is invariably 'Dear Ms Lyons', and is modelled on my form of signing off (I always sign myself 'Ms Lyons'). When she signs off

for herself (and for her teddy, Plonk), small variations occur, as in the
following examples:

> *Goodbye for now,*
> > *Katy and Plonk*   (Letter 3)
> *Goodbye till next time love*
> > *Katy and Plonk*   (Letter 4)
> *Goodbye for now,*
> > *Write back soon*
> > > *love from Katy and Plonk*
> > > x x x   (Letter 7)

Katy also knows what it is not appropriate to include in a letter. Or at
least, she exhibits certain notions about what is and is not appropriate.
In the first 12 letters of our correspondence she never once writes a story
for me despite my repeated requests that she do so, (since I had much
enjoyed reading her stories as her teacher).

One of the most interesting features of the letter-writing form is
that it permits interaction between correspondents as they alternate in
the writer and reader role. This occurs characteristically in Katy's letters
in the questions she directs at me, and in the answers she gives to
questions I ask her. This can give a particularly lively quality to the
writing, as in the following example. After Katy's description in her fifth
letter of being given spellings to learn by her mother, I asked:

> *Did you know that the English language has got four or five
> times as many words as French or German?*

Katy replied:

> *No I didn't know that the English Language had four or five
> times more words than French or jermen. But people say that
> you learn a new thing every day.*

Later in the same letter, on a different topic which she has introduced,
she asks:

> *When you get home from a day's work what do you do then?
> Do you put your feet up and have a cup of tea?*

Writing about the 'written conversations' a Los Angeles teacher
got her class of 11- and 12-year-olds to write with her, Joy Kreeft Peyton
draws our attention to the way in which this kind of writing can act as a
bridge between the back-and-forth interplay which is a normal part of
conversation and the stand-alone quality which must be achieved in
writing (Kreeft Peyton 1988a). She sees the use of questions in dialogue

writing of the kind considered here as crucial in enabling this kind of writing development to happen (Kreeft Peyton, 1988b).

THE SENTENCE GRAMMAR OF ENGLISH

I now want to turn to the question of Katy's knowledge of the sentence grammar of written English. Does she know about the relationship of subject, verb and object? Can she compose sentences which contain these elements grammatically expressed? And to what extent can she handle the kind of clause structure within a sentence which is characteristic of written as against spoken English? I'm going to look at some of the long sentences that appear in Katy's journal entries to show that when it comes to looking at her syntax – that is, the structure of the sentences she writes – what she can do is truly astonishing. I turn first to clause structure.

Clause structure

A sentence which is to go beyond a simple single clause structure must have connectives, such as 'and', 'when', 'if', 'because'. The connective most commonly used by children as they first attempt to write at length is likely to be 'and'. The use of 'and' is generally seen by teachers as a kind of primitive connective which needs to be discouraged if children are to make progress with their writing. Certainly 'and' is a sign of clausal co-ordination, the structure which is particularly characteristic of speech, although this is no reason in itself to forbid its use in writing. In general, the written sentence (especially in discursive writing) is characterised by clausal subordination.

An increasing incidence of subordinate clauses has been widely seen as an indicator of development in children's writing. What do Katy's letters show us about a nine-year-old's knowledge of clause structure?

Let us look first at a long sentence that Katy writes in her second letter.

> *Tomorrow on Wednesday morning some of the forth years will have a project in fro[n]t of them in the hall and first they will tell us what they have been doing and information and then we will go up too one of them and ask them questions and say how nice you think the topic was if you did think it was nice.*

At first sight this seems to exhibit the characteristic 'chaining' that indicates an immature command of the syntax of written English. Further analysis however reveals that its structure is considerably more complex than meets the eye. It consists essentially of five co-ordinate clauses joined by 'and'.

> *Clause 1*   *Tomorrow on Wednesday morning some of the forth years will have a project in fro[n]t of them in the hall*
>
> *Clause 2*   *and first they will tell us what they have been doing*
> *Clause 3*   *and then we will go up too one of them*
> *Clause 4*   *and ask them questions*
> *Clause 5*   *and say . . . etc. (to end)*

However, the sentence also includes clause subordination. The second co-ordinate clause has a subordinate clause embedded in it.

> Clause 2
>   *first they will tell us* x
> |
>   Clause 2a
>   *(what) they have been doing and information*

'What' in clause 2a is in brackets because it is counted as a relativiser (Quirk *et al.*, 1985).

The final complex clause contains no fewer than four clauses, in an intricate syntactic relationship with one another.

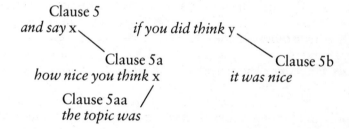

In this analysis, the 'if' clause is taken as an adverbial element of clause 5. This example shows Katy successfully handling the syntax of a long written sentence which exhibits both the chaining which is characteristic of early attempts to compose written English sentences, and the embedding which is the syntactic mode she will need to learn to handle if she is to become a fully fluent writer. Katy's success here may be masked by the charm of the visible stylistic immaturities which the adult reader may sentimentalise since they engage her attention and enlist her sympathies. This is a feature Carolyn Steedman helps us recognise in her study of young girls' writing and adult responses to it (Steedman, 1983). But we should not allow ourselves to lose sight of the fact that the sentence reads perfectly comprehensibly; nowhere does Katy lose control of the grammatical intricacies she creates as she writes.

Further long sentences occur later in the correspondence. In letter 6 Katy writes:

Mum was teaching me words beacuse she thinks that if people knew more words and were more educated then they would be able to understand each other more easily so we would not have so many wars or quarells with other countrys.

What is immediately apparent about this sentence is that the chaining device is gone. Hereafter Katy successfully produces long written sentences in which there are many complex subordinated clauses.

Clause 1
Mum was teaching me words beacuse she thinks x

Clause 1a
(that) if people knew more words and were more educated they would be able y

Clause 1b
to understand each other more easily so we would not have so many wars or quarells with other countrys.

Both clause 1 and clause 1b contain adverbial elements:

beacuse she thinks (Clause 1)

so we would not have so many wars or quarells with other countrys (Clause 1b).

It is not only in the long sentence that Katy displays her command of complex syntactic structures. Her second letter displays several short sentences that show her firmly in control of syntactic embedding. The following is a good example:

Clause 1
I wasn't very pleased when Mr. Brooks said to me x
just because I had done seven pages

Clause 1a
(that) I went rambiling on in my stories

Phrase Structure

Once a sentence is analysed into clauses, each clause in turn can be analysed into its various units or phrases. I follow the framework of analysis adopted by Crystal (1987) or Quirk *et al.* (1985) in which these

units are given functional labels such as Subject (S), Verb (V), Complement (C), Object (O), Adverbial (A). The order SVO is often taken to be
the characteristic basic structure of the non-interrogative sentence in
English. There are however five basic patterns: SVO, SV, SVOO, SVC,
and SVA (Crystal, 1987 p. 95).

To what extent do Katy's sentences conform to these patterns?
Let us return to two sentences whose clause structure has been discussed
above. The first is from Katy's sixth letter. Five of its six clauses display
the basic phrase structure SVO, with some variation.

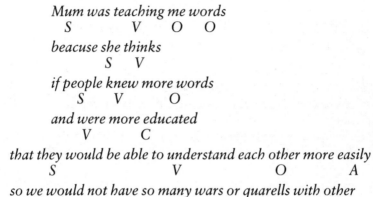

> *Mum was teaching me words*
>   S   V   O   O
> *beacuse she thinks*
>   S   V
> *if people knew more words*
>   S   V   O
> *and were more educated*
>   V   C
> *that they would be able to understand each other more easily*
>   S   V   O   A
> *so we would not have so many wars or quarells with other*
> S V   O
> *countrys.*

What is especially worthy of notice in the following sentence is the
complexity of Katy's main clause structure.

> *What mum has been doing is giving us spellings which I'v never*
> *heard of, and then my sister and I have to look in a dictionary*
> *how to spell the word then write the word in our book and copy*
> *the definition. (Letter 5)*
> *What mum has been doing is giving us spellings which I'v*
>   S   V   C
> *never heard of*

It has a noun clause as a subject ('what mum has been doing') followed
by the auxiliary verb 'is' followed by 'giving us spellings etc.' as the
complement of 'is giving'.

What has been described here shows I hope that Katy already
possesses a great deal of knowledge about the sentence grammar of
English. What she does not possess is a language in which to talk about
it. Katherine Perera (1987) acknowledges that 'words like "verb" and
"noun" provide an economical way of referring to whole classes of
words that share certain grammatical characteristics' and that 'words

like "subject" and "object" make it possible to talk about relationships between different parts of a sentence'. She envisages a kind of talk between children and their teachers where 'the economy of these labels' is useful to teachers, who may use them in much the same way as they use 'sentence', 'phrase' and 'word'. This kind of talk about language in the context of their own writing, as recommended in the NCC Consultation Report (NCC, March 1989), can be seen as a drawing out and naming of what Katy and other young writers already know. But we also need to be wary of reducing the whole exercise to a simple 'naming of parts'.

THE SPELLING AND WRITING SYSTEM OF WRITTEN ENGLISH

Spelling

Katy's mother worries about her spelling. (It is certainly not 100 per cent accurate by the end of her second year in the junior school). In the fifth letter we learn how her mother has been trying to help her improve it at home.

> *What mum has been doing is giving us spellings which I'v never heard of, and then [my sister] and I have to look in a dictionary how to spell the word then write the word in our book and copy the definition.*

This suggests that it is long words or less commonly used items of vocabulary that are the problem. But is this true? What do Katy's spelling errors show that she knows about the grapho-phonic logic (and illogic) of written English? In Table 10.1 opposite I give a complete list of all the spelling mistakes Katy makes in her journal between January and July in her second year in the junior school, alongside a selection of correctly written vocabulary items from the same source.

One of the first things we detect is a firm knowledge on Katy's part of sound/symbol correspondence. Errors such as 'jermen', 'rambiling' and 'monotonus' show this since they are clear attempts at phonetic spelling. Other misspellings indicate the visual memory at work interfering with an attempted phonetic rendering. 'Reckonise', for instance, suggests a childish articulation accompanied by visualisation of the word 'reckon'. 'Rediculous' has a phonetically rendered first syllable but shows knowledge of the spelling of its suffix which can only have been visualised. It is in some of the most commonly used words that a transposition of letters occurs ('beacause', 'puzzels'), or a misremembering of which of the mid-word consonants should be doubled ('tommorrow', 'quarells'), or simple omission of a letter ('brillant', 'hapster'). Little slips and difficulties of this sort can try even seasoned

Table 10.1 Incorrect and correct spellings from Katy's journal, January to July

	Misspellings (all)	Correct spellings (selected)		Misspellings (all)	Correct spellings (selected)
Letter 1	brillant i'll hapster (hampster) inclueding presants coulour ext (etc) unfortully tommorrow forth (fourth) frout (front) too (to)	imagine honestly information questions topics	*Letter 4* *Letter 5*	reckonise I'v	ear-ache haven't wrong valentine although newspapers slightly dictionary definition
Letter 2	i topices luchboxes Rebbeca rambiling (rambling) personely stuidents	register colouring	*Letter 6* *Letter 7*	temperture i'v monotonus jermen beacuse quarells countrys l arguement puzzels puzzels probaly	headaches language educated express answer malinger
Letter 3	tommorrow tryed i	divorced chocolates housekeeper pranced knickers married brochure	*Letter 8* *Letter 9* *Letter 10*	favorite rediculous solisitor	actually pampered authors relative DHSS famous adjourned appeal I (×8) organised journal

writers of English; I myself have just had to correct my first draft spelling of 'omission' in the previous sentence (I first wrote 'ommission'). The most important thing about Katy's errors is that none of them hinder the reader's understanding of her meaning. Words like 'brochure', 'dictionary', 'language', 'adjourned' and 'journal' appear to present no problem. Her errors point to an as yet imperfect visual memorisation; her recollection of what words look like is not always stable, as can be seen in her spelling of 'topics' and 'colour/colouring' in letters 1 and 2. There is however evidence in the whole sequence of letters of a previously insecurely fixed item becoming committed to memory: the writing of the word 'I'. The regular use of the lower case 'i' may seem a surprising error for such a competent writer as Katy to make. But she does make it, in all her first three letters. By her fifth letter 'I' is in upper case, by her tenth letter it appears eight times, written correctly on each occasion.

Punctuation

Similar progress can be observed in Katy's use of that troublesome piece of punctuation, the apostrophe. It first appears not as the conventional symbol in the shape of a figure nine, but as a short flat stroke written over the letter preceding its correct place, e.g. wasn̄t. There are signs that Katy knows this isn't quite right; already in the second letter, another form of apostrophe is used, though still not the conventional one. The conventional form does also appear for the first time in this same second letter, and is used consistently in the following three letters. In the sixth letter, the non-conventional form is reverted to, as it is in the ninth letter. The positioning of the apostrophe in its conventional form is correctly made in letters 2, 3, 6, 8 and 9, but not consistently. Quite clearly Katy has a growing awareness of the use of the apostrophe in written English, has made progress in self-correction and is now ready for some intervention from a more experienced writer to help her get it right.

WHO NEEDS TO KNOW ABOUT LANGUAGE?

Recently I told 54 assembled student teachers that I was going to give them a grammar test. They all looked alarmed. I promised them that they would all pass. The test was as follows. I told the students the following joke, and asked them to raise a hand at the end of it if they had not understood.

> *A passer-by went into a shoemaker's workshop to watch the shoemaker at work, and said: 'What's that you've got there?' The shoemaker looked up from the last and said: 'Hide!'*
> *'Hide?' repeated the passer-by, puzzled. 'Hide! Hide! A cow's outside!' said the shoemaker, irritated.*

The passer-by was even more puzzled. 'Why should I hide? I'm not afraid of cows . . .'

No-one raised a hand. I complimented the students on their knowledge of English grammar. Following the joke depends on an ability to distinguish nouns from verbs, adverbs from nouns and the possessive suffix '-s' from the abbreviated third person singular of the verb to be. Yet most of my students did not know that they knew this.

Where does this take us? In its chapter on linguistic terminology, the report of the Cox Committee devotes five paragraphs to the question of children's writing development and its relationship to an explicit knowledge about language. The reader's attention is drawn to some commonly held but confused assumptions about this relationship. One of these assumptions is that 'the sole or primary use of linguistic terminology is to help children's writing development' (DES, 1988a p. 20). The report comments:

This is certainly important, but it is not the only purpose, and perhaps not even the main one' (ibid., p. 21).

It goes on to draw attention to quite specific features of languages use where discussion can help performance: 'the match between language, situation and purpose', for instance, and 'elements larger than individual sentences' (ibid., p. 21). The main justifications for teaching about language however remain 'quite apart from the debate over the relation between grammar teaching and writing development' (ibid.).

As I hope I have shown, at nine years old Katy already knows a great deal about the structure and grammar of a sentence. She is already developing a competent command of the spelling and writing system of English, drawing on her knowledge of how things are said, and how the sounds of words can be represented in written English (though this can result in some unconventional renderings). In commenting on her struggles with the apostrophe, I have already drawn attention to a suitable occasion for some direct teaching. Are there any other occasions that present themselves in her work as suitable for teacher intervention?

As Katy's teacher rather than her correspondent I might do well to draw her attention to her increasing control of the long written sentence and to her grasp of the difference in usage between writing and speech. I could acknowledge her phonically based attempted spellings, and what they tell me about what she knows. And I could speak of those features of her writing which might need a convenient label for reference (nouns and pronouns, for instance) in much the same way as I might speak of the process of writing using appropriate terminology, such as drafting and re-drafting, editing and publishing.

It seems to me that there is a case to be made for a greater degree of awareness, particularly on the part of teachers, of the increasing elaboration and sophistication of the child's handling of written English, which all too often can go quite unremarked. Writing here about Katy's letters to me, I'm glad I know a bit about language, enough at least to have been able to show you something of what she can do.

NOTE

This is a revised and updated version of a paper which first appeared in *Language and Education* Vol. 2, No. 3, 1988.

ACKNOWLEDGMENTS

Special thanks to Jenny Cheshire for her guidance on the grammatical analysis of Katy's sentences, and to Patricia McNulty for her advice and help in editing.

REFERENCES

Crystal, D. (1987) *The Cambridge Encyclopedia of Language*. Cambridge: Cambridge University Press.

DES (1988a) *English For Age 5 to 11* (the Cox Report). London: HMSO.

DES (1988b) *Report of the Committee of Inquiry into the Teaching of the English Language* (the Kingman Report). London: HMSO.

Kreeft Peyton, J. (1988a) 'Dialogue Writing – Bridge from Talk to Essay' in *Dialogue Journal Communication: Classroom, Linguistic, Social and Cognitive Views*, Staton, J., Shuy, R., Kreept Peyton, J. and Reed, L. Norwood, NJ: Ablex.

Kreeft Peyton, J. (1988b) 'Why Ask? The Function of Questions in Dialogue Writing' in Staton, J. *et al.* (*op. cit.*).

National Curriculum Council (NCC) (March 1989) *English 5–11: National Curriculum Council Consultation Report*. York: NCC.

Perera, K. (1987) *Understanding Language*. Sheffield: NATE.

Quirk, R., Greenbaum, S., Leech, G. and Svartvik, J. (1985) *A Comprehensive Grammar of the English Language*. London: Longman.

Steedman, Carolyn (1982) *The Tidy House: Little Girls Writing*. London: Virago.

On Literacy and Gender

JANET WHITE ———————————————————————◇

Boys are more to do with practical work and experiments and girls are more to learn and listen and enjoy writing. (15-year-old boy)

Learning language, learning gender

What connections are there between the ways children learn language in school and questions of gender identity? As soon as we start to ask questions about language and gender, we come across certain anomalies in the way in which 'literacy' is acquired in school. Despite an apparent equality of provision, boys and girls learn to be literate in different ways (Martin and Rothery, 1984; Gilbert, 1989) and with different degrees of proficiency (Gorman *et al.*, 1988). Furthermore, the experience of language in contemporary schooling does much to polarise spoken and written modes of communication for girls and boys alike (Kaplan, 1983), with boys typically able to trade off their poorer performance in literacy by means of their sheer volume of talk (Spender, 1980; Buswell, 1984; Swann and Graddol, 1988). Literacy likewise becomes something that can be detached from 'practical work' (as we can see in the comment of the teenage boy quoted above), and even from intellectual effort (Stanworth, 1983; Whyld, 1983; McRobbie and McCabe, 1982), although language is just as systematically concerned in the making of meaning in mathematics and science as it is in the study of literature.

One of the abiding ironies in the present schooling ethos is that, for all the public and professional promotion of 'literacy' as the touchstone of educational success, in the day-to-day encounters of the classroom it is the quiet girl reading and writing with untroubled competence who is thought to be merely passive and probably dull, while the boy who can barely write his own name is excused on the basis

The views expressed in this chapter are those of the author, and are not necessarily shared by the National Foundation for Education Research or the Assessment of Performance Unit.

of having 'flair', of being 'bored . . . not because he is not clever, but because he just cannot sit still, he has got no concentration . . . very disruptive . . . but quite bright' (ESRC, 1988).

Disparities in language learning

While many educators point to significant changes in their practice with respect to a diversified curriculum, a greater amount of pupil involvement in learning, and a wider range of purposes for all modes of language use, it is still the case that one nineteenth-century ideal persistently re-emerges in the outcomes of schooling for girls: that of the genteel educated female, 'literate, with a smattering of foreign languages, a future in an office, and the holder of the religious conscience' (Marland, 1983). If teachers are to counter the gendered outcomes of schooling, they need to be prepared to intervene in the literacy development of pupils with a clear, explicit knowledge of the way language works at all levels of meaning creation. The generic structures of speech and writing shape and create the knowledge of school subjects, but they simultaneously shape the identities of speakers and writers. Without a knowledge of how meanings are made through language, teachers are liable to unconscious collusion in the repetition of sex-stereotyped educational practices, often carried out in the name of more enlightened pedagogies, in which great stress is laid on 'starting from the experience of the child' or 'the process of learning' as being in some way distinctly more valuable than the 'product'.

Approaches which espouse such views tend to overlook disparities in the actual language experience of children, with respect to variables of race and class as well as gender (Heath, 1983; McNamara, 1989). Diminished scrutiny of the products or outcomes of learning, however dynamic the processes which lead up to these may have been, is an abrogation of responsibility on the part of anyone who seeks to redress such imbalances. As Blanchard points out, 'often what is not dynamic, in this view, is the content of the curriculum' (1988: 32); this criticism is developed later on with reference to the narrative writing of children involved in process-oriented classrooms.

GENDER DIFFERENCES IN LITERACY DEVELOPMENT

Links between reading and writing

Writing depends on reading, and what is often overlooked, as the emphasis in literacy development turns to children's 'own writing', is that children can write only those texts which they know how to read. Over the past decade numerous campaigns have been mounted through subject associations to counter sex bias in reading materials, but these initiatives are slight when weighed against the mass of print and televisual media encountered by children. Occasional light pruning of the school's bookshelves and conscientious revisions of worksheets do little to address the question of what it is that children read *for pleasure* and hence what they are most likely to turn to for inspiration when they start to write.

In the UK, for example, a series of Assessment of Performance Unit (APU) language surveys conducted between 1979 and 1983 (Gorman *et al.*, 1981 *et seq.*) has provided a clear picture of the literacy orientations of pupils aged 11 and 15, specifically connecting reading and writing habits. This research has noted that both boys and girls enjoy reading various kinds of fiction in the primary school (with preferences differing along gender lines), but that boys rather than girls have clearly developed interests in a range of 'hobbyist' magazines (for example, fishing, cycling, model making, stamp collecting, etc.). Girls are, in general, more avid readers, whereas boys prefer to watch television, and both have positive cases to put for their preferred medium.

By age 15, these differences are accentuated, with many more boys than girls stating a preference for books and magazines 'which give accurate facts about hobbies or how things work'. It is clear that boys and girls are looking to reading material to provide different forms of knowledge, with girls stating that they read to 'help understand their own and other people's problems' such as those to do with sex, love and marriage. While a great deal of this reading material (love stories, comics, specialist magazines) is not the subject of official study at school, there is more coincidence between the themes of girls' preferred reading and courses in English literature. There are similarly direct links between the technical reading consumed by boys and scientific/mathematical areas of the curriculum. (See also national survey data from both the UK and the USA which relate pupils' leisure interests to their takeup of science subjects (Johnson and Murphy, 1986).)

The reading predilections of each sex group are equally evident in their writing. The voluntary writing of girls in primary school comprises often quite voluminous correspondence with pen friends, contrasted with boys who write the 'odd letter' or, in about one in three cases, never put pen to paper outside school (White, 1987).

Boys who do write fiction for their own enjoyment choose themes such as plane crashes, murders, thrillers or war exploits – poles apart from girls' interests in 'things I would like to happen to me', fairy stories of stories about horses. At age 15, girls continue to give preference to writing which is self-reflective or empathetic in character, in contrast to the practical, informative bias of boys' writing. Increasingly, boys' self-directed literacy is associated with the microcomputer, further extending earlier interests in graphics, tables and symbolic displays (EOC, 1985).

CONSEQUENCES OF STEREOTYPICAL READING/WRITING HABITS

Who is disadvantaged?

There seems to be a general consensus that the narrowing of girls' interests to genres of writing which are easily marginalised puts them at a disadvantage educationally:

> *Telling fairy stories, even telling good fairy stories very well, for all that has been said about the importance of fantasy in psychological development, simply doesn't count. The real positions of power and influence in our society necessitate command of genres for which boys' educational experience provides an appropriate preparation and girls' does not. (Poynton, 1985, p. 36)*

The other genres which Poynton has in mind are not just the written ones concerned with exposition and argument, but their counterparts in talk. Many a feminist critic would be in agreement with that position, and take up the challenge: '. . . speaking up, at home, at school, on the stage, always seemed to involve a sense of danger and challenge, which I fed on' (Kaplan, 1983, p. 52). Individual solutions aside, the advantage/disadvantage lines are not so easily drawn. Firstly, there is the question of what girls are in fact doing with the narrative forms they know so well. Secondly, there is the abiding tension between schools' official criteria for excellence in literacy, and the dispensability of these practices for many rewarding occupations in the world outside (White, 1986). Thirdly, there are many questions surrounding the nature of the 'power' boys learn to wield so early on – is it an equivocal advantage?

Resistance from within

Two recent studies of girls' writing (Gilbert, 1989; Moss, 1989) have shown how a conventional narrative form of romance can be, if not subverted entirely, then at least pulled and pushed by the force of the female writer's underlying resistance to depicting a passive heroine, waiting for a princely solution to her fate. It is undoubtedly the case that closer reading of the written outputs of other classrooms would alert us to similar writings of resistance, not only from girls. Boys too are positioned in conventional roles by much of the fiction they consume: he-man, daredevil, invincible hulk; constantly challenged to reconfirm their supremacy. Neither the all-conquering hero nor the stay-at-home princess fit the lived realities of childhood or adolescence, nor suggest the most desirable alternative.

In fact, girls have far more flexibility in written language than is generally assumed; the question remains, though, to what extent could they do better if their abilities as writers were recognised and developed across a full range of subject areas? And how would the technocratic subjects have to change in order to accommodate the humanistic and socially responsive interests of girls, assuming girls ever became a pressure group to be reckoned with? By contrast, the performance of boys measured in relation to that of girls indicates underachievement on a scale that would be utterly disabling were it not for two factors in their language development experience: promotion of competence in oral language and the nature of their out-of-school reading. The trade-off between oral and written language modes serves not merely to excuse boys' indifference to school standards of literacy, but actually operates to ensure a different kind of success and power in the dynamics of the classroom (Swann and Graddol, 1988; Mahony, 1988).

Boys' voluntary reading

The most cursory glance at the range of comics and magazines which are consumed by children reveals fundamental differences in the uses of language favoured by the writers of girl- and boy-directed material.

Boys of primary school age and beyond are practising reading on texts which are distinguished not simply by their themes of violence and terror, but also by their complex visual formats in which explosive actions interrupt the linearity of narrative sequence, and stylised representations of sound effects engage a more sensory, if less reflective, reading than is the case with 'classical' descriptive narration.

The fantastic world of science fiction with its attendant tales of mythical quests introduces a distinctive and at times untranslatable vocabulary: Blusteroids, Chelnov, Excisus, Shinobo, Gryznov, The Monad, etc. Such vocabulary, however ludicrous to the adult eye, has a pedigree of scientism about it, and arguably plays its part in familiarising the young reader with a whole range of textbooks in which the vocabulary is similarly opaque but just as authoritative. Even when there is resistance to reading such textbooks, we might assume they will be more tolerable to readers accustomed to depersonalised uses of language than to those who have been led to anticipate meaning and relevance from the printed page. Very helpfully, the writers of boys' comics print in bold their 'technical terms': 'My **mystic explosion** has trapped the fool on that plant world. The plants have no machines so he-man will not be able to **rebuild a teleportation machine**.' Conventions of capitalisation are used in standard expository texts to highlight key words and concepts: on this level too, reading comics may be a useful preparation for learning some of the conventions of school textbooks.

A variety of reading positions is available within a comic which might comprise an adventure story, a detachable subtext of mechan-

isms of conquest, a riot of graphic elaboration, and a form of dialogue –
or speechifying – which is archaic, formal and coded in a way the
vernacular of interpersonal relations is not, this latter offering another
possibility of distance from the narrative. These are not modes of
reading which are emphasised in initial literacy schemes, nor indeed in
traditional English literature classes (Barnes, 1987; Belsey, 1980). They
are important though in coping with a mass of texts, literary or not, in
subjects other than English and in the world beyond school. Indubi-
tably, these modes of reading are hard to acquire and rarely taught
explicitly, but they are some of the 'advantages' which boys may derive
from their out-of-school reading – in the long term. In the short term,
boys swell the ranks of remedial readers, unable to cope with such texts
as schools insist they do read, and presumably struggling with portions
of unsupervised reading as well.

The *disadvantages* of such a diet of reading material lie in its
power to generate and validate a view of experience which gives short
shrift to matters of personal reflection, humane responsibilities, or the
exigencies of living in a social context – areas of experience which are
borne in upon girls through their 'chosen' leisure reading as much as by
their school work. The remainder of the discussion highlights ways in
which these contrary world views surface in the extended writing
produced by boys and girls under the auspices of the new pedagogy of
the process classroom.

GENDER STEREOTYPING AND SKEWING IN CHILDREN'S WRITING

Pedagogic assumptions underlying story writing for younger readers

For many teachers and pupils, a project in which an older class writes
stories for a younger one on the basis of outline plots dictated by the
younger children is the most appealing way to realise numerous ideals
for enhancing the experience of composition. Pupils can work in
collaboration at many stages of the project; there is a real audience in
prospect; the commitment to a specific reader is thought likely to
sustain an extended process of drafting and revision; while the production of a finished book gives more insights into the technicalities of
publication and 'real authorship'.

Other teachers, parents, and the wider community tend readily to
support these initiatives because of their spin-off in terms of better
liaison between schools, whose pupils get to visit one another's classrooms two or three times; the potential for enhancement of spoken and
written language alike seems considerable under these circumstances.
In so far as the genre of writing is deliberately chosen, there seems to be
an assumption that story form is sufficiently familiar to provide security

yet likely to be further illuminated by several weeks' work (despite the
fact that the choice of 'story' is among the most problematic and least
analysed factors in the scheme).

This type of work has been one of the most popular options
generated by the National Writing Project in the UK, and one project
coordinator puts the case for story writing in the following strong
terms:

> *Here [the older children] were on an equal footing with adults.
> The fact that their audience was even younger must also have
> boosted their confidence and helped them to develop a sense of
> control over the writing, the courage to claim authorship, to
> learn the lesson that writing is about power . . . One can only
> speculate on the possible effects of this experience on their
> future development as writers and learners. (Wallen, 1986)*

A closer look at assumed ideals

While it seems to be generally true that children involved in extended
writing projects grow in confidence as writers – at least for the duration
of the project – partly because they turn out work of a high technical
standard (groaning at times about the sheer length of time it all takes), it
is far from clear what they are learning about power. What is clear when
we read their work closely and attend to what they have to say about
their audience, is that pupils are perplexed by the requirements to write
stories according to the specifications of children of the opposite sex,
and to what lengths they will go to pull these schemata back into the
confines of their own gendering. Case studies conducted in two classrooms illustrate these points. One class contained about 35 pupils aged
nine to ten who wrote for readers aged seven to eight; a second class of
23 12-year-olds also wrote for readers aged seven and above.

The child-writers' perspective

In some cases, the children chose their reader on the basis of an
introductory letter; in other cases, the readers were randomly paired
with writers. After the event, (in the two classrooms studied) the
children were asked whether it was, or would have been, easier to write
for someone of the same sex as themselves. With few exceptions they
stated that they would prefer to write for a reader of the same sex,
because 'you can remember what you were like at that age'. Writers
who did not feel they had to adjust to sex-specific genres, even though
writing for a member of the opposite sex, were those who had drawn a
reader whom they defined as atypical. For example, one boy with a girl
reader commented, 'my story is more of a boy's story – perhaps she's a
tomboy'. These comments were made despite the fact that the writers
were proud of the work they had done, 'I didn't know I was capable of

writing a story so well'; 'It is the best thing I have ever done'; 'I'm glad that I've achieved writing a book and that it looks quite nice' (comments from children aged 12 whose finished stories were often over 1000 words in length).

The children's remarks reveal a very strong awareness of sex stereotyping in reading materials, and an equally strong expectation that their role as writers is to continue in the same tradition. In this respect, they are imbibing a lesson in conformity: far from learning that writers – sometimes – have power because they are able to challenge the way linguistic artefacts structure the world, they are instead doing their best to replicate those structures. The conformism is perhaps exacerbated by the very fact that these children are commissioned to write for readers younger than themselves. In this situation, the claim that the children are on 'an equal footing with adults' reveals a further layer of problems for the young writer: what is an 'adult' role in relation to readers still younger than oneself? For the majority of girls, the parental/maternal role is most likely to be evoked, whereas for boys, unencumbered with caretaker responsibilities, to write stories for girls presents openings for a different order of power play, as we shall see in the examples which follow. By inviting children to adopt their implicit conception of an adult role as they compose stories, are we simply redoubling the opportunity for them to produce material gendered along stereotypical lines?

Nine- to ten-year-olds writing for seven- to eight-year-old readers

This class project began with a less common feature: subject matter for the stories was prescribed in advance by the teachers. All stories were to be about animals. Unfortunately, the ready availability of scenarios filled with anthropomorphised animals provides a quick and easy route into some of the most traditional sex-stereotype images encountered by young children, whether as readers or television viewers. The animal theme suggested itself to the teacher as a potential help to 'getting the children started' without any thought as to what the topic might bring in its wake. In itself, this is graphic testimony to the low level of consciousness which matters of gender have in the minds of even the better language teachers.

How far did the children work within or beyond the conventions at their disposal?

The comparison of the first drafts of many stories (from dictation and notes taken down in discussion with the younger child), with the completed word-processed versions showed that revisions in the hands of older children working in same-sex pairings resulted in the firming up of stereotypical elements to a remarkable degree.

Common to many stories was the theme of animals lost, stolen, or out adventuring on their own. In the hands of boys writing for boys, these scenarios were typically expanded between first and final draft to incorporate still more serialised adventures, but with little in the way of details concerning setting or motivation beyond the minimum needed for comprehension. Where dialogue was introduced, this most frequently appeared as a way of speeding up the action (the quick exchange of instructions prior to a raid or capture), or as a means of incorporating peer-group humour of a knock-about kind. There was no dwelling on emotions nor apprehension about danger: one draft containing the statement 'I was afraid', uttered by a dog about to swim across a blazing stream, was revised by the older boys without reference to any such faintheartedness. Models underlying these stories seemed to be contempory television or cartoon genres, which take for granted the reader's familiarity with the 'story so far', and the characters who populate it.

The girls' stories, on the other hand, took a quite different source of inspiration: the genre of traditional nursery tales, with their overlay of moral homily concerning correct behaviour and appropriate attitudes towards danger. Thus when older girls were presented with an outline concerning a creature out on its own in the woods, the androgenous possibility was rewritten, and the animal provided with a mother – or a husband – to make sure that domestic and moral obligations were not flouted. Far from being free to rush from one adventure into another, the girls' characters were developed within one story frame, allowing for reflection on the significance of the action. Girls' stories also showed more use of literary narrative conventions, such as descriptive characterisation and settings, and clearly resolved plots (for further discussion, see White (1990)).

On the evidence of such stories, what is it that boys and girls have learned about 'power'? Perhaps the real lesson lies in the subliminal rehearsal of gendered sterotypes for the edification of even younger children. The more competent writer has the power to control the text, and to persuade the reader who commissioned it in the first place that the outcome is more desirable than the sketchy brief from which it started. In view of the lengths to which the older girls have gone in rewriting the first drafts in order to trim ambitions of personal liberty, such projects are the reverse of empowering. Instead of being set the task of displaying their knowledge of nurseryland fiction by emulation, girls could well be encouraged to explore the larger social context of printing and publishing that guarantees the circulation of fiction scarcely superior to their own.

For boys, on the other hand, there is possibly a different case to argue, and it has to do with understanding a range of fantasy other than that derived from contextless threats or challenges. The prospect of a long-term project in which boys and girls not only wrote for each other, but wrote differently in different genres, would be one way of getting out of the impasse of reconfirming the stereotypes. The value of such a project would depend on highly skilled teacher intervention and a determination to continue the 'process' of writing and reading beyond the point where a 'product' is handed over to its apparently unique reader. The pedagogy which confers on children's texts the status of adult compositions ought not to back off from questions of adult scrutiny.

Gender skewing in children's writing: 12-year-olds writing for seven- to eight-year-old readers

Many of the stories written by girls for boys and vice versa show signs of gender skewing as their authors struggle to elaborate a given storyline to suit the presumed demands of the younger reader. Interestingly, although the children were conscious of the problem posed in working with unfamiliar/uncongenial subject matter when questioned about preferred audience, their notion of linguistic difficulty was conceptualised only in terms of vocabulary and sentence structure, 'finding words that they would understand', 'writing it simpler than I normally write'. Yet when we look at how the stories are elaborated, we can see that major revisions and interpolations have been made to the familiar genres of children's fiction.

Girls writing for younger boys

In the hands of girl writers, science fiction and piratical adventures acquire an overlay of domesticity and morality; a boy hero, soon to be the intrepid rescuer of his football club's trophy, is firmly controlled by his house-proud mother, for whom he spares an anxious thought in the midst of his night of Bond-like exploits. The extracts quoted in Texts 11.1–11.3 illustrate these features.

Text 11.1 was written by a girl who commented, 'I didn't know a thing about robots and I didn't like the subject'.

Text 11.1 Extract from story by girl writer for younger boy reader

CHAPTER 9

Tail-break got to Electron and Camero (who was still on the floor) safely Electron was in the middle of the operation.

Bomber-bot took to the air firing downwards at Camero. Tail-break shot back to protect them.

Then something awful happened bomber-bot started falling to the ground The shots had hit him and the robots were looking very scared. Murder was a criminal offence and they didn't want Tail-break to be put in prison. 'Oh no', he cried 'What have I done? I aimed so I would not hit him.'

No-one was blaming it on him but the facts were Bomber-bot had been hit maybe killed and the shot had been fired by Tail-break.

The girl author of text 11.2 stated 'I know more about what young girls did than about boys'.

Text 11.2 Extract from story by girl writer for younger boy reader

> *By now Captain Nick's crew were*
> *on the deck. They knew Dark Mark and*
> *his men were trouble so they planned to get*
> *them off their ship in the quickest way possible.*
> *'This is your last chance! Give*
> *me that map or we will fight you*
> *to the death!' screamed Dark Mark.*
> *'Then we shall fight you,*
> *and you will loose.' There was*
> *a fight then, but only a small one*
> *because Dark Mark's crew got scared. They*
> *ran off Captain Nick's ship onto their own and hid.*

Girls don't like to write about mindless fighting and killing – the resistance is captured in the deliberately retarded action of the wounded body which 'started falling to the ground', not 'slumped' or even 'fell' – and consequently seek to minimise such episodes in their stories, going so far as to invoke legal sanctions against wrongdoing. Domestic sanctions against disruptive behaviour are similarly close to the surface as text 11.3 shows, and throughout these stories the male heroes are depicted in uncharacteristically self-reflective, even self-doubting, moods, a long way from the free-floating careless adventures of classic boy-oriented fiction.

Text 11.3 Extract from story by girl writer for younger boy reader

I walked home and as soon as I walked through the gateway, my Mum saw me. She went mad, absolutely mad and I was not surprised. My football kit and tracksuit were filthy, my whole body was caked in mud and I had walked all over her nice clean carpet and dripped mud all over it. Oops!
Mum sent me straight upstairs for a bath while she got the dinner ready. After my bath I crept downstairs and sat in front of the TV. I thought she hadn't heard me come down but she had and she stormed into the living room.
'I want a word with you,' she said. 'Next time you go

training, I don't expect to see a single bit of dirt on your tracksuit, alright?'

   'Sorry Mum,' I answered meekly.

[Later, at the crisis of the story:]

'Gosh!' it's morning and I was supposed to be home by 6 o'clock last night! My mum will be mad. She'll kill me!' I wailed.

[The trophy is finally recaptured and the boys are taken to the police station:]

. . . our parents were waiting and we poured out the whole story over a nice hot cup of tea. They all said that we were very brave but we shouldn't have trespassed.

In the girls' stories which feature boys as heroes, mothers appear to have far more potential to terrify than the rather unsubstantial villains who populate the tales. The ways in which these girls represent 'mothers' display the girls' own understanding of language, and in particular of maternal language, as a force of social control which will subdue and regulate the picaresque wanderings of small boys' fantasies. As teachers we need to ask: do girls need yet another 'dummy run' for their conventional future as keepers of the social conscience? Texts such as those quoted suggest that boys and girls alike need to be critically alerted to how little the social conscience is seen as a matter for joint construction.

Boys writing for younger girls
When boys are writing for girls who have suggested an adventure story with a female heroine, they feel no compulsion to lock the heroine into a family context – that is not where they think control lies. One such tale ends with the girl back home in bed only to find her poetry book open at a page which reads as text 11.4.

Text 11.4 Extract from story by boy writer for younger girl reader
   In the park or in the streets,
   Not quite knowing who you could meet.
   Going to the local Park,
   The ones that's scarey in the dark.
   The gates reveal a whole new place,
   Just think to yourself 'This is Ace'.

The little poem encapsulates the tale already told, and holds the promise of further adventures to entice the child across the scary threshold – very different from the containment of cups of tea in the police station. Beyond that, the poem contains a frisson of delighted fear, as the boy writer anticipates the anxiety the girl subject presumably feels at 'scary' and 'dark' places made fearful by his own sex (as we might guess he is perfectly aware); thus in his writing he enjoys both threatening and being threatened.

In the stories boys write for them, girls are allowed to participate in practical jokes, such as putting whoopee cushions on teachers' chairs and other varieties of teacher baiting, in a familiar 'Beano' comic style. Such girls take in their stride escapades which endanger life and limb (not to mention clean clothing), and in text 11.5 the mishap of a complete drenching is passed off with a laugh, far from the world of maternal reprimands.

Text 11.5 Extract from story by boy writer for a younger girl reader

Elizabeth mopped her forehead with her hand and quickly launched herself out the window. But she slipped on the ledge and started to fall headfirst. She managed to catch hold of an old flag pole (which is one of those ones which sticks out of a wall) and sighed a sigh of relief. She had sighed too soon because there was a tiny creak and then a crack, the pole was nearly in half! It was now hanging on by a thread and Elizabeth went hurtling down to earth. There was a gigantic splash as Elizabeth landed in a barrel of water. She spurted a mouth full of water out and clambered out of the barrel.

'Unlucky, Elizabeth!' shouted Helen who was now laughing.

'OK, OK. Let's get going!' answered Elizabeth.

Girls are almost inscribed into boyhood as such moments by virtue of being written into boys' roles. The resulting tomboys are reminiscent of certain adult authors' attempts to write about girls in a more lively way (the adventures of Tyke Tyler or Pippi Longstocking are examples of the genre). Yet in none of the boys' stories is the heroine commanding; her gender is skewed in the direction of masculinity, but no further than the boy writers have been taught to expect or want from their peer group of girls.

Typically, the heroines have to be rescued from magician or peer group gang by *deus ex machinae*, or by total gaps in the narrative; in the boys' equivalent of these predicaments, a hero might be expected to draw out the ray gun or recite some coded formula. Even as 'Elizabeth' and 'Helen' enter the Evergreen Forest on the trail of the promised treasure, they are ambushed by a trio of boys disguised as ghosts (text 11.6).

Text 11.6 Extract from story by boy writer for younger girl reader

The boys then dropped the white sheet down on them and rattled some chains, just to mock the girls. Still laughing they ran off to find the treasure.

The ambush illustrates, as did the poem in text 11.4, the entry of the writer as both the threat and the threatened, a sign of the control boys feel they can exert over girls' freedom of manoeuvre. The controlling force or power here is not through appeals to social or moral order but quite simply by assumption of male superiority and physical supremacy.

THE PROBLEMS IN REVIEW

The focus of this chapter has been on gender, but the scripts quoted also carry within them the subtexts of race and class. As we read children's versions of nurseryland stories, we might ask: Which culture uses tales of domesticated animals to socialise its young? Which class relies most on women as home-and-hearth bodies, and represents them as such in children's fiction? There is now a growing recognition that books provided for children to read ought to be inspected for bias of gender, race and class – my argument is that the 'free' writing done by children themselves needs similar scrutiny.

The 'new literacy' brings with it additional demands on the teacher. Not only do teachers need diverse managerial skills to sustain changing group structures within their classrooms but, more crucially, they must be thoroughly informed about the teaching of writing. Knowledge of teaching writing must take into account the complex roles of literacy in the wider uses of language in education and society. It is never sufficient to rest content with the notion that children are empowered simply because they accomplish tasks with enjoyment; we have to be confident that the tasks themselves are worthwhile. In the case of language, we need to ask: What purposes are being served by specific occasions of language work in school? How are children being helped to understand, practise and question the forms of language which currently hold sway in our society? Which genres of written language in particular do children most need to control? How are forms of resistance likely to show themselves when children begin to rewrite or reread traditionally gendered texts?

There is nothing new in the suggestion that language is a form of social control, but there is a poignant irony in the fact that when children are encouraged to draw on their 'own' resources as language learners, they may come to identify still more closely with the controlling systems from which we seek to free them. Gender identity is constantly rehearsed and reproduced in language; given precise knowledge of the ways in which this happens, teachers' guiding interventions in children's language development may indeed be powerful.

NOTE

This is a shortened version of a chapter which first appeared in Christie, F. (ed.) (1990) *Literacy for a Changing World*. Victoria, Australia: ACER.

REFERENCES

Barnes, D. (1987) 'The politics of oracy', in Maclure, M., Phillips, T. and Wilkinson, A. (eds) *Oracy matters: The development of talking and listening*. Milton Keynes: Open University Press.

Belsey, C. (1980) *Critical practice*. London: Methuen.

Blanchard J. (1988) ' "Glaciation, symmetry, etc.": Finding an insider curriculum', *English in Education* 22, 2, pp. 31–34.

Buswell, C. (1984) 'Sponsoring and stereotyping in working-class English secondary school', in Acker, S., Megarry, J., Nisbet, S. and Hoyle, E. (eds) *World yearbook of education 1984: Women and education*. London: Kogan Page.

EOC (Equal Opportunities Commission) (1985) *Girls and Information Technology*. Report of a project in Croydon to evaluate guidelines for good practice in the IT curriculum, Overseas House, Manchester.

ESRC (Economic and Social Research Council) (1988) *Girls and mathematics: Some lessons for the classroom*. London: Girls and Mathematics Unit, Institute of Education, University of London.

Gilbert, P. (1989) 'Stoning the romance: Girls as resistant readers and writers', in Christie, F. (ed.) *Writing in Schools* (B.Ed. course Reader). Geelong, Victoria: Deakin University Press. Paper originally presented at the ANZAAS Congress, James Cook University of North Queensland, August 1987.

Gorman, T. P., White, J., Orchard, L., and Tate, A. (1981) *Language performance in schools: Primary survey report No. 1*. London: HMSO.

Gorman, T. P., White, J., Orchard, L., and Tate, A. (1982a) *Language performance in schools: Primary survey report No. 2*. London: HMSO.

Gorman, T. P., White, J., Orchard, L., and Tate, A. (1982b) *Language performance in schools: Secondary survey report No. 1*. London: HMSO.

Gorman, T. P., White, J., Orchard, L., and Tate, A. (1983) *Language performance in schools: Secondary survey report No. 2*. London: HMSO.

Gorman, T. P., White, J., Hargreaves, M., MacLure, M., and Tate, A. (1984) *Language performance in schools: 1982 primary survey report*. London: DES.

Gorman, T. P., White, J., and Brooks, G. (1984) *Language performance in schools: 1982 secondary survey report*. London: DES.

Gorman, T. P., White, J., Brooks, G. MacLure, M., and Kispal, A. (1988) *Language performance in schools: A review of APU language monitoring, 1979–83*. London: HMSO.

Gubb, J., Gorman, T., and Price, E. (1987) *International studies in pupil performance. The study of written composition in England and Wales*. Windsor: NFER-Nelson.

Heath, S. B. (1983) *Ways with words: Language, life and work in communities and classroom*. Cambridge: Cambridge University Press.

Hough, J. (1984) *Deprivation of necessary skills*. Paper presented at The Girl Friendly Schooling Conference, Manchester Polytechnic (mimeo).

Johnson, S. and Murphy, P. (1986) *Girls and physics: Reflections on APU survey findings*, APU (Assessment of Performance Unit) Occasional Paper No. 4. London: DES.

Kaplan, C. (1983) 'Speaking/writing/feminism', in Wandor, M. (ed.) *On Gender and Writing*. London: Pandora Press.

Mahony, P. (1988) *Schools for the boys? Coeducation reassessed*. London: Hutchinson Educational.

Marland, M. (ed.). (1983) *Sex differentiation and schooling*. London: Heinemann Educational Books.

Martin, J. R. (1989) *Factual writing: Exploring and challenging social reality*. Oxford: Oxford University Press.

Martin, J. R., and Rothery, J. (1984) *Choice of genre in a suburban primary school*. Paper presented at the ALAA conference, Alice Springs (mimeo).

McNamara, J. (1989) 'The writing in science and history project: The research questions and implications for teachers', in Christie, F. (ed.) *Writing in Schools* (B.Ed. course Reader). Geelong, Victoria: Deakin University Press.

McRobbie, A., and McCabe, T. (1982) *Feminism for girls, an adventure story*. London: Routledge and Kegan Paul.

Moss, G. (1989) *Unpopular Fiction*. London: Virago.

NWP Theme Pack. (1990) *What are Writers Made Of? Issues of Gender and Writing*. Thomas Nelson.

Poynton, C. (1989) *Language and gender: Making the difference*. Oxford: Oxford University Press.

Spender, D. (1980) *Man-made language*. London: Routledge and Kegan Paul.

Stanworth, M. (1983) *Gender and schooling: A study of sexual divisions in the classroom*. London: Hutchinson Publishing Group in association with The Exploration in Feminism Collective.

Swann, J., and Graddol, D. (1988) 'Gender inequalities in the classroom', *English in Education*, 22(1), pp. 48–65.

Wallen, M. (1986). 'Finding and teaching an audience: Writing and learning 8–13', *Dorset National Writing Project Newsletter, No. 1*, Dorset County Council.

White, J. (1986) 'The writing on the wall: Beginning or end of a girl's career?' *Women's Studies International Forum*, 9(5), pp. 561–574. Oxford: Pergamon Press.

White, J. (1987) *Pupils' Attitudes to Writing*. Windsor: NFER-Nelson.

Whyld, J. (ed.) (1983) *Sexism in the Secondary Curriculum*. London: Harper and Row.

12

Rocks in the Head: Children and the Language of Geology

BEVERLY DEREWIANKA ⎯⎯⎯⎯⎯⎯⎯⎯⎯⎯⎯⎯⎯⎯⎯⎯◇

This paper describes an action research project involving a class of seven-year-olds at a country school in Australia. Their teacher, Fran Egan, had been introduced to Michael Halliday's functional grammar and was keen to try applying her new insights about language in her classroom.

Although Fran was delighted with the children's progress and attitude to writing in their 'whole language/process writing' classroom, many of the whole language activities had become isolated exercises – retellings, cloze passages, shared book, and so on – divorced from the 'real' language happening in other curriculum areas. How to get language out of 'the language block' and into the curriculum? How to promote purposeful interaction between speaking, listening, reading and writing?

In her language programming, Fran widened her perspective from the individual activity to a whole thematic unit. The focus became *language for learning*, fostering an explicit consciousness in the children of how language functions in the learning process.

In particular, Fran was interested in Halliday's notion of Register. Register is a way of describing how the *context* influences the language produced in a particular situation. In the classroom situation it is essentially the teacher who controls the context. The ways in which he or she constructs the classroom context can help promote the sort of language which contributes to learning. The following pages describe the ways in which Fran programmed to create certain contexts and how these contexts influenced the language of the classroom.

PLANNING THE CONTEXT

According to Halliday, there are three main variables which determine the Register of any particular context – the Field, the Mode and the Tenor. We could represent this diagrammatically (see Figure 12.1). Let's look at how each of these influenced Fran's programming.

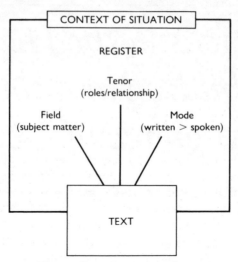

Figure 12.1 Register and context

The Field

In basic terms, Field refers to 'content'. The content of any learning is ultimately embodied in language. To learn content is to learn language. The class had developed an avid interest in rocks and Fran decided to build on this, taking 'Why We Study Rocks' as the theme of the unit. In a broad sense then, the Field which Fran was planning to develop was geology, and in particular 'rocks'.

Fran acknowledged the children's existing knowledge of the field of 'Rocks' and was concerned with extending the field in both planned and unplanned directions. One of the functions of education is to help children to explore and make sense of their world and language is a major resource in this endeavour as it is through language that we represent our world. Language enables us to express the relationships we perceive between phenomena in the environment. The children's understanding of the field would be developed not only through the labelling or naming of various rocks, but through the identification of relationships within the field.

Fran therefore planned for opportunities for the children to develop and use the language needed to observe, describe, define, compare, contrast, group, classify, and generalise. The children's knowledge of the field then would hopefully grow during the unit from their fairly random, everyday 'commonsense' knowledge about rocks to a more explicit, systematised, integrated knowledge.

This might sound like a rather onerous, sobre undertaking for such young children, but Fran didn't want to patronise them. She had high expectations and so did they. They were eager to 'name their world' in ever-increasing detail, to discover how it is organised and how it functions. And to do that they needed the appropriate language tools.

The Mode

Learning can take place through the oral mode or the written mode. Fran was interested in the different roles these modes played in the learning process.

We could look upon learning as a gradual 'distancing' process – from an involvement in the detail of the here-and-now to stepping back, reflecting, seeing the bigger picture, relating and consolidating and putting things in perspective. And in fact Halliday talks of a variety of modes – each playing a part in this distancing process. He plots these modes along a continuum, ranging from the sort of language that accompanies action to the sort of language employed in reflection. At the 'action' end of the continuum the language tends to be oral – the sort of exploratory, interactive language used when coming to grips with the world. Stepping back further, one might reconstruct the action by telling someone what happened or writing a recount of it. Further towards the 'reflection' end of the continuum, we can exploit the 'frozen' nature of the written mode as it invites us to play around with the thoughts captured on paper – to shape and refine them, to extend them, to make connections between them. At each step backwards, choices are being made to select significant aspects of the experience/subject matter and order them coherently.

ACTION ←————————————————————→ REFLECTION
e.g. language → commentary → reconstruction → construction
     accompanying the action

Fran decided to use this Mode continuum as the guiding principle in her programming. She would let the children explore the content first in the oral mode – interacting, sharing, bouncing off each other, with all the hesitations, unpredictability, backtracking, and approximations typical of spoken language. Then she would gradually move them along the continuum, shunting backwards and forwards as necessary, until they were able to reflect upon their experiences and understandings and pull them together in the written mode.

The Tenor

Fran was aware however that the learning power of the various modes could only be fully utilised if the Tenor in the classroom situation allowed for this to happen.

Tenor refers to the relationships between the participants and the roles that the participants engage in. The traditional classroom relationship between teacher and pupil is one in which the balance of power is very unequal, with the teacher in control of the knowledge and the patterns of classroom interaction. The sort of language which flows from such a relationship is typically long slabs of teacher monologue, punctuated by routines of pseudoquestions, programmed answers, evaluative comment by teacher, with the occasional regulatory outburst.

More conducive to learning might be the sort of language which reflects a more even balance of power – where children feel comfortable to contribute information, to hypothesise, to admit ignorance, to ask questions, to make suggestions, to give opinions, to initiate topics, to take responsibility. Fran planned therefore that, at appropriate stages during the unit, the children would enter into a variety of relationships – teacher/class, teacher/group, parent/child, child/child, child/group, child/class – each relationship enabling the child to interact and learn in a particular way.

Another closely related aspect of Tenor which she took into account was the *roles* adopted by child and teacher. At times these were deliberately structured into the programme according to the learning activity at the time. The teacher's role would range from 'knower' to 'co-learner', while the children became 'geologists', 'lapidarists', 'builders', 'researchers', 'authors', 'apprentices', 'experts', etc. They were expected to live the role, posing the sorts of questions and making the sorts of observations that such a role would demand. The adopting of these roles aimed at empowering the children, encouraging them to see themselves as responsible learners, apprentice members of the discipline, moving from a tentative grasp of the field towards a more definite, confident control.

The unit was designed not only to develop knowledge about rocks, but also to provide opportunities for the children to learn the sorts of roles necessary to become independent learners.

In summary, we can see learning language (and even learning itself) in terms of the mastery of a wide range of Registers. Each of these Registers is characterised by a particular Mode, Field, and Tenor.

Figure 12.2 is an attempt at describing how a number of Registers were developed over the three-week unit, starting at the 'action' end with physical engagement with rocks, employing a variety of modes as the children worked towards the 'reflection' end with the production of a written text – a jointly composed 'Big Book' drawing together what they had learnt about rocks. It represents the learning process as a spiral with no definite beginning or end.

PUTTING IT INTO PRACTICE

By now Fran had designed a programme which consciously structured the learning context in terms of Mode, Field and Tenor:

◇ The Mode would range from oral/active through to written/reflective as the unit progressed.

◇ The overall Field involved an ever-increasing knowledge of 'Rocks', deliberately introducing an awareness of how the

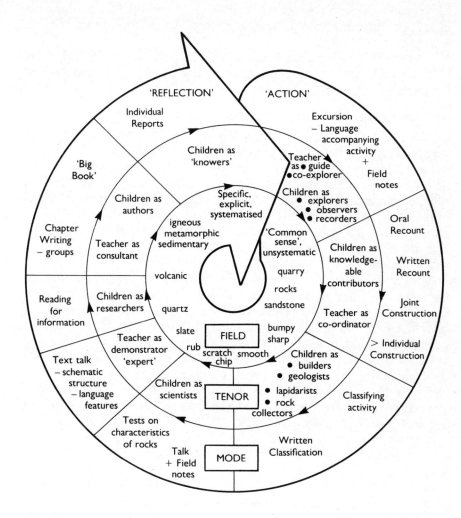

Figure 12.2 Diagrammatic description of a three-week unit of work

Field is constructed through comparing, contrasting, classifying, etc.

◇ The Tenor would reflect the various roles and relationships engaged in by teacher, children (and parents).

Now Fran was curious to see whether this structuring of the context did in fact produce the sort of language which we would associate with learning.

In the following pages, we will trace through the stages of the unit as described in the spiral diagram, giving examples of the typical language produced at each stage.

a) Language Accompanying Action

To initiate the children's formal study of rocks, an excursion into the surrounding countryside was organised, with a number of parents volunteering to drive the children around. To a certain extent the activity was planned – they would visit a variety of sites where different types of rocks could be observed, and it was suggested that the children note rocks in their natural state and rocks that had been used in construction. But otherwise the 'content' was determined by the children themselves, the open-ended nature of the activity allowing them to relate current knowledge to new information.

They first stopped at some old rock walls, previously just part of the landscape but now seen through new eyes. While they speculated on the origin of the rocks, parents recounted tales from local history about how the walls were constructed by Irish immigrants. Then on to a cutting where the freeway was slashing its way through a hillside. The children observed the layers of rock telling their stories of different geological eras. Nearby was a rock platform at the beach where they saw how the molten lava from nearby extinct volcanoes had solidified at the ocean's edge. Then around to the harbour with its pebbly shore and smooth rounded rocks. And finally the local quarry surrounded by stately walls of columnar basalt.

Along the way, the children had noted four sandstone churches, several stone walls, the rock fences in the paddocks, a few houses and a school made of basalt, the retaining walls of the harbour, the road surface, a couple of stone park benches, and a number of other rock constructions, including of course their own sandstone school building.

Mode

The language, captured on audiotape and video, was primarily oral: very much 'language accompanying activity' – the language of observing, exploring, coming to terms with the here-and-now. The written mode also played a minor role in its function of recording, capturing fleeting thoughts for later retrieval. The field-notes represented more than mere 'memory-joggers' however. They were early attempts at identifying significant details from the wealth of experiences surrounding the children (see the example on the opposite page).

Field notes

o ROCKS   M-warby
cins of rocks
homes
weve past the   Sandstone
Cheroh and head-   Brick
ing to wers   ~~rock~~ stone
saddlback monn
·ROCKS are evere
were on Hill.
parsing poney club
parst rock wall.
gone past tree   ·cins of rock
farm. Pasting   honeycome ~~rock~~
covit stone wall   Sandstone
dont kown troth   Brick
Lots of moss and
roots wet moss as
well. Nest stop
little blow holl.
pasted brige
work. Nest stop
park of resles

Tenor

The relationship between the adults and children in this context was more of an 'equal status' nature, allowing the children the freedom to make discoveries along with their teacher and parents. The children themselves were asking the questions, sharing information and giving instructions . . .

> 'Come and see this!'
> 'This one's got holes.'
> 'Look – sparks!'
> 'Why have they got that column shape?'
> 'It's sort of crumbly.'
> 'I know why it's smooth.'

They believed themselves to be apprentice geologists and their language reflected this role.

Field

Their command of the field at this stage was a mixture of everyday terminology ('moss rocks', gravel, orangey rocks, stones) and more specific terms (quartz, basalt, quarry, sandstone). In context, and in response to their questions, terms such as igneous, latite, columnar basalt, etc., were introduced.

b) Recount

Mode

On their return to school, the class shared their experiences in the form of an oral recount. This was intended not only as a pooling of information, but as an initial 'distancing' from the action of the excursion – putting things in perspective, selecting significant aspects, ordering them in time.

This was followed immediately by a written recount of the day's outing in the form of a 'joint construction'. With the teacher acting as scribe using the overhead projector, the class, drawing on their shared experience, jointly composed the text. Within this functional context, questions arose regarding sequence, tense, singular/plural, spelling and punctuation. Most of these were initiated and worked through by the children themselves, though Fran explicitly guided them to a recognition of the typical features of the Recount genre:

◇ an opening *Orientation* (putting the reader in the picture – who took part? when? where?) followed by a series of *Events* sequenced in time, finishing with a *Reorientation*;

◇ the use of conjunctions of time to link up the events (first, firstly, then, next, then, then, next . . .);

◇ the use of location indicators (in the Jamberoo, Jerrara and Kiama areas, out of the school yard, at Jerrara, on the top of the fence, on the rocks, at the new bridge work, in the rock cutting, at the base, at the top, out of the hole, into Kiama, etc.);

      ◇ individual, named, known participants (Year Two, Nicole, we, Jamberoo school, the Little Blowhole, Kiama, the Quarry);

      ◇ action verbs in the past tense (we walked, we touched, they wiggled, we stopped, we travelled, we talked, we went, we finished).

Here is the 'joint construction' text:

Year 2 Excursion to Observe Rocks

Year Two became interested in studying rocks when one of the classmembers (Nicole) talked about a rock book she had read in Silent Sustained Reading. Year Two and their class teacher Miss Egan decided to go on an excursion in the Jamberoo, Jerrara and Kiama area.

As we walked out of the school yard we noticed the Jamberoo School Infants building is made out of sandstone. Our first stop was at Jerrara where we could observe rock fences. We observed lots of things here. Firstly we saw how the rocks were not stuck together properly. Then we touched them – they wiggled. Barbed wire was placed on the top of the fence. There was dried coloured moss on the rocks. The colours were green, grey, white and light orangey brown. There were different colours in the rocks.

Next we stopped at the new bridge work. The bridge was made out of cement. We saw mountains of rock that had been cut through. We saw little lines in the rock cutting. These were left by big building drills (Jackhammers).

There were fragments of rock left at the base. At the top there was a stack of rocks left by the workmen.

From the bridge we travelled down to the Little Blow Hole. We noticed the rocks here were sharp and they had little holes in them. We talked about how the igneous rocks were formed long ago.

At the Blow Hole there was a dark hole. It's sort of a hole with cracks in it. When big waves come the water spurts out of the Hole.

Then we went into Kiama. We observed how a bridge's foundations were being turned (changed) into cement. Then we went to the Kiama Infants School and saw it was made out of basalt.

Next we went to the Kiama Harbour shore. We noticed there was black sand from the volcanoes. The rocks here were mainly round and smooth. We saw cunji on the rocks.

From here we went to the Quarry. We saw column shaped rocks. This was called latite. We also noticed that tar is shiny sticky stuff with sparkling minerals in it.

> *We finished up our excursion by climbing on a huge pile of rocks at the Quarry. It was interesting to observe and find rocks.*

Tenor

Because they had all participated in the excursion, the children came to the writing task with something to say – the experience had been shared and each participant had something to contribute. The teacher therefore withdrew to the role of scribe, allowing the children to debate which points they felt were worthy of inclusion in an account of the outing. The teacher did not always play a passive role however. The scribe can in fact exercise a great deal of power, and when necessary the teacher used this power to guide the children towards a more effective text – reminding them of their audience, pointing out inconsistencies in tense, pronoun reference, helping with the overall structure, and so on.

Field

Generally the Field of a Recount is 'What went on' and tends to emphasise events. This Recount however is not simply an itinerary of the excursion. It also records the observations made by the children. (This is reflected in the high incidence of verbs such as 'we noticed', 'we observed', 'we saw'.) We could represent the Field of the Recount by drawing up strings of related phenomena from the text:

Table 12.1 Field of Recount

Human Participants	Locations	Rocks	Constructions
Year Two	Jamberoo	rocks	Jamberoo
Nicole	Jerrara	sandstone	PS Infants
Miss Egan	Kiama	cement	School
	the school yard	mountains of rock	
	Jerrara	rock cutting	rock fences
	the bridge	fragments of rock	
	Little Blowhole	stack of rocks	bridge's
	Kiama	sharp rocks	foundations
	Kiama Harbour	igneous rocks	
	the Quarry	basalt	Kiama PS
		black sand from volcanoes	Infants School
		round rocks	
		smooth rocks	
		column-shaped rocks	
		latite	
		'tar' – minerals	
		huge pile of rocks	

From the 'Rocks' string we can see that at this stage the children's knowledge about rocks is still expressed in everyday terms, with the occasional technical term creeping in (igneous, basalt, latite, minerals). As yet there is not much evidence of the children attempting to bring order to the Field, but this is understandable, as the purpose of a Recount is simply to tell what happened.

c) Classification activity

Mode
At this point we 'shunted' slightly backward along the Mode continuum towards the 'action' end. The children had brought back their rock samples and were now going to classify them. The small-group discussion, while fairly reflective and orderly, nevertheless allowed the children to question, interject, change their minds, react to feedback. This oral give-and-take led to rather unsophisticated written classifications in diagrammatic form (see Figure 12.3). The ability to summarise in a precise, logical way is an important function of the written mode and was a significant step along the continuum.

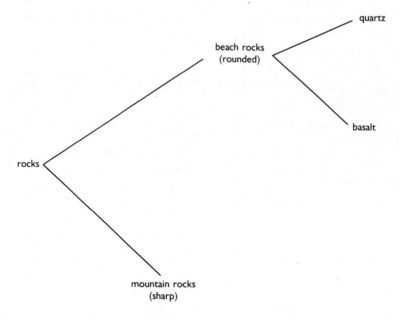

Figure 12.3 'Geologist' group classification

Tenor
Roles were quite deliberately structured for this activity. The children were able to choose whether to be geologists, builders, lapidarists or

rock-collectors according to their interest and knowledge. The children looked for the particular characteristics in the collection of rocks which would be of interest to their group:

◇ The geologists examined the features of each sample, noted the location where it was found and hypothesised as to its origins, justifying their decisions.
◇ The builders considered the different attributes of the rocks and classified them according to their possible uses.
◇ The lapidarists grouped their rocks with an eye to aesthetic qualities.
◇ The rock-collectors classified their samples according to idiosyncratic criteria – shape, colour, size, etc.

In each group the children took their roles very seriously, genuinely trying to tackle the problem from the specialist point of view.

The peer/peer relationships of the small groups permitted the children to interact as equals, without the 'expert' adult inhibiting their attempts. For example:

P1 *I think this comes from down in the earth because it's all got kind of bits of dirt in it.*

P2 *I don't reckon this is glass. It doesn't feel like it.*

P3 *I know, cause it's been washed around.*

P4 *Geologists can tell what . . . they can tell what is what and which is which because they've got these special tools and stuff like that to open them up and see what they're like . . .*

   this man and then he polishes it and stuff like that and then he sells it for a lot of money and . . .

P1 *I think this one comes from the mountain because it's got all like it was buried in the ground . . . like . . . cause it's got all grassy patterns on it.*

P3 *They've come from the sea because they're all smooth and they've got . . . um . . . sort of like sea patterns and they're real real clean and that one's got all green on it and it's really really smooth – like a giant button.*

P4 *The blue rocks . . . people might think they're from the sea and the water made them blue, but Kirsty said they're from the fishpond.*

Field

The children made a valiant effort at the classifying activity (see opposite), but whilst they learned a lot about the process of classifying, (i.e. going from the most general to increasingly specific classes, according to particular attributes) they were frustrated by the lack of a more detailed knowledge of rocks and their attributes. This awareness of their limited knowledge of the Field is reflected in their later write up.

Classifying activity

HOW DO YOU GROUP ROCKS?

When our class studied rocks we collected rocks and put them into groups. Here's an example of the names we gave them,

smooth rough shining dumpy   sharp   Precious

Little   Vauable   Underground.

until we found the **scientific** names for them. The scientific names for them were

ICNEOUS. SEDIMENTARY. METAMORPHIC. Igneous rocks means volcanic rocks.   Sedimantary rocks means layer rocks.   Melamorphic means

Changed rocks. Geologists can make up more groups of rocks because they know more about rocks and minerals then we do.

d) Experimenting

Mode

Still towards the 'action' end of the continuum, the children carried out a variety of experiments on their rock samples in order to come to a more detailed understanding of the attributes of different types of rocks. The dominant mode was oral, although again the written mode played an ancillary role as the children dictated their observations to a group scribe. These notes were later shared with the whole class.

Tenor

In their role as 'scientists', they chipped and hammered and rubbed and scratched. Their language reflected a sense of responsibility for their own learning – an expectation that they would ask the sorts of questions and make the sorts of observations one would expect of a scientist . . .

> 'The crystal cr . . . smashed up in three goes.'
> 'That's why I'm experimenting with it.'
> 'I'm gonna experiment with this one.'
> 'You get a little bit on your finger and dab it onto the paper and it makes a sort of red colour.'

The small group resulted in a peer relationship which encouraged the children to participate on an equal footing. The following transcript shows children utilising the oral mode to negotiate meanings about rocks, empowered by their roles as respected, knowledgeable equals:

> *Hammering Test*
>
> P1   *What happened to it?*
> P2   *Nothing. It's a bit hard.*
> P1   *What is it?*
> P2   *Too hard to smash up.*
> P1   *What name of the stone? . . . Igneous . . . firestone.*
> P2   *No. It's too hard . . . too hard . . . too hard.*
>   *(Spontaneously consult named rock collection)*
> P1   *Probably be that one.*
> P2   *Check with this.*
>   . . .
> P2   *Feels as though it's crushed. And it is. I know it is. It has to be.*
>   *You're not allowed to pick them up and keep them.*
> P3   *I'm not . . . I'm just having a look at them.*
> P1   *Doesn't matter what rock.*
> P2   *These look as though they came from a cave . . . a sort of a cave. See. Cause Jenolan Caves . . . that kind of thing.*
>   . . .
> P2   *There. I crushed it up easily in three goes.*
> P1   *'The crystal crushed up . . .'*

P2   *Easily! No, 'the crystal cr . . . smashed up in three goes'.*
That one's too easy.

P1   *I know. That's why I'm experimenting with it.*

        . . .

P2   *Try this. Try this. Slate. A piece of slate.*
That's slate. See how it's the same.
Crush up some slate. We know the name . . . we know the
stone's name . . . Try it with the sharp end.

P1   *That should do.*

P2   *Bet you it isn't — it would be crushed up.*

P1   *Slate didn't get crushed.*
I'm gonna experiment with this one.

P3   *That one will crush.*

P1   *It has to be wrapped . . .*

P2   *Try it wrapped.*

        . . .

P2   *Do this . . . Try this and see what colour it makes! What*
colour it makes! What colour it makes.

P1   *Hang on. Watch this.*

P2   *. . . yellow. See what it makes up with the yellow.*

        . . .

P2   *Check it out with this one.*

P1   *That will be shale. It could be shale.*

Field

The Field was one of *doing* ('smashing', 'crushing', 'experimenting', 'squashing', 'watching') and of discovering *attributes* ('very sharp edges', 'a bit too hard', 'too hard to smash up', 'crushed', 'orangey'). The group was also keen to find out the names for the various rocks ('What's the name of the stone?' 'Igneous. Firestone.' 'Crystal.' 'Sandstone'.) They regularly compared their samples with those in a labelled rock collection ('That's slate. See how it's the same? . . . We know the name – we know the stone's name.')

By this stage the children had had plenty of opportunities to explore the subject of rocks in the oral mode – using familiar terminology but gradually acquiring more specific terms at the point of need. Every so often, they employed writing to preserve their observations. Now Fran started to exploit the power of the written mode to start ordering their experiences. All their understandings about rocks were to be brought together in the form of a 'Big Book'. The children decided which aspects they were particularly interested in and formed themselves into groups to produce a chapter on their chosen topic. We were now moving towards the reflective end of the mode continuum – going from the multitude of specific details to more generalised, orderly reflection.

e) Text talk

Mode

The emphasis now shifted to written texts, although oral language still played an important interactive role. Fran chose a short expository text on Rocks. Using the overhead projector, she guided the children to engage with the text by identifying and underlining various features (schematic structure, major 'participants', the use of exemplification, etc., as well as layout aspects such as headings, illustrations, captions, glossary).

This demonstration was aimed at helping the children develop strategies for locating information in written texts. It also served as an explicit model for the children's own writing. (See below for model text and indication of the sorts of features identified by Fran and the children.)

— Heading

ROCKS

Scientists group rocks into three main types: **Igneous, sedimentary** and **metamorphic**.
] *Opening Classification*

IGNEOUS rocks are produced by white-hot material deep inside the earth which rises towards the surface as a molten mass called **magma**. If the magma stops before it reaches the surface, it cools and forms rocks such as **granite**. If the magma erupts, it forms a red-hot stream called lava. When the lava cools it becomes rock. One of the most common lava rocks is called **basalt**. Igneous rock is used in the formation of the other two main types of rocks - sedimentary and metamorphic.

explanation

technical terms e.g.

Description
• *Types of rocks*

- *igneous*

SEDIMENTARY rock is formed by small particles or **sediments** such as sand, mud, dead sea animals and weathered rock.   These are deposited in layers and become solid rock over millions of years as they are squeezed by the weight of other deposits above them.

- *sedimentary*

The word **metamorphosis** means 'change'. Rocks which have been changed by heat and pressure are called METAMORPHIC rocks.   They are formed deep inside the earth. **Slate** for example is formed from compressed mud or clay. **Marble** is another type of metamorphic rock. It is produced from limestone which has undergone change through heat and pressure

examples e.g.

- *metamorphic*

Tenor

In this activity, the teacher took on the role of 'expert', sharing her knowledge of text with the class. The children, however, were not passive recipients, but were invited to actively participate in an unthreatening, supportive environment.

Field

The written text presented the Field in an organised manner – filling in gaps in the children's knowledge and drawing out relationships, in particular the class/subclass taxonomy:

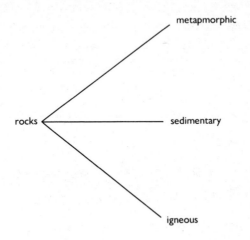

Figure 12.4 Presentation of Field in written text

f) The big book

Mode

By now the class was well into 'the writing process'. The oral mode was still important as the groups pooled their knowledge and collaborated in researching and constructing their joint texts. But it was the written mode that took precedence as they sought information from books, jotted down their notes, organised their knowledge, drafted, redrafted, edited and finally published.

The children also worked on individual reports, summarising what each one now knew about rocks.

Tenor

The children assumed the roles now of researchers and authors and were learning the skills to make them competent in these roles. Most of the interaction was at the peer level as they shared their information, asked each other questions, made suggestions and came to decisions. Because of the constant and explicit modelling by the teacher (e.g. text talks, joint constructions, public editing, shared book) the children were able to be independent and productive in their small groups.

Sample writing from 'the big book'

Rocks

Rocks are found everywhere. We live on rocks all joined together with pressure. There are Billions millions and trillions of rocks. In rocks there is precious stones which lapidarists cut a way to see if they can polish the stone. There are three kinds of rocks a sedimentary igneous and a metamorphic. A sedimentary rock is made up of lots of layers. An igneous rock is a Fire rock because it comes from a volcano. When the lava met the sea it cooled down and was called it a volcanic rock. A metamorphic rock is a sedimentary rock and an igneous rock pres sured for a very long time and it makes a metamorphic rock. Rocks have patterns and lots of colour in them.

Before publication, the class was fortunate to be visited by a real-life editor of children's books, who took on the role of expert to answer their questions about what an editor does. They also had discussions with a group of Indonesian geologists visiting the area who were quite taken with the way that the children took seriously their role of 'apprentices' in the field.

Field

A perusal of the published 'big book' reveals a well-developed knowledge about the field of rocks. The children appeared to be quite comfortable with the three major classes of rocks and happily took to the terms 'igneous', 'sedimentary', 'metamorphic', defining them in their own words ('fire rock', 'a rock made up of lots of layers', 'two rocks pressured for a very long time'). They also became aware of an extensive variety of subclasses (quartz, crystals, gems, slate, shale, marble, latite, sandstone, pumice, coal, columnar basalt, blue metal, etc.). They had started to look at the composition of rocks and had an inkling about minerals. They had a good knowledge of the characteristics of various rock-types and the uses of different rocks (see the extract 'Rocks' opposite, for example).

Best of all, they did not see the acquisition of such knowledge as 'difficult' or 'a bore', as evidenced by the fact that many weeks after the theme had finished, their enthusiasm had not diminished and they kept bringing samples to class and making collections at home.

A detailed analysis of the transcripts and written texts has since revealed that Fran's planning had in fact produced the kind of registers which we would associate with learning, the children engaging purposefully with a variety of modes from active through to reflective; experiencing a number of different roles within a supportive environment; and gaining an increasing control over the field in question.

13

Grammatical Differentiation between Speech and Writing in Children Aged 8 to 12

KATHARINE PERERA ⸺⸺⸺⸺⸺⸺⸺⸺⸺⸺◇

Primary school teachers often complain that their pupils 'write as they speak'. In an earlier study (Perera, 1986), I attempted to show that, in fact, young children's writing shows more evidence of differentiation from their speech than that lament would suggest. The study took published corpora of data and compared the speech of 53 12-year-olds with the writing of 28 12-year-olds and 48 nine-year-olds. This comparison yielded some useful information but, because of the way the data were presented, it had the limitation that it was not possible to compare the same children as both speakers and writers. This paper, therefore, presents a smaller follow-up study, comparing the speech and writing of 48 monolingual English-speaking children in Wales. The data come from a language development project at the Polytechnic of Wales: the speech samples are published (Fawcett and Perkins, 1980); the writing samples by the same children are, as yet, unpublished, and I am grateful to Robin Fawcett for providing access to transcripts and writing. The 48 children come from three groups, aged eight, ten and 12, with 16 in each group; each contains eight boys and eight girls, from four different 'classes of family background'. When recorded, the children were within three months of eight, ten or 12. So a reference to 'eight-year-olds' encompasses children between 7.9 and 8.3.

For the collection of the spoken data, the children were tape-recorded as, in groups of three, they made a construction out of Lego bricks. They were then interviewed individually by Perkins, who asked them to describe what they had made and to talk about other games they played. For the writing task, the children had to write about the Lego construction they had built.

The data for this study come from a grammatical analysis of the first three pages of the transcript of the adult–child interview for all 48 children and from an analysis of the 48 pieces of writing they produced. So the corpus consists of language samples from the same children talking and writing about the same topic. It is a small amount of data, on a limited topic, so the findings can only be tentative, but, because they are generally in accord with the results of the earlier, larger study, I believe they may have some general applicability.

CONSTRUCTIONS TYPICAL OF SPOKEN LANGUAGE

Differentiation between speech and writing by children works in two ways. On the one hand, as they get older they use in their writing grammatical constructions that are more advanced than those they use in their speech (O'Donnell *et al.*, 1967); on the other hand, they use in their speech an increasing proportion of specifically oral constructions. This section will examine the oral constructions that the children in the study used in their speech, because such an examination throws some light on what they are doing in their writing.

Excluded from the analysis are all those constructions that are heavily dependent on the situation in which the speech occurs: deictic items like 'this', 'that', 'here' and 'there', that the children use when they point to things in the room; expressions like 'you know', 'isn't it' and all other question forms, since they seem to require the presence of a listener; and the false starts, redundant repetitions and ungrammatical sequences that are a result of the pressures of producing spontaneous speech. Even after excluding all of these, there are still in the spoken data eight different constructions that we think of as characteristically oral. In the examples that follow, the name and age of the speaker are given, together with the volume and page reference in Fawcett and Perkins (1980). Although the oral constructions are illustrated from the speech of children, it is important to emphasise that all these expressions occur frequently in the spontaneous speech of adults – there is nothing immature about them.

The first is the clause initiator 'well'. This is so familiar that it needs only one example:

1 'well *I de'cided to put the gàrage on*/

(*Andrew (8); II, 24*)

This is by far the most common oral expression in the data. Between them, the 48 children use 137 instances of 'well'.

The next most frequent type of oral construction is the use of 'this' and 'these' for specific indefinite reference; that is, when the speaker has a specific person or object in mind which has not yet been introduced to the listener. (This use is different from deictic 'this', because it is not referring to something physically present in the situation.) For example:

> 2 *well there's* 'this *bùmpety thing*/
>
> > *(Sarah (8); II, 57)*

> 3 *they* 'had *to run* 'under *this* 'dark *tùnnel*/
>
> > *(Rachael (10); III, 59)*

> 4 *it's* 'got 'these '*things that* 'catch *the márbles*/
>
> > *(Peter (12); IV, 20)*

In more formal contexts, including writing, 'this' and 'these' would be replaced by 'a' and 'some', e.g. 'They had to run under a dark tunnel', 'It's got some things that catch the marbles'.

The third type of oral construction is the group of 'vague completers'. They include expressions like 'or something':

> 5 *it* 'might *be a* 'children's *hòme* or something/
>
> > *(Andrew (8); II, 24)*

and 'an all that', as in:

> 6 *we was* 'looking *for pièces* an all that/
>
> > *(Neil (10); III, 182)*

They have been described in studies by Dines (1979, pp. 13–31) and Scott (1983) under the general heading of 'and stuff'. The most famous adult use of one of these vague completers was probably in the film where Groucho Marx said to his leading lady, 'let's get married or something' and she replied, 'Let's get married or nothing'. Sadly, the example of 'or nothing' in 7 is not a witty riposte but simply a non-standard version of 'or anything':

> 7 *they* 'wouldn't *let him óut* or nothing/
>
> > *(Sarah (12); IV, 306)*

These completers seem to be used when the speaker feels that more could be said but that perhaps it is unnecessary to be more explicit. There is quite a range used by the children, from the highly colloquial 'and that' to the more formal 'and things like that'.

The fourth category is the recapitulatory pronoun. In this construction, the speaker uses a noun phrase at the beginning of the sentence and then abandons it syntactically, filling its grammatical slot with a pronoun, for example:

> 8 *well my* 'nan 'she *got some bóoks*/ *from the library*/
>
> > *(Sharon (8); II, 266)*

9 *wèll/ Néil/ you knów/* he *'started 'building a well he 'put the 'bottom of the 'house by thére/*

(*Jason (10); III, 193*)

10 *'this mán/* he . . . *was 'selling ícecreams/*

(*Jane (12); IV, 220*)

In more formal styles, the initial noun phrase would serve as the subject of the sentence and the pronoun would not appear at all, for example: 'My nan got some books from the library'.

The fifth set of examples features the word 'like'. There are uses of 'like' which are perfectly normal in non-colloquial contexts, such as: 'She looks like her mother'. The only instances included here are those like 11 and 12 which are clearly not part of the formal language:

11 *we were 'going to make 'like a 'big 'house with a pòrch/*

(*Martyn (10); III, 87*)

12 *'like there's 'these two 'rubber bánds/*

(*Peter (12); IV, 20*)

Similarly, 'sort of' and 'kind of' have both a neutral and a markedly colloquial use. The neutral use is where the meaning is 'a type of', as in 'Stilton is a sort or cheese'. In this use, the expressions occur between a determiner and a noun. It is not always possible with the construction, 'It's a sort of x', to tell whether it is being used literally or colloquially. Therefore, conservatively, all such constructions are excluded from the analysis, leaving only those like 13 and 14 that are clearly colloquial:

13 *we 'kind of 'lean on a trèe/*

(*Richard (8); II, 237*)

14 *we 'sort of ran óut of these/*

(*Rachael (10); III, 57*)

The sixth type of oral construction is the tag statement, which speakers seem to use for emphasis:

15 *it's the 'one we 'do in jàzz band/* it ís/

(*Nicola (8); II, 171*)

16 *it's hàrd* it is/

(*Neil (10); III, 182*)

17 *'that was 'going to 'be like a dànger spot*/thát was/

(*Martyn (12); IV, 185*)

The last of these oral constructions is the amplificatory noun-phrase tag. In this construction, the speaker uses a pronoun first and then, as if aware that the reference of the pronoun may not be clear to the listener, adds an explanatory noun phrase at the end:

18 *we 'sort of ran óut of these/'these* the 'red brícks *sort of
    thing/*

(Rachael (10); III, 57)

19 *the 'girl who cálled her 'sister out of it/* the'fire

(Andrea (12); IV, 250)

Table 13.1 gives the occurrence of these oral constructions in the corpus of children's speech. In order to take account of the different number of words used by each age group (given at the top of the table) all the figures are presented as occurrences per hundred words; the actual number of instances is given in brackets. The figures for the totals reveal the most striking aspect of this analysis: that there is a dramatic increase in the use of these colloquial constructions between the ages of eight and ten, from 1.86 per 100 words to 3.46, an increase of 86 per cent. All of the constructions, apart from the recapitulatory pronoun, show an increase from age eight to ten. Those that reveal the greatest gain are: the tag statement; vague completers; 'well'; and 'this' and 'these'.

The figures in Table 13.1 provide evidence that, far from dying out of children's speech, oral constructions are becoming much more prominent.

The fact that they hardly occur in writing is, therefore, that much

Table 13.1 Oral constructions in the speech of children aged 8–12 (occurrence per hundred words, with number of instances in brackets)

Construction	8 yrs (no of words = 3010)	10 yrs (no of words = 3926)	12 yrs (no of words = 3768)
well	0.86 (26)	1.71 (67)	1.17 (44)
this/these	0.40 (12)	0.76 (30)	0.53 (20)
vague completer	0.23 (7)	0.46 (18)	0.27 (10)
recapitulatory pronoun	0.17 (5)	0.13 (5)	0.11 (4)
like	0.07 (2)	0.13 (5)	0.19 (7)
sort of/kind of	0.10 (3)	0.13 (5)	0.08 (3)
tag statement	0.03 (1)	0.13 (5)	0.03 (1)
amplificatory NP tag		0.03 (1)	0.05 (2)
Total	1.86 (56)	3.46 (136)	2.42 (91)

more remarkable. Because that is the case. In the 48 pieces of writing produced by these same children, there are only two examples – both in the same sentence:

20 *We used* these sort of *tiles for the roof.*

(Bryan, 12)

This can be contrasted with the 283 instances in speech, produced by 45 of the 48 children. The virtual absence of oral constructions in the children's writing is not a freak result: in 90 unpublished pieces of writing by nine-year-olds in the Bristol Language Development Project there are only these three examples (I am grateful to Gordon Wells and Barry Kroll for access to this material):

21 Well *have a guess.*

(Mary, 9)

22 *But then he saw* this *elephant.*

(Philip, 9)

23 These *men were cannibals.*

(Philip, 9)

It is tempting to think that there is something in the constructions themselves that inhibits their use in writing. But a search through many hundreds of pieces of children's writing does produce occasional examples – and indeed adults sometimes use them in personal letters in order to establish a warm, friendly tone of voice. Here, from a variety of sources, are examples of some colloquial constructions occurring exceptionally, in writing:

24 *When we arrived at dover we saw the white cliffs* and everything.

(12 yrs, Handscombe (1967, p. 42))

25 *The boy's father* he *has a job and family to take care of.*

(adult, Shaughnessy (1977, p. 67))

26 *We arrived on top of a flat hill* kind of

(12 yrs, Handscombe (1967, p. 56))

27 *In the morning they both went out* the two eldest.

(11 yrs, Burgess et al., (1973, p. 124))

28 *The skin has got* like *pimples on.*

(11 yrs, Rosen and Rosen (1973, p. 134))

So there is nothing inherent in these constructions which prohibits their use in writing; rather, children have learnt, highly successfully, that they are not a normal part of the written language. They can only have learnt this from the reading they do, and from the stories that they have had read to them. This means that, as young as eight (almost as soon as they can write independently), children are differentiating the written from the spoken language and are not simply writing down what they would say.

There are a number of reasons why we may not always be aware, perhaps, of the amount of learning that is involved in children's avoidance of these constructions in their writing. First, it is a negative virtue to leave something erroneous out – we are more conscious of errors that are present than of signs of learning marked only by absence. Secondly, as adults we are so used to written language that we think it is somehow 'natural' that these constructions do not occur; whereas, in fact, such knowledge can be acquired only through considerable exposure to written language. And thirdly, we are probably not aware of how frequent these constructions are in speech: they rarely feature in grammatical descriptions and when they do get mentioned it may be in disparaging terms, as if they are errors of some kind.

CONSTRUCTIONS TYPICAL OF WRITTEN LANGUAGE

We can now consider the written texts in the corpus, because the other side of the differentiation coin is children's use in their writing of constructions that occur rarely or never in their speech. There are two main reasons why writers use structures that are uncommon in speech: first, they are able to use psycholinguistically complex constructions because, unlike speakers, they have plenty of planning time; speakers who spend too long planning their utterances tend to be interrupted and to lose their speaking turn altogether. Also, writers can pause in the middle of a construction without losing their way because the first part is already safely trapped on the page and can be re-read as often as necessary. (However, re-reading while writing is a skill that has to be learned. Research by Graves (1979, pp. 312–19) shows that beginning writers do not take advantage of the physical presence of their chosen words but rather compose additively, one word or phrase at a time, often with disjointed results. So it is not surprising that some of the more demanding constructions, which will probably require the young writer to re-read while composing, do not appear with any frequency in children's writing until the age of ten or 12.)

The second reason for the occurrence of specifically literary constructions in writing is that writers have a need for grammatical variety. This necessity arises from one of the most fundamental differences between speech and writing – the fact that writing cannot convey the expressive features of the spoken voice. Speakers can vary their rate, volume, pitch height, rhythm and intonation patterns, partly to relieve their speech of monotony but also to place emphasis appropriately on the important parts of the message. Because writers have none of this variety available, repetitive grammatical patterns are more noticeable and more boring in writing than they are in speech. So, to achieve a pleasing style, writers have to vary their grammatical constructions.

Writers also need to manipulate grammatical structure in order to get the emphasis in the right place. It is possible to indicate emphasis in writing by underlining or capitalisation but such devices are not approved of in formal styles and, interestingly, none of the children used them.

Another difference between speech and writing is that writing is, on the whole, more formal than speech. We have already seen that children reveal an early awareness of this by their avoidance of informal constructions in writing. In addition, a few of the older children in the sample use in their writing some notably formal constructions that do not occur at all in their speech at this age, for example:

29 *When one person had finished he sent for the next one,* and so on.

(Huw, 10)

30 *We used blocks to make a fridge, beds* etc.

(Stuart, 12)

These examples seem to be formal equivalents of the vague completers used in speech. In his spoken account, Stuart uses a vague completer for a similar purpose:

31 *we . . . 'put in 'pieces of légo/ for 'different óbjects/ 'like a frídge* or something/

(Stuart (12); IV, 26)

His selection of 'etc.' in writing, rather than 'or something', shows a sensitivity to the different requirements of the two modes. In 32, Peter, aged 12, attempts an appositive noun phrase:

32 *We had the test in the Library and we* (Alan and Stewart) *made a house.*

In speech, such an idea may well be expressed by an amplificatory noun phrase, tagged on at the end of the sentence: 'we made a house – Alan and Stewart and me'. It is apparent that Peter does not get the formal construction quite right; in his brackets he should have written 'Alan and Stewart and I' but, of course, mistakes are especially likely to occur in a construction that is new to the user and still in process of being acquired. Such errors can be seen as a sign of growth.

One aspect of the formality of writing is the tendency to make the links between ideas more explicit than would be necessary in speech. Sharon demonstrates this with her use of 'for instance':

33 *We kept adding different ideas,* for instance, *kitchen windows, gates, trees, doors.*

(Sharon, 10)

In speech, such specification is often simply added, without any overt indicator of the relationship. Sharon's friend, Janet, provides an example of the typically implicit spoken form as they play with the Lego together:

> 34   *well 'you got some 'funny idéas/ gátes/ shútters/*
> *(Janet (10); III, 242)*

Another type of linguistic formality is illustrated by ten-year-old Richard in a letter about his Lego construction:

> 35   *If you meet an architect interested in our farm we would willingly give* him or her *the plans.*

He shows here that he can use the singular pronoun after a non-specific singular noun. That this is a rather formal construction is apparent from the fact that, colloquially, many adults would use the plural 'them' instead: 'we would willingly give them the plans'. In addition, Richard seems surprisingly mature in being aware that if he had used generic 'he' and written 'we would willingly give him the plans', he could have been accused of sexism.

As well as being more formal than speech, writing also tends to be less redundant. One of the grammatical ways in which redundancy is decreased is by the use of non-finite rather than finite subordinate clauses. There are some types of clause that are normally non-finite, even in speech – for example, adverbial clauses of purpose (such as 'he went home to rest'). But most non-finite adverbial clauses are more typical of written than spoken language, for example:

> 36   After constructing the kitchen *I started on the car.*
> *(Janet, 10)*
> 37   *Janet had the most amusing idea of building a multi-coloured wall,* first of all using red, then blue, then yellow.
> *(Sharon, 10)*

The finite version of the adverbial in 36 would be:

> 38   After I had constructed the kitchen *I started on the car.*

Similarly, non-finite relative clauses are generally more common in writing than in speech. Examples 39 to 41 show how some of the children use them in writing:

> 39   *I was one of the children* chosen to take part in the project.
> *(Siân, 10)*

40 *We made the windmill out of ten Lego bricks* piled on top of each other.

(Ann-Marie, 12)

41 *Amanda's house had one little person* walking up to the front door.

(Heidi, 12)

The more redundant, more speech-like version of **39**, for example, would be:

42 *I was one of the children* who were chosen to take part in the project.

In the corpus studied there were approximately twice as many of these two non-finite constructions in the children's writing as in their speech. The figures are given in Table 13.2. The difference between the two modes is much more marked in the 12-year-olds than in the two younger age-groups, suggesting that the children are becoming increasingly aware that lower redundancy is preferable in written style and are acquiring the grammatical means that enable them to achieve it.

We know that writing lacks the intonation features of speech. An important function of intonation is to signal the *focus of information* in a clause. The unmarked position for the focus is the end of the clause, where we most often put those parts of the message that are either new or important, or both. However, any part of the clause can be made prominent by the speaker; but the writer, in contrast, generally has to make sure that the focus of information coincides with the end of the clause. If the normal clause order of subject, verb and complementation will not achieve end-focus, then there are grammatical devices the writer can use. One is to move a normally final place adverbial to the front of the sentence, as in **43** and **44** (over the page):

Table 13.2 Redundancy-reducing constructions in children's speech and writing (occurrence per hundred words, with number of instances in brackets)

Speech		Writing	
8 yrs.	0.10	8 yrs	0.14
(no. of words	(3)	(No. of words	(2)
= 3010)		= 1414)	
10 yrs.	0.31	10 yrs	0.45
(No. of words	(12)	(No. of words	(12)
= 3926)		= 2677)	
12 yrs.	0.24	12 yrs.	0.60
(No. of words	(9)	(No. of words	(20)
= 3768)		= 3348)	

43   *On top there was a chimney.*

(Gary, 8)

44   *Outside the garden I put a little bus-stop sign.*

(Kathryn, 10)

For Kathryn, in **44**, 'the little bus-stop sign' is the most important part of the sentence. If, more prosaically, she had written, 'I put a little bus-stop sign outside the garden', it would have been hidden in the middle of the sentence and would have lost its prominence. In example **45**, there are two kinds of word-order alteration:

45   *By the side of it we put a bus-stop where stood two children.*
(Siân, 12)

   In the first clause there is another instance of adverbial fronting, which allows the focus to fall on the new information, 'a bus-stop'; and in the second clause the verb is fronted, causing the subject, 'two children', to occur, unusually, at the end of the sentence. The result is rather awkward but it does show that Siân is striving to achieve effects which she knows can be obtained.
   For writers, then, the last position in the clause is the most salient. The next most important position is the beginning. The first element in the clause, the point of departure for the utterance, is called by many grammarians, including Quirk *et al.* (1972, p. 945), the 'theme'. The skilful handling of successive themes is essential in writing because a major way in which written and spoken language differ is that the writer, unlike the speaker, has to produce a sustained, coherent discourse, without help or intervention from a conversational partner. This means that sentences have to have a structure which is not only internally consistent but which also links smoothly with the preceding text. The theme generally expresses *given* information – information that has already been introduced. If new material keeps appearing at the beginning of the clauses, the result is a very jerky disjointed passage which is uncomfortable to read. So, being able to maintain thematic continuity is a necessary skill for a writer. Examples **46** and **47** show these young writers using unusual grammatical constructions in order to maintain continuity. Kathryn links the second sentence in **46** to the first by taking up the theme of the garden:

46   *While Louise and Rachael built the bungalow, I made a*
     start on the garden. In the garden were two trees and
     around the garden I placed a fence.

(Kathryn, 10)

If she had written 'two trees were in the garden', she would have had new material at the beginning of the clause, and given material at the end – the reverse of the pattern she needs. By using adverbial fronting, she is able to achieve thematic continuity and appropriate end-focus at the same time. In example 47 Stuart clearly wants 'we' to be the theme of his second sentence (taking up the idea of 'two other boys and myself' from the first):

> **47** *Last Monday the 3rd two other boys and myself did a test for the Polytechnic of Wales, building with lego bricks.* We *were given a choice, we could either build a small individual thing ourselves or build one big thing all together.*
>
> *(Stuart, 12)*

To achieve his chosen theme, he uses a passive verb phrase: 'we were given the choice'. If he had used the active verb phrase which would be more likely in speech, he would have had to write something like 'A man called Mr Perkins gave us a choice', which would have introduced a new and unwanted theme.

On the whole, most of the children in the sample are very good at maintaining thematic continuity in their writing; but to show what can go wrong, here in the opening of one of the very few pieces that are less successful in this regard (each theme is italicised):

> **48** *The house* was big and *I* lived in it. But *the bridge* was big. *The gate and a door* was red and *the cars* were blue. *The dog and the pig* were pink.
>
> *(Sharon, 8)*

In six clauses each theme is new, with not one taking up an idea already mentioned. The stilted language this produces seems strangely reminiscent of some reading schemes.

A much more common problem occurs when thematic continuity is maintained by repeating the same theme over and over again. This gives thematic continuity without thematic variety, for example:

> **49** *I* made a garden with flowers in it. *I* did a fence. *I* was going to do a bus stop. *I* did a table outside and a chair. *I* put a cake on the table. *I* put an egg on the table.
>
> *(Jennifer, 8)*

Such repetition of a pronominal theme is common and unremarkable in speech:

> **50** wéll/ we *de'cided 'first of áll/ to 'do the hòuse/ 'so we 'started to 'build the hóuse/ and we 'thought we'd 'make a 'little gárden/ to go wíth it/ and we 'thought we'd 'have some péople/*
>
> *(Sheryl (10); III, 289)*

However, to be successful, a writer has to create thematic variety while maintaining thematic continuity and getting the focus in the right place. In 51 and 52 there are examples which suggest that their writers might be aware of the need for thematic variety.

51 *We used blocks to make a fridge, beds etc. We then built the roof which was flat. We then put a fence round and put a tree and flowers and made a garden.* A bus stop *was put outside.*

(Stuart, 12)

52 *We built the house because it was very simple and we had a lot of bricks to build it with.* Around the house *we put a fence and three gates in it. We built a bus stop outside the house with three people waiting for a bus.* Inside the fence *we put two trees.*

(Sarah, 12)

Stuart has used 'we' three times and then starts the fourth sentence with 'a bus stop'. This is not entirely successful since it sounds rather clumsy; and, being new information, 'a bus stop' really needs to go later in the clause. But if Stuart had not used the passive and had written instead 'we put a bus stop outside', he would have repeated 'we' for the fourth time. His choice of an unusual construction indicates perhaps that he is becoming sensitive to some aspects of the overall structure of a piece of writing. Sarah, in 52, manages rather better by using fronted place adverbials. 'Around the house' and 'inside the fence' both take up ideas already mentioned so thematic continuity is maintained. If she had used normal sentence order, all five main clauses in this extract would have begun with *we*. Some of the older writers in the sample show that they are able to sustain both thematic continuity and thematic variety over several sentences, for example:

53 *In the Lego boxes there were hundreds of different pieces. Some had only one hole. Others went up to twelve. They had arch shapes, straight lines and some had a circle shape. Nearly everything was used to make our mansion.*

(Ann-Marie, 12)

From examples 43 to 53, it is apparent that end focus, thematic continuity and thematic variety are interrelated. So when an unusual construction, such as adverbial fronting, is used, it is rarely possible to associate it definitively with just one of the three stylistic factors. Adult writers use a number of grammatical constructions to achieve focus, continuity and variety. (A description is given in Perera 1984, chapters 4 and 5.) In this corpus of data, there are three that seem to be being used by the children for these stylistic purposes, though it is important to

stress that there is no suggestion that the children are consciously aware
either of the effects or of the means they use to achieve them. The three
discourse-structuring constructions they use are passive verb phrases,
fronted place adverbials and reordered clause constituents. Although
these constructions do occur in their speech, they are much less common
than in their writing; the figures are given in Table 13.3. The figures for
speech do not alter very much between the ages of eight and 12, whereas
for writing they increase considerably from eight to ten and more than
double between ten and 12. This suggests that by the age of 12, at least
some children are becoming aware of the grammatical resources they
can exploit in their writing. Some of the children make errors in using
the literary constructions; this underlines the fact that these new forms
are still in the process of being acquired. For example, the repetition of
the adverbials in 54 and 55 indicates a certain lack of faith in the fronted
versions:

54 *And* in the garden *I put little seeds* in it.

(Nicola, 8)

55 In the front of it *we put a tree* there.

(Siân, 12)

The figures in Tables 13.2 and 13.3 give the occurrence of
typically written constructions across whole age-groups. Like this, it is
not possible to see how far they reflect typical usage for the group and
how far they derive from just a few exceptional subjects. Therefore,
Table 13.4 shows how many children out of the 16 in each age group are
using in their writing the three main types of literary construction that
have been described.

The figures show there is an increase, with age, in the number of
children using the constructions, not just in the number of constructions
being used.

Table 13.3 Discourse-structuring constructions in children's speech
and writing (occurrence per hundred words, with number of instances
in brackets)

Speech		Writing	
8 yrs.	0.17	8 yrs.	0.28
(No. of words	(5)	(No. of words	(4)
= 3010)		= 1414)	
10 yrs.	0.23	10 yrs.	0.49
(No. of words	(9)	(No. of words	(13)
= 3926)		= 2677)	
12 yrs.	0.21	12 yrs.	1.11
(No. of words	(8)	(No. of words	(37)
= 3768)		= 3348)	

Table 13.4 Number of children in each age-group using literary constructions in writing

	8-year-olds	10-year-olds	12-year-olds
'Formal' constructions	0	3	3
Redundancy-reducing constructions	2	7	7
Discourse-structuring constructions	4	8	11

It is necessary to emphasise that there is no intrinsic merit in the constructions that have been illustrated: they are valuable only in so far as they enable writers to express their intentions more clearly, concisely and elegantly than they could have done without them. Further, I do not believe there is any value in teachers setting exercises for children to make finite clauses non-finite, to move place adverbials to the fronts of sentences, or to turn active sentences into passives. The use of these constructions will be learned most naturally by reading, and by drafting and redrafting sustained pieces of writing.

We know that for a written text to be successful it is necessary for there to be links between sentences. But such links alone are not sufficient. It is possible to make up pseudo-discourses where each sentence is linked impeccably to the preceding one and yet there is a lack of global coherence. Writers have to impose an overall pattern of organisation on their work as well as taking care of local connections between sentences. (There is some evidence (Atwell, 1981) that global coherence is harder to achieve.) The global structure may be chronological, spatial, logical or a combination of these. It is well known that the chronological pattern is by far the easiest and is the one that young writers use most often. Many of the children in the sample organise their account of making a Lego construction in a chronological way. Table 13.5 lists the time adverbials that they use as one means of achieving this overall structural coherence. The most striking thing is the much greater variety of adverbials in the written accounts. In speech they often sequence their actions simply with 'and' or 'then', for example:

> 56 *well we 'started to make the hóuse/ then we 'thought that it would 'be a bit bìg/ . . . 'then we 'started just to 'build thàt bit/ the 'little hóuse/ and 'then we all thought 'well we 'might as well 'put a gàrage there/ on the sìde/ and 'then we 'found all the féncing/ so we de'cided to have the fénce/ and the trées/ and 'then we had the dóor/*
>
> *(Suzanne (12); IV, 207)*

There are written accounts rather like that from some of the eight-year-olds but generally the ten- and 12-year-olds use a wider range of

Table 13.5 Time adverbials in children's speech and writing

	Speech			Writing		
	8 yrs	10 yrs	12 yrs	8 yrs	10 yrs	12 yrs
then	+	+	+	+	+	+
when + finite clause	+	+		+	+	+
first		+	+	+	+	+
first of all		+	+	+	+	+
at/in the end			+		+	+
after + finite clause				+	+	+
after that				+	+	+
after + NP				+		
soon				+		
at the start				+		
last of all				+		
secondly					+	
next					+	
sometimes					+	
in time					+	
at the time					+	
straight away					+	
to begin with					+	
while + finite clause					+	
after + non-finite clause					+	
in the beginning						+
afterwards						+
eventually						+
finally						+
at last						+
on the third go						+
before + finite clause						+
once + finite clause						+

structuring devices. Again, there seems to be a realisation among the older children that special effort is needed to establish a coherent written text.

I have already suggested that we may not notice that children are editing oral constructions out of their writing. Similarly, we may not be aware that they are using in their writing constructions that they rarely use orally. The reason for this is chiefly that they are such simple constructions that educated adults probably use many of them in spontaneous speech. But it seems fair to hypothesise that it is the pressure writing imposes to produce an extended, coherent piece of language that forces children to start experimenting with these constructions. As the new forms of language become more familiar, and as a widening range of speech situations present themselves, then young people may extend their oral repertoire by 'borrowing' some of their newly acquired literary constructions when the need for them arises.

This small-scale study has shown that even though the language of children's writing at the age of 12 may still seem simple and speech-like to adults, the fact is that it is not really like children's speech at all.

CONCLUSION

Finally we can consider the implications of this research for the teaching of writing. Being aware that children are doing something different in writing from speech may alert teachers to signs of development: instances of constructions that show a sensitivity to discourse structure, for example, may gleam through a piece that is badly written, poorly punctuated and atrociously spelt – and provide encouraging evidence that something is being learnt. Such awareness will allow teachers to make a differential response to errors – treating differently those that arise from haste or carelessness and those that suggest the writer is trying out a new construction but has not got it right yet.

The fact that some of the grammatical developments in writing seem to arise from the need to structure a discourse coherently points to the importance of encouraging children to write continuous passages from an early age. Writing one-sentence responses to questions will not provide the stimulus necessary to develop these constructions. As children generally do not use many of the more typically written constructions in their speech, it follows that they need to learn them by reading extensively. It also highlights the value of the teacher reading aloud to the class, throughout the junior years and beyond, because, in this way, children are able to absorb structures of sentence and discourse organisation from written material that would be too difficult for them to read themselves. This is particularly important for weaker readers. If their only experience of written language comes from the rather stilted prose of remedial reading schemes, then it is no wonder that their own writing is flat and dull.

We know that different types of writing have different patterns of organisation: that narratives are structurally different from descriptions, and so on. Therefore, it follows that children need to read and hear read not only stories but also as wide a range as possible of non-fiction, so that they have developed a feel for the necessary linguistic constructions before they are required to use them in their own writing.

Finally, [. . .] I know it is not necessary to make a case for writing – but elsewhere there are people who argue that with the advent of telephones and tape-recorders the need for writing has greatly diminished. Quite apart from the practical disadvantages of dependence on such machines, I believe that the argument is seriously flawed. Writing is not merely a way of recording speech, a kind of inefficient tape-recorder, but a different form of language in its own right which can lead to different ways of thinking. Because written language provides different opportunities from speech and imposes different requirements, it forces the writer to use language in different ways. These different experiences of language are then available to be fed back into speech. So, for some children at any rate, writing is not just a reflection or a record of their oral competence but is also an important agent in their language development. This suggests that it is dangerous to adopt a narrowly functional approach to the teaching of writing. Even if, as adults, we were to do no more writing than signing our Christmas cards, learning to write fluently and extensively would still be important because of its influence on both language and thinking.

REFERENCES

Atwell, M. A. (1981) 'The Evolution of Text: the Interrelationship of Reading and Writing in the Composing Process', Ed. D. thesis, Indiana University.

Burgess, C. *et al.* (1973) *Understanding Children Writing*. Harmondsworth: Penguin.

Dines, E. (1979) 'Variation in Discourse – and stuff like that', *Language in Society*, 8, pp. 13–31.

Fawcett, R. and Perkins, M. (1980) *Child Language Transcripts 6–12*, II–IV. Pontypridd: Polytechnic of Wales.

Graves, D. H. (1979) 'What Children Show Us about Revision', *Language Arts*, 56, pp. 312–19.

Handscombe, R. J. (1967) 'The Written Language of Eleven- and Twelve-year-old Children', Nuffield foreign languages teaching materials project, reports and occasional papers, no. 25, The Nuffield Foundation.

O'Donnell, R. C., Griffin, W. J. and Norris, R. C. (1967) *Syntax of Kindergarten and Elementary School Children: A Transformational Analysis*. Champaign, Illinois: National Council of Teachers of English.

Perera, K. (1984) *Children's Writing and Reading*. Oxford: Blackwell.

Perera, K. (1986) 'Language Acquisition and Writing' in *Language Acquisition*, Fletcher, P. and Garman, M. (2nd edn). Cambridge: Cambridge University Press.

Quirk, R., Greenbaum, S., Leech, G. N. and Svartvik, J. (1972) *A Grammar of Contemporary English*. London: Longman.

Rosen, C. and Rosen, H. (1973) *The Language of Primary School Children*. Harmondsworth: Penguin.

Scott, C. M. (1983) 'You know and all that stuff: acquisition in school children'. Paper presented at ASHA Convention, Cincinnati.

Shaughnessy, M. P. (1977) *Errors and Expectations: A Guide for the Teacher of Basic Writing*. New York: Oxford University Press.

14

Young Children's Writing: From Spoken to Written Genre

FRANCES CHRISTIE ────────────────────────────◇

The study I intend to report on here commenced as an investigation into the processes by which young children learn to write.[1] The focus was upon 55 children who entered the preparatory year, aged five years, and I studied them intensively for a period of three years, up to the point at which they completed year two. In undertaking the study I was initially very much indebted to the work of Martin and Rothery (1980–1981; Martin, 1984; Rothery, 1984), who out of their investigations proposed a typology of genres young children appear to learn to write. I sought to use their description, but specifically, I sought to do something I believed they had not sought to do in their original two reports: namely, to examine where children's written genres come from. That is to say, my focus has always been upon the curriculum context – upon the teaching/learning episodes which teacher and children negotiate, and out of which, as it were, the children are ultimately caused to produce written texts.

The search for a means of talking about the curriculum context has proved an interesting one, because it has, in a sense, taken me away from considerations of writing. Much more than I had foreseen in undertaking the study initially, it has caused me to focus upon the nature of the spoken discourse of the classroom. Specifically, I have sought to identify some means by which I can describe and account for the relationship between the patterns of spoken discourse used in teacher/pupil interaction, and the patterns of written discourse produced by the children. Central to the methodological tools I have sought to develop to this end, is the notion of the 'curriculum genre'. Using this notion, I would now argue (i) that it is quite impossible to understand the nature of the written texts children produce without an understanding of the curriculum context in which they are generated, (ii) that in significant ways much early childhood curriculum practice seriously underestimates what young children can do, with unfortunate effects for their writing development, and (iii) more specifically, that where the 'content' of the learning activity around which writing develops is of a limited kind, so too are the written texts the children produce. Since the notion of 'genre' is so central to the argument to be developed, it will be necessary to offer some definition of the term as it is to be used here.

GENRE DEFINED

The term 'genre' as I shall use it, owes most to the somewhat varying but related usages of Kress (1982), Martin (1984) and Hasan (1989), and it is in fact currently used by a number of people who work in systemic linguistic theory. The term 'curriculum genre' was one I myself coined originally at a Discourse Analysis Workshop, held at Macquarie University, Sydney in January 1983 (Christie, 1985a). Most of us have encountered the term 'genre' in the course of literary studies. A literary text, so one was taught for example in the degree in English which I completed some years ago, was representative of some genre or other, having some characteristic overall shape or pattern, or, to use a contemporary term, 'schematic structure'. The ballad, the sonnet, or the ode, for example, come to mind, all of them in some sense 'prestige' literary forms. The issues which made the contemporary linguistic interest in genre somewhat different, are firstly, that it focuses upon what might be termed 'non-prestige' as well as 'prestige' forms, and secondly, that it recognises generic patterns in speech as well as in writing.

Both Hasan (1985) and Ventola (1984) have shown that even such relatively casual conversations as service encounters have an overall linguistic pattern or shape, justifying us as seeing these as examples of genres: linguistically patterned ways of behaving for the achievement of certain socially determined goals. For my purposes, Martin's definition of genre (1984:25) is most useful 'a staged, goal oriented, purposeful activity in which speakers engage as members of our culture'.

The term 'curriculum genre' refers to any teaching/learning episode which may be said to be structured and staged in this sense. It will involve participation of teachers and students in some activity which seeks to establish for the children understandings and/or tasks of various kinds. To illustrate the point quickly, we may refer to the Morning News genre, the function of which we are told in educational discussion, is that children are given opportunity to 'learn to talk'. In the creation of a text which is representative of the Morning News genre, a morning news giver is nominated, that person comes to the front of the group of children, and a formal exchange of greetings takes place, after which the morning news giver offers some item(s) of news, involving the reconstruction of some aspect of personal experience. The teacher and other pupils may comment and/or ask questions during this phase and finally, the morning news giving is brought to a close, sometimes because the teacher says so, and sometimes because the child indicates he or she has finished.

Close analysis of the kinds of linguistic behaviours children are required to produce in order to be judged proficient in the Morning News genre, reveals that they need to offer a series of observations about personal experience. The mood choice for the morning news giver will thus be declarative (while that of the teacher, by contrast, is frequently interrogative, for she in particular may ask questions), and, somewhat surprisingly, no evaluative comment upon personal experience will normally be offered by the child. It seems that the function of offering evaluation is that of the teacher, a significant measure of the authority accorded her, even in a situation in which the child is supposed to be encouraged to talk (Christie, 1989). Thus is an aspect of the ideology of schooling – more specifically, of the kinds of values associated with the roles of teacher and children – realised in the linguistic choices made in the production of a classroom text.

Ideologies or values, not only to do with the role of teacher and pupils, but also to do with the kinds of knowledge children will examine, are, as we shall shortly see, also important elements of the Writing Negotiation genre. They have important implications for the language used both by teacher and by children, and hence for the kinds of capacities in writing the children are enabled to develop. In fact, as I hope to demonstrate in the curriculum activity I shall be examining, there is a very intimate relationship between the limited nature of the content dealt with and the limited nature of the written genres the children produce. As I shall further suggest, the terms of the curriculum activity are such that the children are constrained to do no more than produce aspects of personal experience in talk, and, just as there is no significant mental challenge involved in such an undertaking, so too, there is little challenge to significant learning in the writing task undertaken.

The values to education of identifying and talking about educational practice in terms of 'curriculum genres', are several. Firstly, the notion enables us to concentrate upon just how it is that we structure, organise, and hence regulate teaching learning experiences in schools. Secondly, because it obliges us to think about language in behavioural terms, it can enable us to identify the kinds of linguistic behaviour children need to master in order to be successful in their learning. Thirdly, because it becomes apparent that the practice of patterning experience in language, and of creating genres, is a feature both of speech and of writing, we are enabled to focus directly upon the relationship of written genres to spoken ones: that is, we are able to trace the relationship of the patterns of the written genre to the patterns of spoken discourse in which the actual task of writing was negotiated.

I propose now to turn to one Writing Negotiation genre, generated when the children involved were in year two. I shall firstly discuss the curriculum genre, indicating one way in which a systemic linguistic analysis (Halliday, 1985) can illuminate several aspects of the ways meanings are realised in the text. Secondly, I shall go on to discuss a sample of the written texts produced by the children. I shall argue that the analysis demonstrates both how limited is the quality of the learning actually involved in the curriculum genre, and how this in turn explains the limited nature of the written texts produced.

A WRITING NEGOTIATION GENRE

The lesson it is proposed to discuss was one in a series which constituted a major unit of work, or 'theme' on Food. Typically, in curriculum practice in the junior school, learning activities in language arts, science and social science will be developed around such a theme. The unit of work on Food lasted eight weeks, and the particular lesson of concern here came towards the end of the unit, in about the sixth or seventh week. The lesson was undertaken early in the day, immediately after roll call and morning news in fact. Later in the day the children were to make sandwiches with their teacher and eat them at lunch time, and they had all brought in various ingredients before the day's activities commenced.

The content of the lesson was built around the teacher's reading of a children's book, *My Lunch!* (Bambrough, 1982) and, inspired by listening to this, the children were to write texts of their own, under the title, 'What happened to my lunch?' The book is one of a series of basal readers widely used in Australia, and like the volumes from most such series, it is reasonably pedestrian, in that its choice of language is both limited and somewhat stilted. Its 'story' (not in fact a true narrative structure) is developed partly through the text, and partly through the associated illustrations, and it concerns a boy who discovers he has lost his lunch at school. A dog is found to have taken the lunch and the teacher takes the boy to buy another lunch in a shop.

In terms of the overall schematic structure of the lesson, an examination of the total pattern of classroom discourse reveals four major elements: the Task Orientation (TO), the Task Reorientation (TR), the Task Specification (TS), and the Task (T). The pattern of teacher/pupil negotiation – the curriculum genre involved here – is a familar enough one. A course is set by the teacher in the TO: in this phase, some initial perspectives are established, and some basic understandings of the Task established; a TR is intended to develop upon the initial perspectives and understandings. Thence, the Task is specified, and in turn the children are deemed ready to undertake it.

The object of a discussion of any linguistic elements of the text will be to illuminate the ways in which its meanings are negotiated and built up. Hence, we should now turn to attempting some analysis of at least some elements of the text in hand. A functional grammar of the kind that Halliday (1985) has produced is valuable for many reasons, not least that it offers a range of possible ways into analysing a text.

Indeed, the skill is in identifying those elements of the grammar which most usefully illuminate the nature of the particular text in hand. My own investigation into curriculum genres (Christie, 1986) leads me to argue that an examination of Theme is a particularly pertinent way of penetrating and explaining the ways in which classroom discourse builds its meanings. In an interesting paper, another writer (Eiler, 1986) has recently demonstrated the value of an examination of Theme to the study of written discourse and how its meanings are made.

Technically, Theme is 'the element (in the clause) which serves as the point of departure of the message; it is that with which the clause is concerned' (Halliday, 1985: 38). In English, though not necessarily in other languages, Theme is what comes first in the clause. Theme may be of three kinds, following the three sets of meanings Halliday identifies in language: experiential – having to do with the experience or 'content' dealt with; interpersonal – having to do with the relationship of the participants in the discourse; and textual – having to do with the actual role of the language in the overall organisation of the text. Some examples will serve to illustrate how the three types of Theme may be realised in text.

Any clause (with the exception of a minor one) will have an experiential Theme, known as topical, since any clause necessarily has an experiential component, as in the following clauses from the teacher's discourse which introduce the TO phase:

> *well now* these people *are back*
> I *want*
> you *to listen to this little tiny story* . . .

Themes which are interpersonal may be of several kinds, for they may involve the use of a finite as in the first of these two clauses, taken from the TS phase:

> have *you ever had a day when you've had no lunch to eat?*

or they may be vocatives as in the following clause, not actually taken from the text in question:

> Mary, *are you coming out now?*

In addition WH forms (i.e. usually questions headed by *what*, *where*, *why*, etc.), frequent in classroom discourse, are held to be both interpersonal and experiential, since they fulfil both functions, as in

> where's *my lunch?*

Textual Themes may be of various kinds, though two of particular importance in classroom discourse tend to be continuatives and structural Themes. Continuatives, as the name implies, have the function of carrying the discourse forward, linking the different elements together as in the opening clause of the teacher, cited above:

> well now *these people are back* . . .

Structural Themes also have the function of linking clauses together, though in a somewhat different sense, for they include the various conjunctions, which are often used in association with conjunctive adjuncts, such as *then*. The following are also taken from the teacher's opening discourse:

> *you know we had a monster sandwich,* and then
> *we made up our own monster sandwiches* . . .
> and I *want you to listen to it (i.e. the story)* . . .
> because when *we finish reading this story* . . .

In general, whoever controls structural Theme directs the course the discourse takes, determining in particular the kinds of patterns of reasoning encoded in those patterns. Overwhelmingly, it is the teacher in this, as in many curriculum genres, who controls the structural Themes, and the children in fact produce very few. When we examine the nature of the structural Themes produced, we find that most have the effect of building connections between events of an additive kind, so that simple connection is created, of the sort requiring no more than very simple narration of a sequence of events. Furthermore, when we examine the elements of the discourse which the children do produce, we find that their contributions to the text are often so minimal as not to contain any Thematic component at all. However, where they do produce Themes, these are always topical, and of a personal kind, to do with self, a classmate or a family member. Collectively, the effect of these patterns of structural Themes and of topical Themes in the text is to construct a discourse, and hence a pattern of reasoning, which involves the children in the simple construction of personal experience, where that involves reconstruction of actual happenings, or construction of imagined experience.

As a basis for significant school learning, I would argue that recourse to personal experience is essential. However, contrary to much early childhood practice, I would also argue that personal experience should not constitute the entire content examined in a lesson. Where that does happen, I suggest, little learning of a significant kind may be shown to have taken place.

I propose to illustrate and support my observations, with respect to Theme and its significance in the way in which meanings are made in the curriculum genre under discussion, by examining two aspects only of its overall schematic structure. They are, firstly, the teacher's opening discourse, in which she initiates the TO phase, and, secondly, that element of the schematic structure I have labelled the TS, which allows a very good examination of the respective roles and contributions of the teacher and children. Table 13.1 sets out all the clauses in the teacher's discourse, in which she initiates the activity. Since she uses no inter-personal Themes in the discourse, apart from those instances where she uses a WH form, which as noted above, also qualifies as topical Theme, I have created no separate column for this kind of Theme, creating instead only columns for the textual and experiential Themes. Technically, the rest of the clause is known as 'Rheme'.

As Table 14.1 reveals at a glance, there are two instances of continuatives, 11 of structural Themes, and 22 of topical Themes, of which five are instances of the WH form. Of the 11 structural Themes, six are instances of the use of the additive conjunction *and*, either used alone or, in two instances, in association with the conjunctive adjunct, *then*. Their effect is to link events in terms of the simplest form of connectedness, and the other conjunctions of the kind which might for example, suggest causal relationship between event, thereby implying that a different form of reasoning is to be encoded in the discourse, are in the minority. Of the 22 topical Themes in the teacher's talk, 11 deal with teacher herself and class members. Personal experience thus constitutes a significant element in the discourse.

Table 14.1 Theme in the opening of the task orientation

Theme		Rheme
Textual	Experiential	
well now	these people	are back
Cont.	*Top.*	
	I	want
	Top.	
	you	to listen to this little tiny story [[like the one we had yesterday]]
	Top.	
	you	know
	Top	
	we	had a monster sandwich
	Top.	
and then	we	made up our own monster sandwiches
Struc. Conj	*Top.*	
well	today	we've got another simple little story [[which is called My Lunch]]
Cont.	*Top.*	
and	I	want
Struc.	*Top.*	

Table 14.1 *continued*

Theme			Rheme
		you	to listen to it
		Top.	
		what	happened to the little boy's lunch
		WH/Top.	
		who	came
		WH/Top.	
and			took the lunch
Struc.			
and		what	happened to it
Struc.		*WH/Top.*	
and then		what	what happened to the little boy
Struc. Conj.		*WH/Top.*	
after		he	found
Struc.		*Top.*	
		he	had no lunch at all
		Top.	
because when		we	finish reading this story
Struc.		*Top.*	
		something	's going to happen to your lunch today
		Top.	
or		we	're going to pretend
Struc.		*Top.*	
that		it	does
Struc.		*Top.*	
so		listen	
Struc.		*Top.*	
		what	happened to this boy's lunch
		WH/Top.	
and		we	'll think of something [[that
Struc.		*Top.*	could happen to our lunches, our beautiful healthy lunches]]

Note: Cont. = continuative; struc. = structural; Conj. = conjunctive adjunct; Top. = topical; [[ ]] = an embedded clause.

Now it is clear, of course, that because of her position as authority, responsible for what is going on, the teacher will need to use a large number of structural Themes, and it is also clear that references to self and class members are appropriate in the opening stages of the activity. However, it need not follow that such a large proportion of the structural Themes should build simple connectedness of the kind identified. Furthermore, as indicated earlier, while recourse to personal experience is a reasonable point for departure in a learning activity, it should not establish a pattern which is not subsequently broken in the discourse. Such is, however, the case in the rest of this text, as an examination will reveal of that element of the text identified as the TS phase. The object, very clearly, is the reconstruction of personal experience. Note that in setting out the discourse, I have inserted a row of dots to indicate a point at which an element of the text, to do with disciplining a child, has been removed, on the grounds that it does not constitute part of the curriculum genre involved.

Task specification

T: *Now what I want you people to think about is something coming along and taking your lunch, or something happening to your lunch so that you couldn't eat it. Not a dog, that's in the story. Well, you can have a dog if you want, but it'ud be better if you think of something else.*

....

All right put your hand up if you've thought of something that could come and take your lunch, or something that could happen to your lunch.

T: *Have you ever had a day when you've had no lunch to eat? Jodie? (she nods) What happened Jodie, when you had no lunch to eat?*

Jodie: *Mum didn't bring it up. She left it at home.*

T: *Left your lunch at home on the bench, and her mum didn't bring it to school, and she had no lunch. And what happened?*

Jodie: *Found no lunch.*

T: *And then what happened? Who had to ring up your mum and dad?*

Jodie: *Mr H.*

T: *And then what happened?*

Jodie: *My mum brought my lunch.*

T: *And who else brought your lunch?*

Jodie: *Dad.*

T: *She had no lunch to start with, because it was left at home, and she thought her mum was going to bring it at lunch time, and when her mum didn't bring it, Mrs S. rang her mum, and she wasn't at home, so her dad brought her lunch and then her mum remembered she hadn't brought her lunch, and she brought lunch too, so she ended up with two lunches. She ate the lot.*

Joseph:	What did she have?
T:	You had – I can't remember – you had a sausage roll and donut.
Jodie:	I had a very nice lunch. I had a sausage roll and a jam donut and a (indecipherable)
T:	Mm so that was an extra special thing. Who else has ever had no lunch, and then something's happened that they've had a different lunch? Emily? What happened yesterday?
Emily:	My sister left hers on the dressing table.
T:	And what happened when she found that she had no lunch? Was she happy? What was happening to her?
Emily:	She was crying.
T:	She was crying and she came to me, and what did I say?
Emily:	She could have one from the canteen.
T:	What else happened to you?
Emily:	The day I put the lunch in the school bag and brought the other school bag instead.
T:	Mm and what happened that day? Emily had two school bags at home, and she put the lunch in one school bag, and took the other school bag to school. And when she looked in her bag, no lunch. And what happened that day?
Emily:	I got a lunch from the canteen.
T:	You had a special lunch order.

Table 14.2 sets out in summary fashion the distribution of Themes across the teacher discourse and the children's discourse in the text. Since the text makes little use of interpersonal Themes, we will focus as before, on structural and topical Themes.

This analysis serves to demonstrate how completely the teacher dominates the text, in this, the phase in which teachers and pupils are to negotiate some sense of the task to be undertaken. In addition, such an analysis reveals very clearly the kinds of meanings constructed. Of the 39 structural Themes produced by the teacher, 19 are instances of the conjunction *and*, in four places in association with the conjunctive

Table 14.2 The distribution of structural and topical themes in the task specification phase

Structural	Themes	Topical	Themes
Teacher discourse	Pupil discourse	Teacher discourse	Pupil discourse
39	1	51	7

adjunct *then*, and twice in association with the other conjunction *when*. In addition, *when* is used once alone, while *so* and *that* are both used twice. The pattern built up over a stretch of discourse of the kind examined, where there is such a large concentration of the additive conjunction *and*, as well as use of the conjunctive adjunct *then*, and use of the temporal conjunction *when*, is to construct a pattern of reasoning which is essentially anecdotal. That is to say, the requirement upon the children is that they build simple sequences of events drawn from personal experience. In the terms of the discourse which is essentially created by the teacher, the children are not enabled to do more than that.

When we turn our attention to the topical Themes, and we examine instances of such Themes in both the teacher's discourse and the children's discourse, three matters at least are worthy of mention. Firstly, as the table shows at a glance, the teacher uses many more topical Themes than the children. Secondly, a number of her Themes include use of the WH form, while only one instance of a WH form occurs in the children's talk. However – and this is the third matter of note – there is another sense in which Theme in the contributions of both teacher and children is very similar: namely, the fact that they identify primarily class members or their relatives. Some examples include *mum*, *she*, *her dad*, and *my sister*. The 'content' of the lesson is very clearly personal experience. This latter observation causes me to return to an issue I alluded to earlier: namely, the ideologies concerning knowledge and teaching learning which appear to apply in the junior primary school. This will in turn cause me to take up, regrettably rather briefly, two of the texts written by the children, selected on the grounds that they are quite representative of those generally produced by the children in the class.

THE RELATIONSHIP OF THE WRITTEN GENRES TO THE CURRICULUM GENRE

As I earlier indicated, a great deal of early childhood curriculum practice appears to exploit and build upon the familiar personal experience of childhood, and this is in some senses defensible of course. Recourse to personal experience is probably for all of us a necessary first step or point of departure in undertaking new learning. What seems to make much early childhood education somewhat remarkable in this respect, however, is its tendency to view personal experience as a sufficient 'content' in itself for learning, about which children may both talk and write.

The trap in such a view, as I believe my analysis of the above curriculum text using Theme in particular does demonstrate, is that it leads the children into patterns of reasoning and examination of experience of a most limited kind. It requires no more than the simplest construction of event of an anecdotal kind, both in talk and in writing. In the text I have examined, the language the teacher generates actually constrains the children, so that the discourse patterns she and they construct, and hence also the patterns of reasoning encoded in these, involve nothing of the speculation or enquiry which are ostensibly part of the purpose of education. Were such matters to be more centrally part of the classroom discourse, they would be apparent in several ways: in the use of textual Themes whose collective effect was to construct more than simple sequence of event; in the capacity of the children to control and use a greater number of the textual Themes, so that they also exercised some share in the directions taken in the discourse; and finally, in the use of a much greater number of experiential Themes than in the text examined, to do with matters other than the most immediate personal experience.

Let me conclude by citing two of the written texts produced in the lesson I have discussed, both of which, in the terminology Martin and Rothery (1980, 1981) have proposed, are examples of Recounts, the first of which is somewhat more complete than the second.

Text 1
One day I forgot my lunch and Mrs S. hat (had) to ring my mum up to bring my lunch and I got a jam donut and two pese (pieces) of fru(i)t and a sosisg (sausage) roll and a drink. It was yummy. The end.

Text 2
One day I went (to) school and I remembered I forgot my lunch and I rang my mother she brot (brought) fich (fish) and chips.

Recounts – involving the simplest reconstruction of personal experience – are arguably the most commonly produced written genres in junior primary school education.[2] The children in the particular study I undertook, and who included the writers of the two examples in Texts 1 and 2, wrote a very large number of texts using the same basic generic structure throughout years 1 and 2 of schooling. In short, they showed remarkably little advance in their developing control of written genres, though they did admittedly, achieve some greater control of spelling and handwriting.

The children were, in fact, capable of doing considerably more in their writing development than such a finding may appear to reveal. Whenever a deliberate attempt was made to intervene, and to teach more explicitly for a control of other genres, they demonstrated capacity to handle these. We must conclude, therefore, that the persistence of the Recount in writing was a direct response to the demands of the curriculum genres in which they were generated, and which were a very frequent feature of the children's total curriculum experience over the first three years of schooling. In participating in such genres with their teachers, the children were enabled to do no more in the linguistic patterns they generated, both spoken and written, than to revisit and recreate aspects of personal experience. Yet personal experience – the theme of Food is itself a good example – does open up many possibilities for exploration of new experience and information, in ways more consistent, I would argue, with what an education is supposed to be about.

It is time for education – teacher education in particular – to look much more directly at the very intimate relationship between the curriculum context and genre and the written genres children produce. It is time, too, to re-examine some of the basic assumptions about what constitutes useful knowledge for the early years of schooling. Since knowledge, experience and information will be themselves encoded in the various linguistic patterns used, it should be clear that as we seek to change the nature of the knowledge examined, offering more genuine intellectual challenge to young children, we will also necessarily need to change the linguistic patterns, spoken and written, which are a part of early schooling.

NOTES

1 This paper is a very much revised version of another paper, 'Curriculum genres: towards a description of the construction of knowledge in schools', given at a *Working Conference on Interaction of Spoken and Written Language in Educational Settings*, held at the university of New England, 11–15 November, 1985, and organised on behalf of the Language in Education Network.
2 In fact, as the rest of my study has subsequently revealed, the Recount is probably the commonest genre throughout all the years of primary school. The reasons for this, while certainly closely related to the themes discussed in this paper, actually merit another complete paper to do them justice.

REFERENCES

Bambrough, L. (1982) *My Lunch!*, Reading 360 Series. Melbourne: Longman Cheshire.
Christie, F. (1985a) 'Curriculum genre and schematic structure of classroom discourse', in Walker, R. F. *et al. A Knock on the door: an analysis of classroom discourse*, in Hasan, R. (ed.) *Discourse on Discourse*, a Report on a Working Conference on Discourse Analysis, held at Macquarie University, 21–25 February 1983, Applied Linguistics Association of Australia, Occasional Papers Number 7.
Christie, F. (1989) *Language Education*. Oxford: Oxford University Press.
Christie, F. (1986) 'Learning to write: where do written texts come from?' A keynote paper at the Twelfth Australian Reading Association Annual Conference on *Text and Context*, held at the Sheraton Hotel, Perth, 2–5 July 1986.
Eiler, M. A. (1986) 'Thematic distribution as a heuristic for written discourse

function', in Couture, B. (ed.) *Functional Approaches to Writing: Research Perspectives*. London: Frances Pinter.

Halliday, M. A. K. (1985) *An Introduction to Functional Grammar*. London: Edward Arnold.

Halliday, M. A. K. and Hasan, R. (1989) *Language, Context and Text: Aspects of Language in a Social-Semiotic Perspective*. Oxford: Oxford University Press.

Kress, G. (1982) *Learning to Write*. London: Routledge and Kegan Paul.

Martin, J. R. (1984) 'Language, register and genre'. A reading in the Deakin University BEd *Children Writing Course, Course Reader*. Geelong, Victoria: Deakin University Press, pp. 21–30.

Martin, J. R. and Rothery, J. (1980, 1981) Writing Project Reports, Numbers 1 and 2, *Working Papers in Linguistics*. Linguistics Department: University of Sydney.

Rothery, J. (1984) 'The development of genres – primary to junior secondary school', in Deakin University BEd *Children Writing Course, Study Guide*. Geelong, Victoria: Deakin University Press.

Ventola, Eija (1984) 'Can I help you?: A Systemic-functional Exploration of Service Encounter Interaction'. Unpublished PhD thesis, University of Sydney.

15

The Rights of Bilingual Children

HELEN SAVVA ──────────────────────────────◇

Operating in more than one language is *normal*. It is not in itself a problem and it certainly does not constitute a learning difficulty. Yet those of us who live in England live in a country in which monolingualism is still regarded as the norm. This is both a cause and an effect of official attitudes towards bilingualism and bilingual children. Most recently, we have had National Curriculum provisions placed before us which, whatever their good qualities in other respects, are still inadequate regarding the education of bilingual children in England.

Bilingualism is a sensitive issue. It arouses strong emotions in teachers. They can feel defensive, threatened, guilty; they can feel that they are doing their best in difficult circumstances and with very little guidance or support. Quite often when I talk to teachers about bilingualism, some say (and they say it as though they have really caught me out) 'but my parents only want their children to learn English at school' and/or 'but the bilingual children in my class won't *admit* that they can speak another language'. And I always want to ask: 'Well, why do you think that might be? Just ask yourself why'.

LINGUISTIC IDENTITY

Bilingualism and multilingualism are key elements of the language experience of 70 per cent of the world's population and of many of the children we teach. The majority of people in the world operate in more than one language in their daily lives in countries which are officially or unofficially bilingual. Yet in England it's normal to be monolingual and that's official. Traditionally, we have learnt a few 'high status' northern European languages, i.e. French and German (badly). But there is a stubborn and grudging resistance to the languages spoken by significant numbers of children in our schools. That is why children will not talk openly about their bilingualism and that is why their home languages sometimes fall into disuse. Our institutions have ignored and devalued them. Of course parents want their children to have a good command of English, and one of our jobs as educators is to help the children achieve that. But in the course of doing so, the very worst thing that we can do to children is to deny the wholeness of their linguistic and cultural experience and identity.

Why is it that so many bilingual adults of my generation have anglicised names? We anglicised our names to avoid being ridiculed for being different! My name was anglicised by the man who registered my birth. My parents said 'Eleni' and he thought my passage through life would be eased considerably if I was called Helen instead – and Helen it has been. Another incident from my childhood: when I was eight, my mother was strongly advised by my head teacher against taking me on a six-month trip to Cyprus. She was told that it would ruin my education because I would forget my English. My mother took me anyway and immediately enrolled me at the American Academy in Nicosia, where almost all my lessons were in English. However, it was a relatively enlightened institution for those days, and we had two hours of Greek language tuition each week. But I missed the opportunity of going to a local Cypriot primary school where I would have been immersed in the language and would have learnt through the language.

Throughout my schooling in England no-one took the slightest interest in the fact that I spoke another language. So what was there to tell? Of course my parents wanted me to learn English but they were never given the opportunity to decline the offer of Greek lessons at my mainstream schools. So I and many others like me learnt early on that the way to get by was to be like everybody else. We craved assimilation.

For some bilingual children things are a lot better than was my experience and for some they are not. My family and I were 'foreigners' and to understand what it is to be a 'foreigner' – you have to be foreign. Bilingualism isn't only a language issue; it's also a race issue.

ONE CHILD'S BILINGUALISM: POSITIVE PRACTICE AND NEGATIVE ATTITUDES

Satvinder, who is nine years old, wrote the story of Jethro Banks in Punjabi: this version appears (in reduced form) on page 251. She wrote it at the invitation of a bilingual advisory teacher who had been working in her classroom. This was the very first occasion on which Satvinder had been encouraged to use her knowledge of her home language at school. Activities which led up to Satvinder's piece of writing included listening to the story of Jethro Banks being told in English and Punjabi, followed by the class collaborating in groups to re-work the story and present it in dramatic form. In undertaking this work the children were invited to draw upon their whole linguistic repertoire (language/s, accents, dialects). Having written her story in Punjabi, Satvinder produced another version in English. Here it is:

The Story of Jethro Banks

One girl lived with her father. Her name was Emma. Her father wanted Emma to marry a rich man but Emma wanted to marry a poor boy called Jethro Banks. When her father found out, he sent Emma to her uncles house. One day Jethro Banks was working on the farm when a strong disease came, it was called small pox. It was so strong that Jethro Banks died. All the people buried him in the grave. When Emma's father found out he dared not to tell Emma. One day Emma was sitting in her uncles house, when a knock on the door came. Emma opened it. In front of her, there stood Jethro Banks. Emma did not know that he was dead. Jethro Banks had brought his horse, so the two of them rode off to Emma's uncles house. That day it was so cold that Emma tied a yellow scarf around Jethro's neck. When Emma got to her father's house, Jethro dropped her off and went back to his grave. Emma told her father that Jethro had brought her back but her father said, 'No, he's dead'. So her father went to show Emma Jethro's grave. When they got there, they dug and dug, and there lay Jethro wearing the yellow scarf around his neck.

The End

Satvinder explained to her teacher that it would be impossible to write a literal translation since differences in language structures would render the second version nonsensical. She was able to discuss the differences in language structures between Punjabi and English and thus explore her knowledge of two language systems explicitly.

In the transcript which follows, Satvinder and a group of friends in her class discuss their experience of being bilingual with the advisory teacher.

Teacher:	*Do you speak your Punjabi more at home or do you speak it more at school?*
Jaswant:	*I speak it more at home like we come from an Indian family and so we speak it mostly at home cos like they're Indian and they speak Indian so I speak Indian.*
Teacher	*And what about the children in your class, do you speak Punjabi to them?*
Jaswant:	*No.*
Teacher:	*Why is that?*
Jaswant:	*Cos most of them are English and my Indian friends and I don't speak Indian with them like I sort of get shy speaking to them.*
Sharan:	*Yeah. Sometimes like we are talking in the*

Punjabi version

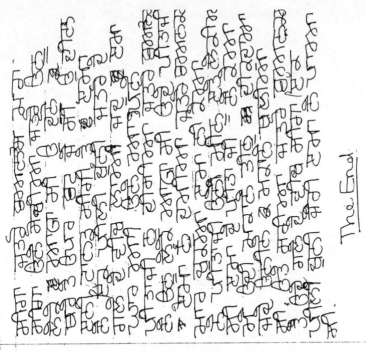

The End

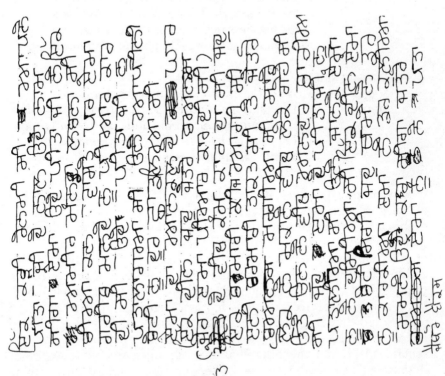

	playground and someone English comes along then like we kind of stop and start talking English 'cos I think I'm going to get the mick taken out of me and things like that.
Teacher:	*Do you get a lot of that?*
All:	*Yeah! yeah! They start saying 'bard, bard' and stuff like that.*
Teacher:	*What do they start saying?*
Sharan:	*'Bard, bard', 'ding, ding' and all that and putting on, making fun.*
Sherekha:	*That's what J- - - - does, she goes 'ardi, ardi, ardi'.*
Sharan:	*They make up stupid words and that, and they swear and that.*
Teacher:	*Do they?*
All:	*Yeah.*
Satvinder:	*Cos they reckon that what you are saying is something about them.*
Sharan:	*They think that if you're talking in Indian and we look at em they start saying horrible things they don't some of them don't even know what we're talking about then they go and tell the teacher and the teacher like they'll say some of the teachers will say don't talk in your own language because other people can't understand it.*
Jaswant and Sherekha:	*Yeah, they say it's an English school.*
Sharan:	*Yeah and the children say to you there is no place for Indians in this school and country and things. They say go back to your own country so that people can understand you.*

It may be that teachers at the school would be both surprised and alarmed to learn about the overt racism which is the shared experience of the children who contributed to the discussion. I would want to say to people who insist that bilingual children won't admit that they speak another language, that we have to provide an environment in which children feel they can. In order to use their whole linguistic repertoire in schools children have to be secure in the knowledge that their languages have a legitimate role to play in their learning. If they come to understand that languages other than English can only ever be peripheral or suspect that racism will be countenanced or ignored, they will remain silent. On the other hand, if we open up our classrooms linguistically and culturally, we will be surprised just how forthcoming bilingual children and their parents can be.

DIVERSITY OF MULTILINGUAL EXPERIENCE

Here is Tacko, a small boy who was four when I knew him. He attended nursery school in Deptford. Tacko and his parents were Kurdish refugees. His mother took him to school every morning. Steve Cummings, his teacher, was genuinely interested in the linguistic and cultural experiences of all the children. Tacko was therefore prepared to share some of his experiences with Steve.

Steve made a recording of Tacko who wanted to sing a song; this turned out to be a Kurdish resistance song which Tacko sang with genuine feeling. A conversation followed during which Tacko revealed a surprisingly sophisticated grasp of the situation in Kurdistan, for one so young.

Steve:	*What do the people of Kurdistan want to happen? Do they want the war to finish?*
Tacko:	*They want to don't fight. Know what? We say 'We shall fight! We shall win! Viva, Viva, Kurdistan!' You know why we said that? Because the soldiers got our house at Kurdistan.*
Steve:	*Does your family want to go back? If they could live in Kurdistan without fighting?*
Tacko:	*No.*
Steve:	*Aren't they going to go back to Kurdistan?*
Tacko:	*No, they won't because the soldiers will kill us. They won't let us into our house, they've got our house as their house.*
Steve:	*What if the soldiers go away and never come back? Would your parents go back to Kurdistan?*
Tacko:	*Yes . . . yes, if there was no fighting . . . all the soldiers killed and in hospital . . . they would go back to Kurdistan, if there was no fighting and get our house back.*

Tacko took the tape home. Two days later Tacko's mother brought Steve a video tape which had been smuggled out of Kurdistan because she wanted him to understand more about the situation there and how it affected her family.

That kind of trust doesn't just happen. We have to earn it. With luck, Tacko will hold onto his very strong sense of personal identity and his commitment to his home language and culture. Meanwhile, his knowledge of the English language and of the interplay of cultures revealed through English will develop and become increasingly sophisticated. Tacko has the right to choose how the languages and cultures which are part of his life should exist and operate in relation to each other. And it is different for each child.

One of the key lessons to be learnt about bilingual children is that they are not a homogeneous group. There is a tendency to discuss them and their needs as though they were identical. Linguistically, socially, culturally, politically, the lives of bilingual children are complex and their experiences diverse. They operate along a continuum of language competencies in English and a home language or languages, ranging from virtual beginners to full competence. Some are literate in languages other than English; others only speak those languages. Some are members of established and organised communities. Others belong to groups in a state of flux: unsettled and on the move. Some bilingual children attend multilingual schools; others attend predominantly mono-ethnic schools where English is the only language recognised; others attend schools where they constitute a linguistic majority.

Two examples will help to illustrate this diversity. The first is from a multilingual school in the east end of London where I worked as co-ordinator of the National Writing Project in the ILEA. It was a school that did more than value linguistic and cultural diversity; it placed it at the centre of children's learning. It was there in the range of languages spoken, on the notices and displays around the school, in the activities of the parents and other adults in the school, in the resources in the classrooms and in the library, and in the children's work.

Here I met Runa and Jharna, two young girls who were constant companions in and out of the classroom. At the age of seven they were fluently bilingual, speaking both English and Sylheti at school. At home they spoke Sylheti with their families. Sylhet is a region in north-eastern Bangladesh whose language is sufficiently different from standard Bengali to be considered a distinct language rather than a dialect of Bengali. Runa and Jharna attended community school every afternoon and there they learnt standard Bengali and, for religious purposes, Arabic. They were linguistically competent and sophisticated at the age of seven. They had that confidence in part because they attended a mainstream school where they were taught by adults who genuinely valued their bilingualism, and in part because they attended a local community school.

Those of us who work in mainstream schools need closer contact with community schools and a clearer understanding of the work they do. Community languages should be taught in mainstream schools and should be made available to all children; but this will never replace the work of community schools. Bilingual children are greatly helped by access to both. Community schools enable children not only to learn the home language, but to learn through the home language about the culture and history of the country of origin. These schools provide intensive cultural experience and a special degree of parental involvement and commitment.

My second example takes us to a sixth-form college in north London where I met Phu, who produced an autobiographical piece of writing from which I quote two extracts:

The days were always sunny and warm, the rainy season was just about to start. I used to play around the streets and I knew everyone on the neighbourhood. The language I spoke and still speak was not English and it was a very very different kind of language. Near the street where I lived, there were many different kinds of languages, different turns you made would lead you to a street which spoke a different language from the one you had just been into. You had to learn the minimum of two languages if you wanted to travel around the country.

I still remember when my dad took me to my grans house, we ate fruit and I played with my cousins. I used to stay out all day and only came home when I was hungry. There was no end to having fun and it did not really cost much. The doors of my neighbours were never closed in the day time they were wide opened and I used to go in and out as if it was my own.

When the Viet Kong 'invaded' South Vietnam everything changed . . .

For nearly a year we waited for our turn to come to Great Britain, while in the camp, there were some English classes and they were taught by two English people with a Chinese/ Vietnamese interpreter by their side. In the time that I was there, all I learned was the name of a country on the World map. Everytime the teacher pointed to an island which is above the middle of the map, I was always the first one to say that it is England.

Occasionally, the class was taken to the seaside where the sands were so hot that you could not stand still and I always got sun burnt when ever I go to the seaside. We were once taken to a very very large park, called 'Ocean Park'. It was not a park but a combination of different things – Zoo, a fun fair, some Dolphins and others.

When I arrived at Heathrow Airport, I felt a breath of cold air and outside was very sunny, I thought that it was the cooling system but I was very wrong when I got out of the airport, it was so windy that I nearly could not walk for fear of being blown away by the wind. Getting used to the English weather was not easy, everyday I had to wear about one inch thickness of clothing and I used to go around looked like Humpty Dumpty.

I went to an English Primary School, I could not understand the pupils or the teachers when they spoke to me nor do they understand me when I spoke to them. They communicated to me by hands and doing other things as an example, I in turn would do the same if I was communicating with them. It was like a chicken talking to a duck, the chicken

can only say coc-coc and the duck can only say quack-quack.
  A year went by, we moved to Bradford, and then to London after a year in Bradford. We have been living in London for more than five years now. When ever I get spare times I usually think about my past and also my future.

Tacko, Runa, Jharna and Phu are examples of the most positive thing that the Cox Report has to say about bilingual children. It appears in Chapter 6:

> *Many pupils are bilingual and sometimes biliterate and quite often literally know more about language than their teachers, at least in some respects.*

If we truly value children's linguistic competencies we will take the trouble to find out what they do know about language. If we don't value their linguistic competencies neither they nor their parents are likely to tell us what they know.

BILINGUALISM AND THE NATIONAL CURRICULUM

I want briefly to discuss the approach to bilingual children taken in the Cox Report and in the National Curriculum for English. Chapter 10 of the Report, entitled 'Bilingual Children', is not about how best to serve the interests as a whole of bilingual children; it is simply about teaching English as a second language. The Report at least gives its support to the now familiar idea that developing bilinguals learn best in the main-stream classroom. But in paragraph 10.10 we discover the sole purpose of this enlightened position:

> *The implications are therefore that, where bilingual pupils need extra help, this should be given in the classroom as part of normal lessons and there may be a need for bilingual teaching support and for books and other written materials to be available in the pupils' mother tongues until such time as they are competent in English.*

It would appear that resources which reflect linguistic diversity should be made available only to bilingual children and then only to those bilingual children who are in need of extra help. In addition these resources should be withdrawn when bilingual children become competent in English.
  This is transitional, not full bilingualism. It is not the development and mutual enrichment of two or more languages and cultures but the idea that development must involve the eventual supremacy of one language and the neglect of others.

In Wales, there is official recognition that bilingual education extends cultural and social choice (not so in England). In Wales, Welsh children have the right to bilingual education (not so in England). We know how hard-won that right was. Research quoted in Chapter 13 of the Cox Report about the growth of language competencies amongst bilingual Welsh and English speaking children tells us:

> *The eventual aim of teaching Welsh and English to pupils in primary schools is a degree of bilingualism which represents a worthwhile educational achievement at the age of 11 and which can be the basis for further progress in secondary school.*
>
> *As a result of these educational and social influences the great majority of pupils in Welsh-medium schools achieve a satisfactory degree of bilingualism by the age of 11 . . . The evidence accumulated over the course of APU surveys suggests that there are no significant differences between the performance at 11 in English of pupils educated mainly through Welsh and other pupils (whether the latter are in schools in Wales or elsewhere).*

It would appear that full, balanced bilingualism does benefit children's intellectual development, at least in Wales. The Cox Report maintains, however, that the positions in England and Wales are not comparable:

> *In Wales, Welsh is an official language and a core subject of the National Curriculum.*

Let us look at the word *official*. It is an officially verifiable fact that 59 per cent of bilingual children in Coventry speak Punjabi. 30 per cent of all children in Haringey are officially known to speak Greek (in a borough where bilingual children form 64 per cent of the school population). These children, and others like them throughout England, do not officially have the right to hold onto their bilingualism. To live in England and to be educated in English schools means that bilingual children must, first and foremost, embrace English at the expense of other languages; what happens to those other languages is a matter of official indifference. If communities want to maintain and develop the language and culture of the home, that is their responsibility. In English state schools, education will be conducted only in English and children's bilingualism will be transitional.

This is now where we stand with the National Curriculum. At a time when the idea has been gaining ground among teachers that mainstream schools should develop children's full bilingualism, we have statutes whose effect could be not just to declare illegitimate any discussion of home languages as media of instruction, but to dissuade teachers from valuing children's use of home languages as instruments of learning in the curriculum at all.

It is a great irony that the Cox Report argues for this position in the name of equal opportunities. English has to be the first language and medium of instruction because 'a good command of English is the key to equality of opportunity':

> We believe that all children should be enabled to attain a full command of the English language, both spoken and written. Otherwise they will be disadvantaged, not only in their study of other subjects, but also in their working life. We note in this respect we are following the path already trodden by the Swann Committee. They stated firmly: '. . . the key to equality of opportunity, to academic success and, more broadly, to participation on equal terms as a full member of society, is good command of English and the emphasis must therefore we feel be on the learning of English'. The Swann Committee had also noted '. . . the views expressed very clearly to us at our various meetings with parents from the whole range of ethnic minority groups that they want and indeed expect the education system to give their children above all a good command of English as rapidly as possible . . .'

It is misguided to argue that the only thing bilingual children need to succeed in their personal, social and working lives is a good command of English. The argument rests on a simplistic and superficial notion of equality. It assumes that we share identical aspirations about education, about our working lives, about our participation in society. Equality of opportunity becomes synonymous with identical provision for all (except in Wales). Thus, learning in more than one language and the maintenance of home languages in mainstream classrooms are seen as potentially divisive. In the pursuit of English we ignore children's home languages on the grounds of equality. What kind of equality is that?

There cannot be equality of any sort if children's home languages are ignored. Unless social and educational policies recognise the rights of bilingual children in England, a process of language loss is inevitable. It is illogical to argue that:

> It should be made clear to English-speaking pupils that classmates whose first language is Bengali or Cantonese, or any other of the scores of languages spoken by the school population . . . have languages quite as systematic and rule-governed as their own. We also believe that 'civilised respect' for other languages is based on the recognition that all languages are able to express complex emotions and ideas.

and simultaneously insist on the supremacy of English.

BILINGUAL CHILDREN AND ASSESSMENT

We ought to look briefly at the question of bilingual children and assessment. We now understand that children who are learning English as an additional language should be actively encouraged to use their proficiency in one language in order to learn the new language and simultaneously learn about other things. Jim Cummins (1984) and others have stressed the creative interplay between languages and have pointed out that although surface features between, say, Gujerati and English are clearly separate, there is an underlying proficiency which is common across languages. This common proficiency makes it possible to transfer linguistic and other knowledge.

This influential idea has had a positive impact on classroom practice. It has certainly helped to quash the foolish notion that bilingual children go about their business in the world in a state of perpetual linguistic confusion. But the interactive development of competence in more than one language takes time – too much time, apparently, for National Curriculum testing procedures.

Currently, teachers have the 'choice' – not really a choice at all – of disapplying bilingual children from the National Curriculum and its testing procedures if they have only the beginnings of English, or accepting, if children are at a transitional stage of learning English, that their test results (their levels) are going, certainly in English, to be lower than those of their monolingual peers, even though they are engaged in essential cognitive activity of a high order.

Statutory orders on assessment arrangements at Key Stage 1 allow children to be assessed in home languages in Mathematics and Science, where circumstances allow. The orders prohibit this in English. We can understand the argument which says, 'English is English. English can't be a language other than English'. The problem lies in the decision not to recognise that for bilingual children, the development of competence in English is complementary to the development of competence in a home language or languages. For this and other reasons (like the inappropriateness of the idea of subject English to most primary-school curricula, and developments in the secondary-school subject which now include within English the study of media and communications, for example), it would be much better to rename 'English': 'Language and Communications' would be an improved alternative.

The government currently proposes that when bilingual children gain lower levels than they would gain if operating in their strongest language, that is simply an indication that they need more support. According to the Cox Report, to record a low level of achievement would not reflect a child's general ability, but indicate that he or she needed 'special help in English language skills' to 'overcome their problems with the English language'. We are presented here with a deficit view of bilingual children and an inadequate model of their language learning and development. No mention is made of the crude, invidious comparisons likely to be made within and between schools as a result.

There is no way round this problem at present. The position of those bilingual children for whom English is still the weaker language, in the face of levels, is unjust and unacceptable. We must make sure, at least, that the systems we develop for teacher assessment during a Key Stage are of the sort which build up an authentic picture of a child's achievements and needs over time, including references to cognitive breakthroughs which a teacher can see developing bilingual children making.

THE MULTILINGUAL CLASSROOM

Much of what I have written, especially about the National Curriculum, has been critical. I have highlighted commonly held misconceptions which can undervalue and obstruct bilingual children's achievements. It is equally important, however, to acknowledge the excellent work carried out in many LEAs, schools and classrooms by teachers who succeed in valuing and extending children's multilingualism. In the hands of informed and imaginative teachers (whether bilingual or monolingual) the multilingual classroom can provide the most challenging and intellectually stimulating environment for all children. In conclusion, I offer three principles which we should adopt in order to construct such an environment, and provide examples in support of them.

> *Create the conditions which enable children to gain access to the whole curriculum by encouraging them to use, as appropriate, their strongest or preferred language.*

Özlem is a bilingual child who is a virtual beginner in English. She attends junior school, where she is the only Turkish speaker in her class. However, Özlem has access to the curriculum and can operate at an appropriate cognitive level because her teacher encourages her to learn through her strongest and preferred language. As well as speaking Turkish, she reads and writes it fluently.

Özlem takes an active part as her class carries out science experiments which test different fabrics. Although she does not understand English yet, she can observe the experiments as they are carried out. The synthesising and internalising of ideas is done in Turkish; so is the recording of data and information, as we can see from her writing on page 261.

Özlem is making connections between and across languages. This ability to reflect on the structure of language has to be advantageous to the learner. Children who are learning English as a second language can enter school at any point in their educational career. The fact that they may not as yet speak, read or write English fluently does not mean that their intellectual development should come to an abrupt

"ÖZLEM
Testing Fabrics for Flammability   10.3.88

Candle   muum
Sand
match   kiprit
Plasticine   pilastik
tongs   mangal
fabric
stop clock

11 çeşit beele, hepsi birbirisind ayrı hepsini denedik ve şöyle oldu.

1. rengi mavi boyu 5s. birde alevlendi veyandı yerini koz halini aldı . 2. boyu 42s yanarken burusuyordu yandı . 3. rengi kırmızı beyaz boyu 40 s. yanarken kırışıyordu . boya da gittikçe kısalıyordu. Sonla yere düştü
4. Rengi açık mavi , cinsi naylon boyu 72s. yanıyordu ama yanıp kopar ya yanarak aşa düşuyordu .
5. cinsi pamup, rengi beyaz . siyah , kırmız boyu 63. s birden tutuşuyor yanarak kıvrılıyor ve yanarak yere düşüyor.
6. Felt - yanarken dumanı çok siyah . Yandında çok mce kalıyor.
7. man made boyu 29s birde tutuşuyor . yanan yer kopuyor ve aşa düşüyor.
8. Satin , yanıyor yanan yer koparak aşa düşüyor. boyu 29s.

9 ret curtain 5s. alevlenmiyor . yanan yer siyahlaşıyor

Autobiographical piece by Loretta

لورتا

شرح زندگی می

اسم می لورتا . . . . است و در تاریخ ۲۴ نوامبر ۱۹۷۵ در تهران به دنیا
آمدم. مادرم مسلمان است ولی پدرم از ارامنه مسیحی بود. وقتی که می بیست ماهه
بودم، پدرم در اثر تصادف رانندگی فوت کرد و یک سال بعد از آن حادثه مادرم مرا به
انگلستان آورد و ما در لندن ساکن شدیم. می درسی سه سالگی به کودکستان رفتم.
در آنجا کم کم زبان انگلیسی را یاد گرفتم، البته اولین یاد گرفتن این زبان برایم
مشکل بود زیرا که می فقط به زبان ارمنی صحبت می کردم و از سن چهار سالگی هم
روزهای یکشنبه به مدرسه ارامنه رفتم تا خواندن و نوشتن این زبان را یاد بگیرم.

در سن پنج سالگی به مدرسه دولتی انگلیسی رفتم و سه سال بعد در امتحان
ورودی مدرسه خصوصی High School شرکت
کرده و قبول شدم و از آن موقع تا به حال در این مدرسه مشغول تحصیل
می باشم.

در سن هشت سالگی به علت علاقه ای که به زبان مادری ام یعنی فارسی
داشتم به مدرسه ایرانی رستم آموگم که در روزهای شنبه تشکیل می شود. در اینجا
بنا نظر داشتن تعلیمی خوب و فداکار و همچنین دوستان ایرانی دانستم در یادگیری
این زبان موفق شوم. با دانستن این زبانها می توانم با فامیل و دوستانم
ارتباط برقرار نمایم.

بنابراین می تمام روزهای هفته را به مدرسه می رویم و شب تکالیف این
مدارس را انجام می دهیم و هفته ای یک روز هم بعد از پایان مدرسه درسی
پیانو دارم و می تا به سال از نشست grade و چهار grade آن را امتحان دارم
و قبول شده ام و در حال حاضر برای امتحان grade پنجم خود را آماده می کنم.
در ضمن از سال گذشته زبان فرانسه و از امسال هم زبان لاتین جزو دروسی
مدرسه ماست که اجبار باید یاد بگیرم. اگرچه تکالیف این مدرسه ها زیاد هستند و
وقت زیادی را از می می گیرند ولی بخاطر علاقه ای که به آنها پیدا کرده ام کوشش میکنم
که بجای تفریح و بازی وقتم را صرف مطالعه و یادگیری این زبانها بکنم. البته
خانواده ام مرا در درسهایم کمک کرده و همیشه تشویقم کرده اند.

Last year in our English history lesson we had
to write a project in the form of a newspaper in partners,
about Henry VII. and the Battle of Bosworth Field. I was
the editor and our newspaper got distinction.

My activities at school are netball, hockey, Gym,
dance in the winter and tennis, rounders and athletics
in the summer. I enjoy these sports very much.

این بود خلاصه ای از شرح زندگی می و امیدوارم بتوانم در آینده با کوشش
بیشتری به همه هدفهای خود برسم.

end. They may, for example, have a great deal of knowledge about mathematics, science or literature. When working in a comprehensive school in the east end of London I was told a story about a fourth-year pupil who had arrived recently from Bangladesh. Withdrawn from his mainstream mathematics lesson, he was taken to work with a small group on 'extra maths'. After completing a series of elementary calculations which the teacher provided, he pushed himself angrily from the table, chalked a complex algebraic equation on the blackboard and said, 'In Bangladesh, me!'

Loretta is a highly competent trilingual speaker, reader and writer of Armenian, Farsi and English. She moves in and out of these languages effortlessly. The autobiographical piece of writing opposite was produced at Rustam Community School and is entitled, 'A description of my life' (see page 262).

Most of the piece, which in English translation begins:

> *My name is Loretta and I was born in Tehran 24 November 1975. My mother is Moslem but my father was a Christian Armenian . . .*

is written in Farsi. At a particular point Loretta spontaneously decides to switch from Farsi to English. It is probably not insignificant that the switch comes when she describes her English history lesson about Henry VII and the Battle of Bosworth. Loretta reverts to Farsi to conclude her piece and writes:

> *This was a brief description of my life and I hope I can achieve all my aims in the future with greater effort.*

Operating in the preferred language is not something which should be confined to children who are in the early stages of learning English as a second language. Many bilingual children operate naturally in this way, switching between languages in speech or writing in response to context and audience.

> *Take every opportunity to promote children's understanding of cultural diversity by presenting a world view through the curriculum and through the materials selected to resource it.*

A class of year 6 children was embarking on a term's topic on 'Communication'. Since mathematics is a universal form of communication and since it owes its development to many cultures, the teacher, Bet Lowe, decided to make it a significant part of the topic. In particular, Bet wanted children to examine some of the contributions made to maths by many cultures. In considering the names of numbers and the way names used could reflect the base used (5 and 10 generally), and why this was so, the children examined the number systems of the Egyptians, Babylonians, Abyssinians and Mayans. Bet Lowe writes:

The Mayan system interested us most – it is a base 360 system, based on a year. It facilitated calculations of the seasons. This made us aware of how closely number systems are bound to culture. We looked at numbers in many languages to see what patterns could be found. From this, children were asked to develop their own counting system, having first decided which base they would use, and to develop names and symbols for their numerals. This was followed by groups of children setting problems for other groups to solve.

The children were thoroughly fascinated by the realisation that numbers and number systems aren't just the ones we know and learn about; there is a wealth of knowledge that we don't acknowledge. All we can do is what others have already done, and there are whole areas of number development that we have forgotten about.

The children developed their own number systems (see two examples on page 265).

Take every opportunity to ensure that the curriculum both reflects and makes authentic use of the linguistic diversity in our schools and the rest of society.

In her infant classroom, Avril Bristow produced dual-text story books with her pupils, their parents and other adults. The children worked on the original text and on the illustrations. The adults participating in the project produced a second version of the text in a variety of home languages (see page 266).

The next sequence of activities was part of a term's work on the theme of texts, designed by Lorraine Dawes and Derek Hoddy for two year 4 classes. They outline here their reasons for planning a cross-curricular theme on this subject.

We wanted a theme that would develop the children's awareness of the multiracial and multilingual society they live in, and develop their ability to think critically. Redbridge Junior School, in the London Borough of Redbridge, is mixed: approximately a third of the children are Jewish, and another third are of Asian origin. Such diversity is only a resource when it is actively utilised; children (or adults) do not spontaneously volunteer information about their cultural, linguistic or religious background unless encouraged to do so, in the confidence that such information will be positively received. How often can ethnic minority pupils think to themselves as they are learning, 'That's my history, that's my language, that's my culture'? The curriculum has to create the climate for discussion that invites all children to share their experience. We wanted to make the most of every opportunity.

[continued on page 268]

Our number System

Num	English	Num	English
On	One	•	1
to	two	••	2
tee	three	•••	3
fo	four	••••	4
fi	five	•••••	5
Sx	Six		6
Sn	Seven		7
Egt	eight		8
nin	nine		9
hundread	hundred		100
thitid	thousand		1000
tethisind	10 thousand	4|||	10,000
mill	million		10,000000
tamill	ten Million		10,0000000

by Gurindar Jagatmis waggas.

Number Systems.

1, zit
2, zoss
3, ery
4, dif
5, twust
6, twust zit
7, twust zoss
8, twust ery
9, twust dif
10, blum
11, blum zit
12, blum zoss
13, blum ery
14, blum dif
15, blop
16, blop twust zit
17, blop twust zoss
18, blop twust ery
19, blop twust dif
20, zobs

by Mahjabeen

Dual language texts

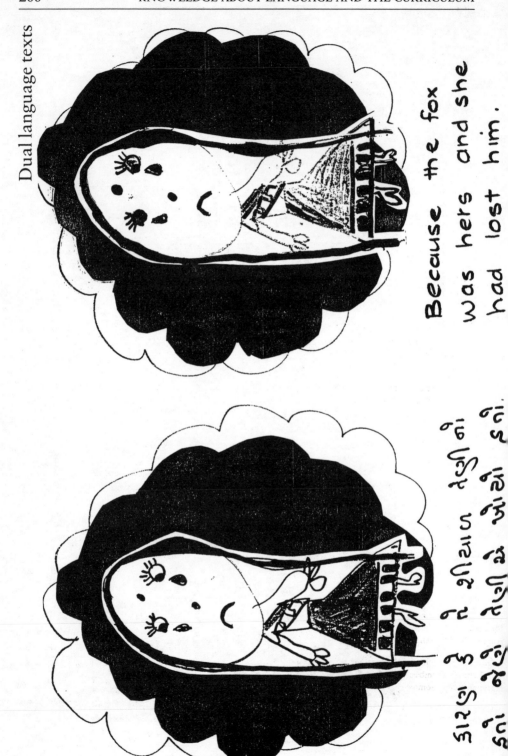

Because the fox was hers and she had lost him.

INFORMATION ABOUT A BOOK
Look inside, near the front of the book

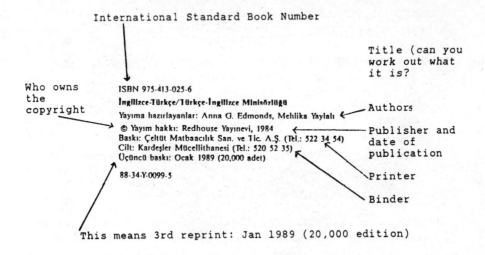

International Standard Book Number

Title (can you
work out what
it is?

Who owns
the
copyright

ISBN 975-413-025-6
İngilizce-Türkçe/Türkçe-İngilizce Minisözlüğü
Yayıma hazırlayanlar: Anna G. Edmonds, Mehlika Yaylalı ← Authors
© Yayım hakkı: Redhouse Yayınevi, 1984 ←— Publisher and
Baskı: Çeltüt Matbaacılık San. ve Tic. A.Ş. (Tel.: 522 34 54) date of
Cilt: Kardeşler Mücellithanesi (Tel.: 520 52 35) publication
Üçüncü baskı: Ocak 1989 (20,000 adet)

Printer

88-34-Y-0099-5

Binder

This means 3rd reprint: Jan 1989 (20,000 edition)

Here are some details about the same book published in Hindi and
English (the dates of publication are not the same).

What city are they published in?

How do you write it in Hindi?

What is Hindi for 4, 1 and 2?

Rs. C.

मूल्य: ६ रु.

©आईबीएच पब्लिशिंग कंपनी, १९८२
प्रथम हिन्दी संस्करण: १९८२

© IBH Publishing Company, 1977

First published : 1977
Reprinted : 1980, 1981

फोटोटाइपसेंटर:
पलकमती प्रिंटर्स प्राइवेट लिमिटेड,
१५ वी मंजिल, नरीमन भवन,
नरीमन पॉइंट, बंबई ४०० ०२१

मुद्रक:
डॉ. जी. मीरचंदानी,
आईबीएच प्रिंटर्स,
मरोल नाका, मथुरादास वसनजी रोड,
अंधेरी (पूर्व), बंबई ४०० ०५९

Printed by A.C. Chobe at IBH Printers,
Marol Naka, Mathuradas Vasanji Road,
Andheri East, Bombay 400 059.

Published by P.C. Manaktala for IBH Publishing Company,
412 Tulsiani Chambers, 212 Backbay Reclamation,
Nariman Point, Bombay 400 021

प्रकाशक:
पी. सी. मानकटाला,
आईबीएच पब्लिशिंग कंपनी,
४१२ तुलसीयानी चेंबर्स, २१२ बॅकबे रिक्लेमेशन.
नरीमन पॉइंट, बंबई ४०० ०२१

> *Another concern was that children tend to accept*
> *everything they read at face value, while subconsciously*
> *absorbing the hidden messages. We wanted to give them the*
> *habit of thinking critically about their reading, by developing*
> *the language they need to manipulate such ideas.*

The activities, spanning several weeks, included a study of how a book is made (incorporating the idea that books are published in many languages). The classes discussed the kinds of stereotyping sometimes found in books, and the ways in which our perceptions of people can be influenced by such stereotypes. They read fairy tales and considered how alternative readings could be achieved by challenging the writers' intentions. They examined newspapers published in languages other than English, both abroad and locally, and discussed the needs of people in Britain for newspapers in their community languages.

On page 267 is an example of one of the information sheets which the teachers devised.

CONCLUSION

There is a sense of community in the successful multilingual classroom. Linguistic and cultural similarities and differences between children are central to the learning that goes on there. It would be simplistic and naive to suggest that tensions do not exist in such classrooms, or that children do not experience conflict and contradiction, or that racism is not a factor. However, I do believe that children are empowered if that which is shared and common, as well as that which is personal and individual, has status in the classroom.

Meanwhile, we have the National Curriculum. On the whole, it fails to provide the positive framework for the successful multilingual classroom that we might have hoped for. However, we must do our best to interpret the statutory requirements in ways which increase bilingual children's sense of achievement and affirmation, and increase all children's knowledge of the linguistic diversity which is a permanent feature of our society.

ACKNOWLEDGMENTS

In writing this article, I have had the benefit of the advice, insights and classroom examples of: John Richmond, Sue Baylik, Avril Bristow, Steve Cummings, Gill Dalley, Ann-Marie Davies, Lorraine Dawes, Diane Drabble, Mary Fowler, Derek Hoddy, Kulvinder Lidder, Bet Lowe, Melissa Marsh, Gnani Perinpanayagam and Shahla Taheri-White. I thank them all.

REFERENCES

Cummins, J. (1984) 'Bilingualism and Special Education: Issues in Assessment and Pedagogy', *Multilingual Matters*, 6.
This paper was first given as a talk to the annual conference of the National Association for the Teaching of English, April 1990.

English Teachers and the History of English

PAT O'ROURKE and MIKE O'ROURKE ⎯⎯⎯⎯⎯⎯◇

THE GHOST IN THE CLASSROOM

Let us imagine, to begin with, one of those rare moments in the classroom when time seems to be suspended and we are able to observe and reflect on what is taking place.

A child is writing. We could list some of the 'variables' that enter into the situation: the relationship of the child to the teacher, the child's experience, the teacher's experience, and so on. But one crucial variable is the nature of the language itself, which the child is struggling to master; within that is another, rather ghostly variable: the history of how that language has been shaped. As the child writes, the traces of that long historical process are present in every moment.

She is patiently forming letters and trying to relate them to sounds and meanings. The letters that she uses were borrowed from the Romans, who, in turn, borrowed them from the Greeks, who, in turn, had adapted theirs from the Phoenicians. The motto seems to be – if in need of a writing system, borrow someone else's. The problem is that someone else's writing system may not fit your language very well. Some of the problems faced by the modern child, then, still stem from the fact that the powerful, literate Roman Empire dominated Europe for hundreds of years and then became the model of literacy for the centuries to follow.

As the child writes, her path is strewn with anomalous and puzzling obstacles. Letters which stand for no recognisable sound: w*h*at, *gh*ost, hi*gh*; or different letters which stand for the same sound: p*ie*, sk*y*, s*i*gn, g*ui*le, b*uy*, *eye*, *I*, and so on. As adults we have often ceased to wonder about these oddities. If we are highly literate, we may even enjoy them as examples of our weird and wonderful language. It is more profitable, I think, to see such words as the bearers of history, small representatives of some strange and winding paths. Some have emerged from certain strong and persistent currents in language; others are the freak results of pure chance.

Many of our spellings are inconsistent because of two conflicting currents at work in historical variation: the natural movement of sound change over the centuries clashes head on with the desire to standardise the system. So spellings which once represented sounds with reasonable accuracy became fixed as the standard form. In the meantime, the sound has moved on.

'Ghost' is one of those words which owes its spelling to a freak of history. After working for years in Holland, Caxton set up his printing press in London, in 1476. He mistakenly assumed that the Dutch digraph 'gh' at the beginning of a word was also an English spelling. He spelt 'girl' as 'gherle' and 'goose' as 'ghoos'. Gradually, most of these changes were dropped, but the 'gh' remains at the beginning of words with unpleasant connotations (for example, ghoulish, ghastly).

So, are we to sit down by the struggling young writer and solemnly explain about Caxton's mistake, perhaps apologising in retrospect for the vagaries of history? Well, sometimes it does, in fact, help to tell children the stories that lie behind some of the anomalies of English. It can help to replace a rather empty sense of mystification with a fuller sense of the mysterious process of language development.

However, the aim of this chapter is to suggest that a knowledge of historical variation is of use to English teachers in a broader and more general sense.

What can English teachers, then, gain from such knowledge?

Firstly, they can gain a clearer perception of the problems faced by young learners when they make the crucial transition from spoken to written English. Writing lends itself far more readily to standardising norms and fixed rules. Speech, especially casual conversation, is, as M. A. K. Halliday says, at 'the leading edge of unconscious change and development in any language' (Halliday and Hasan, 1989, p. 11).

Our pupils are, unwittingly, at the centre of this continuous historical struggle between fixity and movement in language. An understanding of this can help us to help them.

Secondly, teachers can gain from an understanding of the actual process of language change and the causes of that change. This is important for two reasons.

The resistance to linguistic change is a tenacious feature of our society. It is also a potent source of both popular and 'educated' mythologies about language. It is important to understand the nature of this resistance, as well as to discover the all-too-human sources of the myths. Without such an understanding, the myths continue to be transmitted uncritically from generation to generation, and teachers are used, some more willingly than others, as the instruments of that transmission.

The knowledge of how change comes about in language, and why it does, helps us to understand the character of language. We have to confront the puzzling duality of language, for example: at one and the same time, it is a huge system of enormous complexity and ancient lineage, and an instrument available for our personal use. We are both the objects of our language, created by it, and its creators, using it and even changing it, to suit our particular purposes. As English teachers, concerned with the creative abilities of our pupils, and concerned with powerful social phenomena such as bias and prejudice, we need to be aware of the ambiguous character of language. We manipulate it and are manipulated by it. A knowledge of historical variation also helps us to see that many of the features of language use which irritate language purists are simply evidence of long term changes at work. Instead of despising these features, we can learn to interpret them as forces within language. In the following sections of the chapter we will deal in turn with the issues raised in this introductory section, and then go on to discuss some practical classroom implications.

A KNOWLEDGE OF HISTORICAL VARIATION HELPS US TO UNDERSTAND THE WRITER'S PROBLEM NOW

Two important factors of historical variation were mentioned earlier in the chapter: a borrowed alphabet and sound changes over time. As a result of these factors, we have a writing system which contains six letters to represent a sound system of some twenty vowels (not counting the vowel systems of our regional accents). Letters which once re-presented an older sound system fairly consistently, became fixed as spelling was standardised; meanwhile, the sounds moved on. Vowels are more 'mobile' than consonants. They vary more between regional accents and they have changed more over time. Occasionally, a well-meaning and intelligent scholar like Richard Mulcaster (1582) would try to rationalise the system. He tried to reduce the number of unneces-sary letters (like the use of a double consonant in 'putt', 'grubb', 'ledd', for example) and to suggest that a final 'e' should regularly indicate a long vowel ('mat', 'mate') – the 'magic E' of our primary classrooms. But no one system ever prevailed. No one successfully legislated for all, though many were to try. Just to complicate matters, the greatest vowel change of all (the 'Great Vowel Shift', as it is called) took place between 1400 and 1600 'at precisely the same time as the spelling conventions were becoming codified', as Michael Stubbs points out (1980, p. 70). All the long vowels of English moved. The word 'sweet' had been pro-nounced 'sway-te'; the word 'name' had been pronounced 'nah-me'. Words like 'tail' and 'tale', originally quite different in pronunciation, became homophones. The spellings are interesting to historians of language in the same way that Pompeii is interesting to historians of the Ancient World: they are the visible evidence of a great upheaval. But for the writers in our classrooms they constitute a problem.

As adult speakers of the language we are all aware of the cliché that 'English spelling is a bit of a mess', but we can still tend to remain unaware of just exactly where the problems lie, and why. This is because we have learned to perceive our language as somehow 'natural', part of the very air we breathe. The problems of learners, especially slower learners, constantly remind us that it is not. When they hesitate over 'great' and 'grate', 'break' and 'brake', 'leap' and 'sweat', their hesitation has links to an historical chain that goes back to an inexplicable shift in the sound system of English that took place 500 years or so ago.

Another problem confronting the young writer is the divide between 'acceptable' and 'unacceptable' forms. This applies to speech to some extent, but is much more rigorously applied to writing. Many dialect speakers, for instance, use the form known as the double negative ('I don't know nothing about it') or they use verb forms like 'I knows' or 'we was'. As teachers, we are divided in our attitudes towards such forms in written work. For some, they are simply 'wrong', the products of ignorance or laziness. Others feel uncomfortable with the idea of eradicating dialect forms, and with them the identity and self-esteem of their users. But a knowledge of historical variation can break this deadlock by suggesting a third way: we can find out where these forms come from and what kind of forces are at work in language to produce them. The history of 'non-standard' uses of language can be a source of illumination in the classroom, instead of an oppressive social problem. This will be dealt with in more detail in the remaining sections of the chapter.

THE RESISTANCE TO CHANGE AND VARIATION IN LANGUAGE

Change and variation are intimately linked. Linguistic change is possible because of the presence of optional forms side by side in the language. The changeable nature of language is disturbing to many people. It is often described in metaphors of corruption, disease and invasion (by 'Americanisms' or 'Germanisms'). Our attitudes to language are intimately bound up with our social attitudes:

> *Am I right in assuming that in an age tortured by uncertainty with respect to religion, God, family, self, money and property, there is a worldwide collapse of not only the values of the past but of our language which, more and more, tends to be vague, indecisive, careless and often callous? (Quoted in McCrum et al., 1987, p. 344.)*

Such comments form part of a 'complaint tradition' in English which can be traced back to the time of Caxton and further. (Milroy and Milroy, 1987, p. 31.)

Many attempts have been made to 'fix' language by eliminating variations and legislating against innovations. The desire to prohibit change, variety and experiment in language was particularly strong in the eighteenth century and so this period forms an interesting case study for understanding attitudes towards language change.

Jean Aitchison suggests some reasons for the 'puristic' fervour of the time:

> Around 1700, English spelling and usage were in a fairly fluid state. Against this background, two powerful social factors combined to convert a normal mild nostalgia for the language of the past into a quasi-religious doctrine. The first was a long-standing admiration for Latin, and the second was powerful class snobbery. (1981, p. 21)

Three writers were particularly influential in this prescriptive enterprise, forming what Olivia Smith has called 'a linguistic trinity'. These were Bishop Lowth, author of the most popular grammar book of the century (published in 1762), Samuel Johnson, author of the famous Dictionary (1755) and James Harris, author of *Hermes* (1751), a philosophy of language (Smith, 1986, pp. 3–4). Many of our current notions of 'correct' English stem from their work. It was Lowth, for example, who formulated the rule that 'Two Negatives in English destroy one another, or are equivalent to an Affirmative'. What was the nature of their linguistic enterprise, and why was it so successful?

Olivia Smith suggests that a certain philosophy of language helps to account for their influence:

> The political and social effectiveness of ideas about language derived from the presupposition that language revealed the mind. To speak the vulgar language demonstrated that one belonged to the vulgar class; that is, that one was morally and intellectually unfit to participate in the culture. Only the refined language was capable of expressing intellectual ideas and worthy sentiments, while the vulgar language was limited to the expression of the sensations and the passions. Such a concept required making the refined as different from the vulgar language as possible while also requiring that certain types of thought and emotions be advocated to the detriment of others ... The baser forms of language were said to reveal the inability of the speaker to transcend the concerns of the present, an interest in material objects, and the dominance of the passions. Those who spoke the refined language were allegedly rational, moral, civilized, and capable of abstract thinking. By dividing the population into two extremes, ideas about language firmly distinguished those who were within the civilised world from those who were entirely outside it. The complexity of social life was drastically reduced by the denial of the possibility of a moral and intelligent vernacular speaker. (1986, pp. 2–3)

The languages of civilisation were Latin and Greek. Ordinary English, especially spoken English, was 'barbarous'. Grammars were therefore written with the express aim of moving the English of the educated away from its normal cadences and forms. Lowth disliked the use of prepositions at the end of sentences because they were a feature of 'common conversation'; sometimes rules were expressly invented in order to differentiate between spoken and written English, at the expense of the former, or they were invented in order to make English more like Latin. Harris even despised pronouns because they were too particular and concrete; prepositions, on the other hand, were declared pure, because their role was to express abstract relationships (see Smith, 1986, pp. 8–10, 22–3).

Whether or not these linguists had consciously political aims, they contributed to a political climate. The idea of linguistic, and therefore mental, vulgarity or inadequacy was used by the Parliamentarians of the day in their dismissal of popular demands for universal male suffrage.

> *Petitions to Parliament favouring extended or universal male suffrage provoked responses which relied on assumptions about language. Between 1793 and 1818 . . . Parliament dismissively refused to admit petitions because of the language in which they were written. (Ibid., p. 30)*

It is always hard to explain the origins or the motivation of a linguistic movement, but we can show that this drive to finally 'ascertain' the rules of language and preserve them from the normal flux of language change did not arise in a vacuum. If we look at the preceding years, a different picture emerges. At the time of the Restoration a much more open and flexible view of language had briefly emerged. There was a desire to explore English usage, and even to build up a scientific vocabulary based on local English 'trade' terms instead of on Latin. The Royal Society set about collecting words used by English artisans and farmers, many of them dialect words, to see whether they could be incorporated into 'educated' English. In 1674 a 'Collection of English Words not generally used' was published. Dryden, who was later to support the use of Latin and to despair of English, supported this movement and used its terminology. By 1697, however, we find him apologising for his use of these 'cant terms' because they were inappropriate for 'men and ladies of the first quality, who have been better bred than to be too nicely knowing in the terms' (quoted in 'Espinasse, 1974, pp. 359–60).

What had happened to create such a shift of attitude? Margaret 'Espinasse suggests that the decline of the Court as a source of patronage, and the rise of a more powerful middle class had a significant part to play. Writers were increasingly supported by middle class patrons; the class system itself had begun to shift away from its old patterns. This readership brought with it a new kind of social anxiety:

> *This rising middle class would naturally adhere to what they*
> *apprehended as the culture of the upper classes, with zeal and*
> *with anxiety.*
>   *We find a move towards the re-establishment of Latin as*
> *the 'superior' language and the diversion . . . of vigorous*
> *thinking away from the problems of English . . . the disuse of*
> *the inquiring approach to the vernacular as a thing whose*
> *structure may be investigated like that of any other creation.*
> *(Ibid., p. 364)*

The fear of linguistic mobility, then, is linked to fears aroused by social mobility. We cannot control the social upheavals set in motion by an event such as the Civil War, but we can attempt to control language use and turn it into an instrument of social classification. The more people feel themselves to be the objects of social transitions and rapid change, the more they will be tempted to create rigid social demarcations and to seek models of timeless stability. In the eighteenth century, English appeared to many writers and scholars to be chaotic and barbarous. In taking this view, they used language to mirror their feelings about their society. Latin, in contrast, seemed orderly, known, civilised, complete. It also proved to be a powerful means of social division. As teachers, therefore, we need to recognise precisely what we are committed to if we engage in a rearguard action against linguistic variation and change. Dressed up as 'education', we may nonetheless be participating in a profoundly anti-educational and anti-democratic enterprise.

WHY AND HOW DOES OUR LANGUAGE CHANGE?

Language both reflects social change and is the instrument of that change. Sometimes the changes are conscious and deliberate, and we can clearly perceive them at work. At other times they seem to be the unconscious products of a collective social mind, visible evidence of more hidden forces.

   One very visible change in process at the moment concerns the use of the 'generic' masculine pronoun *he*, and the use of terms such as *man* to stand for human beings of both sexes. Many writers are now making a very conscious effort to avoid such usages. This both reflects the desire of women to be given an equal footing in society, and is instrumental in helping to bring that about. The pronouns are a 'closed' class of grammatical words, and so our resistance to changing them is stronger. It can be done, however, as we can see by the loss of *thou* and *thee* in the standard dialect. The sources of that change are more obscure, but Dick Leith suggests that 'middle class insecurity' might once more be the culprit:

> *In sixteenth century urban society, particularly that of London,*
> *social relations were not fixed, which perhaps explains the*

> *Elizabethan obsession with them. With power and influence*
> *increasingly identified with the entrepreneur, there was no*
> *means of knowing who was entitled to* you, *and who to* thou.
> *The best solution was to stick to* you, *which would not offend*
> *... (1986, p. 109)*

In the United States, William Labov has, again, identified social insecurity as a major factor in linguistic changes. Lower middle class families, and, in particular, the women of those families, can produce changes in pronunciation through what Labov calls 'hypercorrection'. Their sense of social insecurity leads them to imitate and insist upon prestigious features of pronunciation (1978, pp. 136–41).

Changes in vocabulary occur more quickly than changes in grammar or pronunciation. We recognise a generation by its characteristic expressions: *ripping, smashing, fab, magic,* and so on. Words change from 'plus' words to 'minus' words, depending on the values of the time. Social battles are often fought out as linguistic battles. In the mid-1980s, for example, we could see an ideological struggle being fought out through words. They became counters in a dispute about the essential nature of society and the individual. From one direction came a drive to promote the image of the individual as a force of unlimited dynamic potential, a restless pioneer, pushing back the frontiers of change. The corollary of such a stance is the idea of society itself as uncluttered virgin territory, free of obstacles to the entrepreneurial spirit. Words like *initiative, enterprise, energy, goal, potential* took on a glow of approval. Society became *the enterprise society.* From another direction came an insistence on the recognition of unpalatable social facts. Words like *community, caring, disadvantaged* took on an extra burden of meaning. Society was to be, or should be, *the caring community.* Even the stars were dragged in. One astrologer tells his readers: 'You cannot wait to grasp life by the throat and fulfil the potential you know is within you.' Now that the sober 1990s have dawned, this advice is tempered with caution: 'Steer clear of get-rich-quick schemes and be discerning about the people you trust' (TV Times, 2–8 June, 1990, p. 81).

As Geoffrey Hughes points out, in periods of recession the minus words of a previous era become plus words:

> *... with the dramatic increase in the price of oil from 1972 to*
> *1984, economy became the major feature. Energy, which had*
> *previously been a commodity to be expended, now became a*
> *resource to be husbanded and conserved. Semantically, the*
> *result was an increasing preference for words which put a good*
> *gloss on the notion of economy, such as* save *and the various*
> *relations of economy.* Thrifty *was brought into play,* lean *no*
> *longer suggests 'emaciated', but 'athletic' and 'efficient'; even*
> mean *and* miser *started to undergo amelioration. (1989, p. 160)*

Over longer stretches of time we can see how such social changes are capable of altering the meaning of a word beyond recognition. In such a way, the Old English word *saelig* originally meant *happy, blessed*. By Middle English times it had become *seely*, meaning *innocent*. In more recent times it became *silly*, meaning *deserving of compassion*, then *weak, feeble*, and finally *foolish, empty-headed* (*Ibid.*, p. 10). We could speculate that a once meaningful social and religious concept, that of the 'holy fool', lost its significance as a more secular society came into being.

More hidden forces are also at work in language, producing changes which may, on the surface, appear capricious and isolated, but often prove to be related elements of a forceful momentum.

At the moment, in everyday conversation, we might find ourselves saying: 'I felt more free', or 'yours was more dearer than the one I got'. When we write, we hesitate over such expressions, and choose the standard forms: *freer, dearer*. We confine the use of *more* to words with several syllables, like *beautiful*. The reason we, or our pupils, feel confusion is not because we are stupid. It is because we are taking part in a movement of linguistic change which has been in process in English for centuries. Nowadays, language change is like a strong, steady current in a river, which constantly flows up against the obstacle of standardisation, seeking to wear it down, or to find a free channel so that it can flow around it.

The main current of movement in English, in process for over a thousand years, is a tendency to change itself from a 'synthetic' to an 'analytic' language. What does this mean? A 'synthetic' language like Latin, or Old English, creates its grammatical meanings largely by changing the shape of particular words, especially word endings. We are used to seeing words with more or less fixed shapes. The typical variations of an English noun are very limited: *girl, girls, girl's, girls'*. But in Old English, nouns changed their endings to denote gender (masculine, neuter, feminine); number (singular and plural) and case (the grammatical role which the word is playing). The word ending (inflexion) would show whether the word was the subject or object of the sentence in which it appeared, or it would show relationships which we now express through prepositions like *of, to, by*. The word endings also showed which declension the noun belonged to.

Synthetic languages, therefore, do not depend so heavily on word order or prepositions. The subject of the sentence can appear after the verb. The word ending will tell us that it is the subject. Dick Leith illustrates the point by using the example of *the boy killed the bear*. In modern English the word order in such a sentence is crucial to the meaning. If we reverse it, the meaning is reversed. In Latin, or Old English, the same sentence could be expressed in a number of ways, but the word endings would ensure one unambiguous meaning for *puer interfecit ursum* or *se cnafa* (knave) *of-sloh þone beran*. Even the definite articles in Old English, *se* and *þone* reinforce the syntactical point (1986, p. 98). There are several possible reasons why English began to move away from the use of word endings towards the use of word order. It is possible that spoken Old English and spoken Latin in fact employed fewer inflexions and more prepositions. We know that the Emperor Augustus was criticised for using too many prepositions in his speeches. He insisted that they were necessary to ensure that he was clearly understood by the public. In spoken English the stress patterns of the language would ensure that many word endings would be inaudible.

It has also been suggested that when Anglo-Saxons and Vikings had to live side by side (i.e. from the ninth century), a process of 'pidginisation' began to take place. Pidgin languages arise when two communities with different languages must contrive some means of communication. In such circumstances 'language is reduced to bare essentials, as it is when we send a telegram; and one of the clearest means of achieving this is to delete, or simplify, some of the patterns in our grammar' (Leith, 1986, p. 24). The loss of word endings would make particular sense in this case, because the Anglo-Saxons and the Danes had many words in common: 'The body of the word was so nearly the same in the two languages that only the endings would put obstacles in the way of mutual understanding' (Baugh and Cable, 1983, p. 103). This process of 'simplification' has been in train for centuries. As Dick Leith explains:

> *What we have seen since Anglo-Saxon times is the gradual erosion, in all dialects, of . . . inflexions. The term which is used to denote this process –* simplification *– does not imply that generations of lazy speakers have merely taken innumerable short cuts in the grammar. The loss of case-endings, for instance, meant that other means had to be found for signalling relations among words in the sentence . . . Prepositions, like* for, of, by, *etc. began to serve those functions; and word order became less flexible. In this, therefore, we see the 'quid pro quo' of much linguistic change: while something in the language may be abandoned by its speakers, something else will emerge as a counterbalance. (1986, p. 100)*

Once the process begins, it is speeded up by 'analogy'. This has been defined as 'the extremely important drift in language through which the exception tends to conform to the rule.' An example of this is the Old English word *gāt*, meaning *goat*, (still present in *Gatwick*). Originally the plural of *gat* was *gaet*. Later a sound change made this into *gōt* and *goot* as we find it in Chaucer. But even before Chaucer's day it was making its plural by analogy with other plurals by adding *s*: *gotes* (Robertson and Cassidy, 1955, p. 115).

The momentum of such processes is very strong and can often be seen most clearly in dialect forms or in everyday conversational English. This is because these are the areas of life that are freest from the demands of standardisation. Speakers who use *more pretty* or *she go* are following an impulse greater than themselves: the impulse to drop inflexional endings, or to make them more uniform by a process of analogy. Once again, standardisation was taking place at the time when these changes were most vigorous, but before they were complete. As a result, a social stigma has attached itself to such forms. They are characterised as 'sloppy' or 'careless'. In fact, like vocabulary changes, they are the bearers of history.

As well as simplification, language also develops new forms of complexity. English has dropped many inflexions, but it has added refinements of tense, mood, voice and aspect in the verb. One such development is the use of the *progressive* aspect of verbs: *he was laughing*. There are some early examples of this usage, but they are not common. It has really taken off since the sixteenth century. The use of the passive only extended to it in the eighteenth century: *the house is being built*. As usual with language changes, this was attacked as 'an outrage upon English idiom, to be detested, abhorred, execrated' (quoted in Baugh and Cable, 1983, p. 293). In the nineteenth century the progressive roles of *be* and *have* as full verbs were extended: *she is being naughty, he is having a party*; and in the twentieth century we have added *have to: she is having to sell the business*. At the present time a new development seems to be underway, in which *being* is combined with another participle: *I didn't see him through* being working *at the time he came*.

Language also refines and extends its uses through additions to its vocabulary – a process which has occurred on a vast scale in English. We have borrowed words wholesale from dozens of languages and created new words out of native and foreign elements. Built into our language are 'productive' systems for adding new words as we need them. Morphemes like *ism* and *ite* allow us to create *monetarism* and *thatcherite*. The loss of the old inflexional endings also means that we can extend the range of a word by using it for more than one grammatical function. Nouns and verbs can become interchangeable: *bore, fall, cheat*. Compounds of old words create new ones: *football, babysitter, wrongfooting*.

CLASSROOM IMPLICATIONS AND ACTIVITIES

The presence of linguistic variety in our classrooms is a resource rather than a handicap – this is the major implication of a knowledge of historical variation in English. All around us we have the evidence of the chequered history of the language, and of its current movements. It is from this recognition that classroom activities can arise. Pupils can be encouraged to research their own dialects, instead of rejecting them. By interviewing older generations of a family or neighbourhood pupils can collect data about changes over a relatively short span of time. Another way to do this is to look at the language of newspapers from 50 or 100 years ago, singling out words and expressions which we would be highly unlikely to find today. One way to detect the changes is to rewrite short sections, substituting modern turns of phrase. Other resources for such research could be children's story books and rhymes, comics and popular songs.

Tracing the history of words and expressions is a source of fascination to both children and adults. We can give such an activity more focus by concentrating on one area of social life, for example, money or 'law and order'. Through changes in word usage, we can trace changes in social attitudes. Looking at innovations in vocabulary can be linked to such research: often the 'new' expressions prove to be older than we might think. As Geoffrey Hughes points out, many of the cult expressions of the 1960s: *freak out, pad* (living place), and *pig* (police-man) are found as underground words in the eighteenth century (1989, p. 23).

The changing sounds of English can be studied by listening to characteristic British voices in films of the 1940s and 1950s. In a short space of time some quite remarkable changes have taken place, not only in the forms of 'Received Pronunciation', but also in the ways in which regional accents and dialects are presented.

The study of historical variation in English has an image of remoteness, mustiness, cobwebs. Yet, like all history, its real role is to illuminate the present. We all act as representatives of the history of the language every time we open our mouths or pick up a pen, and some explicit knowledge of it is therefore a vital resource for English teachers.

REFERENCES

Aitchison, J. (1981) *Language Change: Progress or Decay?* London: Fontana.
Baugh, A. C. and Cable, T. (1983) *A History of the English Language.* London: Routledge.
'Espinasse, M. (1974) 'The Decline and Fall of Restoration Science', in Webster, C. (ed.) *The Intellectual Revolution of the Seventeenth Century.* London: Routledge.
Halliday, M. A. K. and Hasan, R. (1989) *Language, Context and Text: Aspects of Language in a Social-Semiotic Perspective.* Oxford: Oxford University Press.
Hughes, G. (1989) *Words in Time: A Social History of the English Vocabulary.* Oxford: Blackwell.
Labov, W. (1978) *Sociolinguistic Patterns.* Oxford: Blackwell.
Leith, D. (1986) *A Social History of English.* London: Routledge.
McCrum, R., Cran, W. and MacNeil, R. (1987) *The Story of English.* London: Faber and Faber.
Milroy, J. and Milroy, L. (1987) *Authority in Language: Investigating Language Prescription and Standardisation.* London: Routledge.

Robertson, S. and Cassidy, F. G. (1955) *The Development of Modern English*. New York: Prentice-Hall.

Smith, O. (1986) *The Politics of Language, 1791–1819*. Oxford: Oxford University Press.

Stubbs, M. (1980) *Language and Literacy: The Sociolinguistics of Reading and Writing*. London: Routledge.

APPENDIX

This brief glossary is designed mainly for readers outside Great Britain who may not otherwise be acquainted with some of the terms used in conjunction with the National Curriculum in England and Wales.

Glossary of Acronyms

APU   The Assessment of Performance Unit at the DES, set up in the wake of the Bullock Report to monitor on a national basis development in talk, reading and writing, and since extended to cover other curriculum areas

AT   Attainment target, set of descriptions of achievement, divided into loosely age-related levels, for a particular part of the curriculum area, usually narrower than a profile component

CCW   Curriculum Council for Wales

DES   Department of Education and Science (Ministry of Education for England and Wales)

EWP   English Working Party, (the Cox Committee)

ERA   Education Reform Act

GCSE   General Certificate of Secondary Education (16+ School leaving examination, replaces GCE)

HMI   Her Majesty's Inspector (of schools)

INSET   In-Service Education for Teachers

KAL   Knowledge about Language

KS   Key Stage: one of four age ranges specified by the National Curriculum

LEA   Local Education Authority

LINC   Language in the National Curriculum, an in-service programme to develop teachers' knowledge about language

NC   The National Curriculum

NCC   National Curriculum Council, the body appointed by the Secretary of State to administer and advise on the National Curriculum

NSG   Non-statutory guidance (notes for teachers on implementation of the National Curriculum – prepared by NCC)

PC   Profile component; one or more related attainment targets

PoS   Programme of study: the activities required to fulfil the National Curriculum in a profile component

SATs   Standard assessment tasks to be centrally devised

SEAC   Schools Examinations and Assessment Committee, the body appointed by the Secretary of State to administer and advise on assessment and examinations in connection with the National Curriculum

TGAT   Task Group on Assessment and Testing, the committee chaired by Professor Paul Black which constructed the assessment framework of PCs, ATs, SATs, Levels and so on.